TH
ANG
V

THE FIRST ANGLO-SIKH WAR

AMARPAL SINGH

AMBERLEY

Cover illustrations: Front: A nineteenth-century sword from the Sikh courts, inscribed in Gurmukhi: 'Akaal Sahai Nihal Singh' (May God protect Nihal Singh). From the collection of Runjeet Singh (www.akaalarms.com). Back: Brown Bess musket. From a photograph by Antique Military Rifles, under Creative Commons ShareAlike 2.0.

This edition first published 2014

Amberley Publishing
The Hill, Stroud
Gloucestershire, GL5 4EP

www.amberleybooks.com

British Library Cataloguing in Publication Data.
A catalogue record for this book is available from the British Library.

ISBN 978 1 4456 4195 9

Typesetting and Origination by Amberley Publishing.
Printed in the UK.

Contents

Maps

Foreword

Interest in the memorialisation of battlefields goes back some time, but it was during the nineteenth century that past glories were first marked out on the field of battle – sometimes incongruously, sometimes in the wrong place, sometimes marking the wrong dates. Historians left with this legacy have often had to work to understand not only where the battle was fought, but also the background to why the battle was commemorated in the first place.

Over the last decade or so, the new discipline of battlefield archaeology has grown out of a need to reinterpret battlefields, to place them in their correct geographic setting, to understand the events that were played out in past wars, and to consider the level of memorialisation and memory associated with battle sites. Wide ranging in geography and period, battlefield archaeology has moved from Europe and the Americas to Africa and Asia; it has taken in the conflicts of the classical period, considered the wars of empire in the seventeenth and eighteenth centuries, and examined the industrialised conflict of the nineteenth and twentieth centuries. Seemingly, no stone has been left unturned in the quest for knowledge of historical conflicts; and yet, to date, there has been the major omission of a country with a long history of military engagements – India. A complex subcontinent geographically, Indian battlefields must surely present historians and archaeologists a rich archive that will reward detailed study.

India was long considered the 'jewel in the crown' of the burgeoning British Empire, a vast territory of millions of people assembled over centuries of military conquest and commercial development during the decades of the East India Company. Standing in the way of further expansion was the Sikh Kingdom of the Punjab, built in large part by the military actions of Maharaja Ranjit Singh against the Afghans from 1799 until his death in 1839. With the death of the Maharaja came the weakening of the Sikh power base, and the potential for the British to subdue their neighbours. It would not be an easy task in a geographically complex terrain against determined opponents.

In his excellent account of the first war between the British East India Company and the Sikh Kingdom in 1845-6, Amarpal Singh provides the framework for understanding the conflict, its origins, implications and actions; it also provides the basis for the future exploration, study and commemoration of battles that have long been overlooked in the memory of many in the west. With this book in hand, the battlefields of the Punjab come alive once again.

Professor Peter Doyle BSc PhD Cgeol FGS
Battlefield Archaeologist
Co-Secretary, All Party War Graves and
Battlefield Heritage Group

Preface

Sir, I think it my duty earnestly to recommend our retreating to Ferozepore.

— British Army major, Ferozeshah

Never! I'd rather die on the spot.

— Sir Hugh Gough, Commander-in-Chief, British Army in India

The middle of the nineteenth century saw the first serious challenge to the European military predominance that had been firmly established since the decline of the Ottoman Empire two hundred years earlier. By the turn of that century, a new empire had been established on the plains of the Punjab in northern India by Ranjit Singh, ruler of the Sikhs. With British expansion moving northwards towards his domain during the century's early decades, Ranjit had orchestrated in response a rapid change in the Sikh army to face this threat; first importing and imitating western military tactics and weapons, then developing his own, he developed the first modern army in Asia. Six years after his death, the inevitable trial of strength between the two powers on a freezing December night by the nondescript village of Ferozeshah would result in one of the most memorable and dramatic battles in history.

The contest had commenced in the afternoon of that day in 1845, the British army marching out of their base a short distance away to attack the Sikh camp. Bivouac equipment was left behind as the British commander Sir Hugh Gough expected to return the same day after a glorious victory. However, the struggle with the Sikh army turned into a long and vicious battle of attrition extending late into the night with initial British success overturned by Sikh counterattacks as darkness descended on the now burning village. The British force, badly weakened, had split in two with the left wing retreating to a village three kilometres away while the other battered remnants of the army had been forced southwards out of the Sikh camp and into a defensive formation. With their retreat, a relative lull had fallen over the field of battle for the night, prior to the resumption of hostilities at sunrise. The British commander-in-chief now found himself in a most perilous position. Ammunition had been exhausted while thinly clad British soldiers found it impossible to rest without food and water in the subzero temperatures. What had been mooted as a triumphant advance into the Sikh capital of Lahore with only moderate difficulty had turned into a most desperate struggle for the survival of the British Empire in India.

My interest in the subject of the Anglo-Sikh Wars grew several years ago when I researched some firsthand accounts of the battle. The military history of the British East India Company since the Battle of Plassey, a hundred years earlier, had been invariably one of a small, disciplined and well-equipped European army, backed by native sepoys, comfortably gaining victories over more numerous but less organised forces across the subcontinent. The Battle of Ferozeshah was different. Eyewitness accounts written by both British soldiers and officers provide us with graphic descriptions of the privations and hardships suffered during the punishing two-day struggle.

Ferozeshah, Sabraon, Chillianwala and the other battles fought against the British have a powerful hold on the Punjabi people as well. They still have a strong sense of pride in the Sikh army that was welded together by Ranjit Singh. The victory that was declined at Ferozeshah and the duplicity of the Sikh commanders towards their army is a popular subject of discussion across the towns and villages of Punjab. This interest has been translated into numerous books on the wars. Unfortunately, this interest does not as yet extend to the battlefield sites. There are no modern memorials to these great battles. Road maps do not mark these sites as places of interest. There are no signs on highways alerting passersby to the close proximity of these battlefields and no guide books are available. Those books that are available tend to be narratives of the campaign, inadequate to the task of explaining the battlefields. The sketches detailing the battles are just that, hurriedly drawn maps by combatants writing of their experiences after the battle. While invaluable, these maps cover only the most salient points of the battlefield and they miss much of the finer detail provided in written accounts. Just as critically, they lack the changes that the last one hundred and fifty years have wrought on these sites. Over time, new villages have sprung up, new roads and canals now pass through the sites, and other landmarks have appeared or disappeared. Consequently, few visitors walk the banks of the Sutlej at Aliwal or through the fields of Ferozeshah. The area of the Sikh entrenchments at Sabraon, close to the River Sutlej, scene of a great tragedy where thousands of Sikh soldiers died, is a particularly lonely place, frequented only by the occasional farmer or shepherd. Only the British monuments built nearly a century and a half ago alert the passerby of the military significance of these sites. The monuments themselves are quietly crumbling away, victims of the official neglect faced by every ageing structure in the subcontinent. The original plaques on the monuments that boldly declared the names of Mudki, Ferozeshah, Aliwal and Sabraon have long since vanished. In fact, so little is apparent to the uneducated eye that casual visitors would be discouraged from carrying out more than a cursory examination of these sites.

Nevertheless, times are changing. Although battlefield tourism is still in its infancy in India, there is a growing interest in preserving and studying these sites. Many battlefields associated with the Indian Mutiny, the Marathas, and Wellington's wars are already attracting interest, along with the sites of more recent battles such as that of Imphal, in north-east India, where the Japanese were fought in 1944.

I personally found visiting the battlefields of the Anglo-Sikh Wars to be a highly rewarding experience. Small features and details described or mentioned in firsthand accounts and maps gradually begin to make themselves apparent. Ancient *nullahs* (dry river beds) are an important part of the landscape in India and are frequently mentioned in the accounts. Many of the old roads and thoroughfares still exist, either as dirt tracks or as newly tarmaced roads. Ridges of high ground become recognisable as those described. The twists and turns in the passage of the River Sutlej and the exceptionally sandy ground nearby are still as they were during the war. Distances mentioned from villages to the battlefields give vital clues. Descriptions of defences and their locations in relation to villages further aid the process of recognition. Ancient wells marked on British maps of the time either still exist or can be located with the help of villagers. Village lakes mentioned in accounts still survive. Other villages and hamlets used as outposts give a sense of the positions of the opposing armies prior to battle. What initially seems to be the difficult task of interpreting the battlefields becomes progressively easier as one explores the area.

What helps greatly is the availability of satellite and aerial imagery of the battlefield sites. Tools such as Google Earth now give both amateur and professional military historians an unprecedented opportunity to study the layout of a battlefield prior to venturing onto the site itself. Long-vanished roads and tracks, invisible from the ground, make their presence known when viewed from above. Features of the terrain, ridges, dry river beds and disappearing *nullahs* become more apparent. For travelling through these areas, aerial images also make obvious the local village road networks and are preferable to the rather basic road maps which tend to document only the major routes and highways. Distances between villages and other landmarks can also easily be measured. Aerial images are also invaluable in discovering how modernity has affected these sites. The growth and expansion of villages beyond their old walled perimeters is conspicuous, new roads now crisscross the sites, and what was once jungle may now be intensively farmed land. Rivers have shrunk while new canals have appeared. But, most importantly, careful examination can reveal the still surviving traces of battle. The lines of faded trench works, foxholes and dugouts are frequently easier to discern from aerial images.

With the availability of satellite imagery, it becomes readily obvious that the contemporary maps and sketches used in military history books for these battles are more often than not grossly out of scale. To complement the text of this book, new maps drawn to scale are included along with the original firsthand sketches and maps. These new maps give the reader a truer sense of the distances involved. They have also been deliberately overlaid with modern features and reference points to aid visitors to the battlefield sites.

My original intention was to write specifically a battlefield guide. However, as I unearthed new firsthand accounts and previously unpublished documents and data relating to the Anglo-Sikh Wars, the nature of the book gradually evolved to include accounts of the battles themselves. By doing so, my hope is this book provides comprehensive coverage of the First Anglo-Sikh War.

Unfortunately, few Sikh eyewitness accounts of the war have been uncovered to date, and I had to rely almost solely on the account left by Dewan Ajudya Parshad, a high official in the Lahore government, in his work *Waqai Jang-i-Sikhan*. Like the Sikh commanders, Parshad had little affection for the army due to the overbearing and aggressive conduct of the common soldiers at Lahore. This is apparent in his account as he generally portrays the Sikh soldiery in a poor light. He was not an eyewitness at the battles but takes his information from soldiers and officers who were present. (The details of the battles of Mudki and Ferozeshah come largely from S. Ram Singh and Mehtab Singh, brigade commanders who accompanied the army to the battles. There is little information on Bhudowal and Aliwal.) Parshad seems to have been at Sabraon, although not on the south bank of the Sutlej where the battle took place. His account is nevertheless a useful resource, especially in its detailing of the mutinous nature of the troops and how little control the commander and officers really had upon the eve of war.

What we are not short of is British accounts. Considerable numbers of these survive both in published form and in letters, manuscripts, documents, sketches and maps that have gradually surfaced in British museums over the past one hundred and fifty years.

This book is written in two distinct parts. The first part covers the battles of the campaign. A comprehensive account of each battle is given. This being partly a battlefield guide, eyewitness descriptions of the terrain and associated landmarks are intentionally covered in considerable detail to give a more comprehensive vision of the battlefield.

The second part of the book contains battlefield guides that detail locations of interest, both on the battlefield and in related sites and villages. GPS locations of all important locations on the sites are given. Many of these locations or items of interest are large enough to be viewed using satellite imagery on Google Earth. Also included in the guides are descriptions and accounts of early visitors to the battlefield sites. Many of these accounts were left by soldiers marching to reinforce the main British army on the River Sutlej. Several months later, many of these soldiers and other individuals would travel back to British territories after the end of hostilities and pass by the battlefields again. Still others were marching back into the Punjab two years later as the Second Anglo-Sikh War commenced. And others like Lord Roberts, later Commander-in-Chief of the British forces in India and Lord Dalhousie, Governor-General during the Second Anglo-Sikh War, came specifically to tour the battlefield sites. These accounts rarely figure in military books and provide a valuable view of the battlefield and the nature of the fighting from a military perspective, sometimes just a few hours after the battle itself. Part two of the book also details changes to the battlefields since the war, due to both human progress and the forces of nature, notably the frequent flooding of the Sutlej.

Appreciation and preservation of battlefields is important. No other single event can decide the fate of countries and nations in more dramatic fashion than a trial of strength over a few square kilometres of often uncompromising land. Few other events are more galling than the loss of independence suffered after a defeat. On a battlefield are displayed the highest human qualities of bravery, camaraderie and loyalty and also the basest vices of treachery and cowardice. Visiting a battlefield where history was made in such striking fashion is an experience like no other. Some of the places and structures detailed in this book are already in an advanced state of ruin or decay. Other items like the imposing remaining structures in Mudki are being dismantled slowly by locals, their bricks used for more modest projects elsewhere. Other battlefields like those of Aliwal and Sabraon, away from the villages on the banks of the Sutlej, are better protected from modernity. Nevertheless, encroachment is gradually taking place as the population of the Punjab increases and new land is sought. In the last few years, farmers have extended their control up to the Sutlej riverbanks, destroying much evidence of the Sikh army entrenchments and camps at Sabraon and Aliwal. I hope this book will nurture an interest in these sites and encourage battlefield preservation and tourism in its own small way.

My thanks to the many people of Mudki, Lohaum, Ferozeshah, Misreewalla, Bhudowal, Aliwal, Bhundri, Porein, Sabraon and Rhodewalla villages for their help and to the village elders who provided me with information I could never have discovered on my own. My thanks also go to Sukhwinder Singh Hissowal from the Gurmat Bhuvan charity for his considerable assistance in helping research the Bhudowal battlefield and to Parminder Parry Singh Sekhon for helping with the topography of the Bhudowal area. I'm also obliged to Sirdar Buland Singh Pamali of Bhudowal for sharing his knowledge on the Bhudowal battlefield. I'd also like to thank Tara Singh Toor and Jaswinder Kaur for giving me generous use of their car without a second thought which proved so invaluable in my journeys round the battlefields. My greatest thanks go to my parents, my wife Mandeep and my sons Harmeet and Jaspal for their considerable patience during the writing of this book. Finally I'd like to thank you, the reader, for your interest in the First Anglo-Sikh War and the as yet barely explored subject of its battlefields.

Amarpal Singh Sidhu
London, July 2010

Introduction

... all Hindoo India looked to the Sikh army for the expulsion of Christianity from the East.
                              – Herbert Edwardes, aide-de-camp to Sir Hugh Gough

The Sikh soldiery used to assemble in groups round the tomb of Runjeet Singh, vowing to defend with their lives all that belonged to the commonwealth of Govind – that they would never suffer the kingdom of Lahore to be occupied by the British strangers, but stand ready to march or give the invaders battle on their own ground.
                              – W. W. W. Humbley, *Journal of a Cavalry Officer*

Expansion of British Power in India

The eighteenth century was a period of great political upheaval in India. The century which began with the Mughal Empire at its zenith would end with the establishment of a new foreign government, that of the East India Company, as the paramount power on the subcontinent. Overgrown and mismanaged, the Mughal Empire had disintegrated after the gross religious intolerance displayed by the Emperor Aurangzeb. With its demise arose several substantial and numerous minor principalities and independent kingdoms carved out by ambitious Mughal governors and assorted adventurers. In the north, Punjab and Kashmir were occupied by the Afghans. In the east, Bengal broke away from the distant control of Delhi. To its west the province of Oudh became increasingly independent. In central India, a vast empire was carved out by the marauding Marathas. In south-central India or the Deccan, what had been a recently won province became the kingdom of Hyderabad. These along with many other petty kingdoms flowered briefly before being overshadowed by the new power that was the East India Company.

The imperial history of the British East India Company commenced with the acquisition of modest holdings in the coastal regions in the south and east of the country during the early eighteenth century. This changed after the Battle of Plassey in 1757 which gave the Company virtual control of Bengal. The success at Plassey was followed by the victory at Buxar in 1764 against a combined force of the Mughal Emperor Shah Alam II, Shuja-ud-Daula, who was the Nawab of Oudh, and Mir Kasim, the Nawab of Bengal. Altogether a more important victory, it firmly established the East India Company as a major player in the bid for control of the subcontinent. Victory at Buxar meant British control now stretched over a vast area comprised of the eastern states of Bengal, Bihar, Uttar Pradesh and Orissa, which meant huge new revenues for the East India Company. Alongside these gains, the rich province of Oudh in the north-east had now also fallen under its sway. These successes were followed by a string of victories during the next fifty years which enabled the Company to eliminate as rivals the state of Mysore in the south and the Marathas in central India. The trading company suffered none of the internal dissensions, intrigues and personal ambitions that dogged the native courts and powers of India. A further advantage was the superior organisation of an army guided by the military acumen and diplomacy of experienced statesmen and generals. By the start of the nineteenth century, the boundaries of the British Empire had moved northwards to Delhi and beyond.

The small number of Europeans available in India, both for military and for civilian purposes, posed a problem for the British authorities. Direct rule and administration over the huge areas that had been gained was impossible. The everyday control and administration of these states was, out of necessity, left in the hands of locals. Thus a system peculiar to India known as 'Subsidiary Alliance' began to be used by the Company. Power in a state was to be exercised through an advisor or Resident with the local ruler left in nominal control. The local ruler was to allow a

British force to be stationed in his state, ostensibly for protection from aggression by other states, while his own army was gradually disbanded. The cost of this British force was to be paid for by the local ruler, who was also to relinquish all responsibility for foreign affairs to the Resident. In effect, the ruler became the figurehead of a state that continued to function but where ultimate authority rested with the British. The day-to-day running of the state was left to local bureaucracy, thereby freeing the British from a significant drain on their manpower.

Formation of the Sikh State

The only area that lay beyond the control of the East India Company by the turn of the nineteenth century was the north-west of India, comprising the geographical areas of Punjab, Kashmir and Sind. These territories had been seized by the Afghan adventurer Ahmed Shah Abdali during the 1750s as the Mughal Empire crumbled. However, large areas had already been liberated from Afghan control by the Sikh confederacies. These confederacies, called *Misls*, controlled small principalities which, while having a strong sense of community, rarely worked in unison. Warfare among them was as common as against any foreign invaders of the Punjab. While strong enough to wage war against each other and lesser neighbouring powers, they lacked the singular purpose that could bind them together to repel an ambitious and organised power like the East India Company. As with other states in India, petty jealousies and personal ambitions generally played a major part in making it difficult to mount a unified stand against an external threat.

It is beyond the scope of this book to go into the rise of Ranjit Singh, the Sikh ruler or Maharaja of Punjab for nearly forty years until his death in 1839. But it is sufficient to say that through the use of his considerable foresight, powers of diplomacy, and a genius in warfare, he rose from being one among a considerable list of contenders for supremacy in Punjab to establishing by the early years of the nineteenth century a single unified Sikh state to the north of the River Sutlej. But his desire to incorporate into a single Sikh empire the minor principalities south of the river, the Cis-Sutlej states, was thwarted by the British. The Sikh rulers of these minor states, fearful of being dispossessed of their kingdoms, had voluntarily accepted British supremacy over their states during the early part of the nineteenth century.

Ranjit Singh was mindful of his as yet modest strength; he knew his forces, confident but undisciplined, were unprepared to withstand the military strength, organisation and mass artillery of the East India Company. He also knew his own power was not fully consolidated; recently conquered chieftains and vassals who had not yet forgotten their independence could quickly desert their new rulers. Ranjit's dominions and resources were small as yet compared to what the British could bring to the field. If there was to be a trial of strength, it would have to be left for the future and on his terms. He therefore agreed on a pact of non-aggression with the British; a treaty signed at Amritsar in 1809 confirmed the suzerainty of the British up to the River Sutlej.

Yet war was never actively considered by either side. The peace that extended from this time onwards until his death was beneficial to both Ranjit Singh and the British, allowing both empires to further consolidate their gains. The treaty freed Ranjit from any threat of British aggression on his southern border while his rule over the Sikhs in the trans-Sutlej area was still tenuous. Over the next thirty years, in a series of campaigns, he strengthened his grip on the plains and proceeded to eliminate all Afghan control over Punjab up to Peshawar and the Khyber Pass to the west of Lahore. To the east, towards the Himalayas, the Ghurkhas were repulsed and his rule established over the Kangra region in 1809, while the Jullunder Doab, the area between the Sutlej and Beas rivers, was brought under direct control in 1811. To the north, the territory of Kashmir was added to the empire in 1819. To the south-west, Multan with its great fortress was wrested from Afghan control and would define the southern limits of the empire. By 1839, the year of his death, the Sikh kingdom extended from Tibet and Kashmir to Sind and from the Khyber Pass to the Himalayas in the east. It spanned 600 miles from east to west and 350 miles from north to south, comprising an area of just over 200,000 square miles. For a time after Ranjit's death, there was still sufficient momentum and organisation to allow for further expansion. The control of the Ladakh and Leh regions to the east of Kashmir was consolidated, and an ambitious expedition launched into Tibet concluded with the Tibetan and Chinese government suing for peace in 1842.

The pact of 1809 also proved useful to the British, who recognised that the turbulent areas in the north and west would prove a heavy burden for their army. Even if it could be achieved, any potential occupation of Punjab and these frontier zones – populated as they were by unruly Muslim tribesman who would chafe bitterly under foreign rule – would tie up substantial resources. The continual feuding between these tribesmen and any ruling power would also undoubtedly call for a permanent and sizeable garrison likely to sustain a steady stream of casualties. The British recognised the fact that Ranjit Singh acted as a powerful force between their empire to the south and these difficult elements and Afghanistan beyond. With a minimum of force, they could rule over the more placid territories of India while Ranjit Singh, as an ally, could keep these wild tribesmen at bay. In effect, the Sikh empire provided security for the territories of the East India Company at no cost to the company itself.

Modernisation of the Sikh Army

Friendship with the British could be as precarious an activity as enmity. Many Indian states had gradually withered in the embrace of the East India Company as it strengthened its hold over the subcontinent. After an imposed reduction of their armies and with increasing amounts of control exercised by the British Residents, many states survived in name only. Some had already disappeared due to escheat when no male heirs were available while other rulers were quietly deposed in favour of direct rule. If a change in policy by the East India Company directors ever meant an attempted expansion into the Punjab, a reason would surely be found to justify the aggression.

Ranjit Singh had recognised that the independence of his Lahore state could only be guaranteed by a military force prodigious enough that the East India Company would find it difficult to argue for a more expansionist policy north of the Sutlej. With this in mind, he orchestrated a revolutionary change in the structure and organisation of the Sikh army very similar to the changes later forced on the Japanese during western intrusion in the Meiji

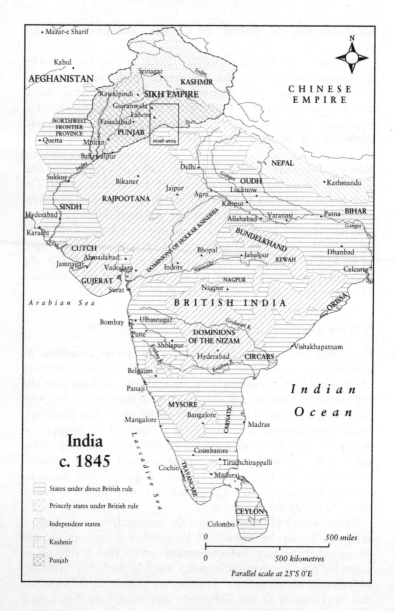

India
c. 1845

Maps labels: Mazar-e Sharif, Kabul, AFGHANISTAN, Srinagar, KASHMIR, Rawalpindi, SIKH EMPIRE, Gujranwala, Lahore, NORTHWEST FRONTIER PROVINCE, Faisalabad, PUNJAB, inset area, Quetta, Multan, Bahawalpur, Indus, Sukkur, Delhi, Ganges, NEPAL, CHINESE EMPIRE, OUDH, Kathmandu, Bikaner, Jaipur, Lucknow, Agra, Kanpur, BIHAR, SINDH, Hyderabad, Allahabad, Varanasi, Patna, RAJPOOTANA, Ganges, Karachi, DOMINIONS OF HOLKAR & SINDHIA, BUNDELKHAND, Dhanbad, CUTCH, Ahmadabad, Bhopal, Jabalpur, REWAH, Jamnagar, Vadodara, Indore, Narmada, Calcutta, GUJERAT, Surat, NAGPUR, Nagpur, BRITISH INDIA, ORISSA, Arabian Sea, Bombay, Ulhasnagar, Godavari R., Pune, DOMINIONS OF THE NIZAM, Sholapur, Krishna R., Hyderabad, CIRCARS, Vishakhapatnam, Belgaum, Panaji, Indian Ocean, MYSORE, Bangalore, CARNATIC, Mangalore, Madras, Laccadive Sea, Coimbatore, Cochin, Tiruchchirappalli, TRAVANCORE, Madurai, CEYLON, Colombo

States under direct British rule
Princely states under British rule
Independent states
Kashmir
Punjab

0   500 miles
0   500 kilometres
Parallel scale at 25°S 0°E

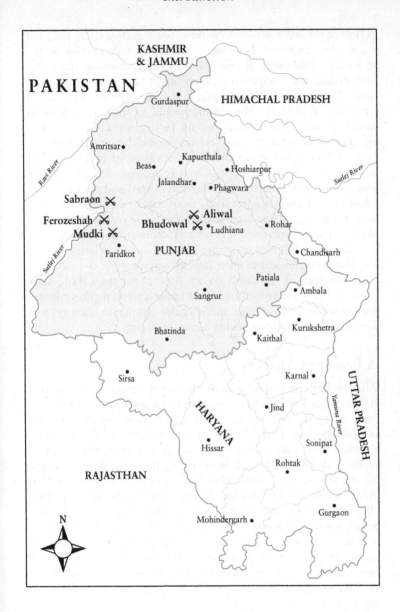

period of the late nineteenth century. The transformation required a complete overhaul. No longer would the Sikh cavalry be the mainstay of the army. Ranjit had seen the devastating effect that well drilled and disciplined infantry could have against a cavalry force. The core of the army would therefore be the infantry backed by powerful artillery. The cavalry would be little more than an auxiliary force. The infantry would be organised and drilled in the European manner. The artillery would be armed with the best cannon, many being of a heavier calibre than any cast by a European power. To aid this transformation, foreign generals and adventurers from the west were welcomed and paid generous allowances. Experienced generals from America, France and Italy with experience of the Napoleonic Wars were recruited and their skills inculcated into the fast evolving Lahore army. Over the years a small army of Europeans, eager for the generous salaries paid by the Maharaja, flocked to enter into his service.

At the time of his death on 27 June 1839, the Lahore state possessed an army consisting of just under 47,000 regular infantry and around 16,000 regular and irregular cavalry, in addition to a formidable artillery comprising almost 500 guns.

A Period of Anarchy

After building an empire with the limited resources at his disposal, Ranjit Singh left his sons a powerful and wealthy state with the finest army in Asia. While he had been alive, his considerable personality had kept the disparate elements in the kingdom together. But none of his successors found themselves capable of the task of guiding and maintaining the state. Kharak Singh, his eldest son, was a poor ruler, lacking in intellect. His son Nau Nihal Singh quickly displaced him, only to die in suspicious circumstances on the same day his father was cremated. Sher Singh, another of Ranjit's sons, ruled for two years but with such a *laissez-faire* attitude that the army quickly became conscious of its position as the ultimate arbiter. Following the death of Sher Singh, power no longer resided in the *durbar* or court but in the military committees called *punchayats* that were elected by the common soldiery.

The descent into anarchy after Ranjit Singh's death was as rapid as the rise in influence of the army as leadership passed violently from one aspirant to another. Each ruler paid handsome bribes to the army in return for their support, only to be discarded when another ambitious individual promised greater reward. The army had little regard for these men, intervening only because a nominal leadership was required to run the state, and generous rewards were available during these interventions. Those in power, however, feared the army. Dependent on the whims of the *punchayats*, they had little room for manoeuvre. The intrigues lasted until September 1845 when Vizier Jowahir Singh, the brother of the Queen Regent Maharani Jindan, was summoned in front of the assembled army at Lahore and brutally murdered in the act of offering a considerable amount of treasure for his life. With the death of Jowahir Singh, the personalities that would steer the state during the coming war with the British now came to the fore.

Around 8 November 1845, Lal Singh, a Brahmin of little ability and an unsuitable candidate given the seriousness of the situation, was given the role of Vizier or Prime Minister by Maharani Jindan, the mother of Dhuleep Singh, now the only surviving son of Ranjit Singh after the years of strife. Lal Singh had previously achieved the lowly position of a *moonshee* (secretary) at the Lahore court. His father had been elevated to a high position by the former minister Dhian Singh before his assassination, and was given the responsibility for managing the tax revenue from Kashmir. Heera Singh, another minister, treated him as a favourite and raised Lal Singh to the role of treasurer at Lahore, also making him Raja of Rhotas and Domelia. But, intriguing with Maharani Jindan against Heera Singh, Lal was among those who orchestrated the minister's death. Largely due to his close relations with the Maharani, he was raised to the highest position in the state.

Alongside Lal Singh, General Tej Singh was made Commander-in-Chief of the Sikh army. Originally from Meerut in British territory, he had joined his uncle Khushal Singh, the court chamberlain in the Sikh state. Tej Singh was quickly raised to the position of General in 1819 and gained considerable military experience over the years in campaigns against the Afghans at Mankera, Leiah and Derjat and in Kashmir prior to being given the post of Governor of Peshawar district. At the age of forty-six, he would now lead the Sikh army.

In Kashmir, power rested with Gulab Singh, a powerful vassal of the Sikh state who had made himself virtually independent during the recent troubles. Gulab had succeeded his father Raja Kishore Singh in 1822 as ruler of Jammu. Having served in many campaigns, notably Multan in 1816, Dera Ghazi Khan in 1821 and at the Battle of Shaid, putting down a revolt organised by the fanatic Muslim preacher Sayyid Ahmed, he had gained a trusted position within the Sikh government. By the age of fifty-three, he had quietly consolidated his position in Kashmir with his own army of 10,000 men.

Curiously, none of this ruling triumvirate of Lal Singh, Tej Singh and Gulab Singh happened to be Sikh or Punjabi for that matter, but they had risen to high office through the even-handed policies of Ranjit Singh. Beyond loyalty to their now dead patron, they had little natural fidelity to the Sikh state itself. The intrigues and personal ambitions of these men and their relationship with the increasingly assertive Sikh army would form the backdrop to the First Anglo-Sikh War.

Across the River Sutlej, changes in the British administration were also taking place. In 1844, Sir Henry Hardinge had succeeded to the post of Governor-General of India replacing his brother-in-law, Lord Ellenborough. Hardinge was an experienced military man, having served in Canada and the Peninsular War, notably at Vimiera, Corunna, Albuera and Vitoria. He was wounded at the battle of Ligny shortly before Waterloo and had thus been absent from that great battle. After the war, Hardinge had entered politics, becoming the Member of Parliament for Durham in 1820. In 1828, he was offered and accepted the position of Secretary for War in the Duke of Wellington's government. Following two stints in the post of Chief Secretary of Ireland, and now aged sixty, he was offered and had accepted the Governor-Generalship of India.

Hardinge's Commander-in-Chief was the ageing but experienced Sir Hugh Gough, who had succeeded Sir Jasper Nicolls. Gough had joined the army in 1794 and had fought in South Africa and the Caribbean before also fighting under Wellington in the Peninsular War in the battles of Talavera, where he was badly wounded, Barrosa and Vitoria among others. Gough reached India in 1837 but was sent shortly afterwards to China as Commander-in-Chief of the British forces after the end of the First Opium

War. He returned to India in August 1843 assuming the role of Commander-in-Chief of British forces in India. Shortly after this, he defeated the Marathas at Maharajpur in the Gwalior campaign. By 1845, Gough was sixty-six years old but still vigorous, although his old-style Napoleonic tactics of a straight bayonet charge would later come into question. Neither Gough nor Hardinge was averse to conflict if circumstances and the preparations of the British army allowed.

Causes of the War

Friendly relations with the British gradually broke down during the times of trouble after Ranjit Singh's death. The internal discord of the Lahore state did little to impress the British and the opportunity for expansion was not overlooked. As early as 1841, a war with Lahore was being mooted. Lord Ellenborough, then Governor-General, raised the issue with the Duke of Wellington, writing: 'I am most anxious to have your opinion as to the general principles upon which a campaign against that country should be conducted'. Sir Henry Hardinge, his successor, wrote to Ellenborough in turn in January 1845, mulling over the timing of any action and the need for a suitable *casus belli*:

> Even if we had a case for devouring our ally in adversity, we are not ready and could not be ready until the hot winds set in, and the Sutlej became a torrent. Moderation will do us no harm, if in the interval the hills and the plains weaken each other; but on what plea could we attack the Punjab, if this were the month of October and we had our army in readiness?

Confident of British military strength, Ellenborough, followed by Hardinge in 1845, launched a series of hostile moves that concerned Lahore territory. In 1843, the British government ordered the construction of sixty iron boats at Bombay designed to be used as a bridge across the Sutlej as and when the British government desired to cross into Lahore territory. All had crews of thirteen *lascars* and were equipped with baulks, chesses, cables and anchors and other gear required for the building of a bridge. Eleven of the boats were armed with cannon. Of considerable size, forty-seven feet in length and twelve feet in breadth, these were designed to provide a double roadway across the river, capable of carrying the heaviest of British artillery. Constructed to allow an interval of twenty-six feet between boats, a bridge as long as 700 metres could be quickly established where necessary. This was in addition to Pasley pontoons complete with wagons collected at Ferozepore near the Sutlej that could be used to build fourteen rafts to aid a crossing. Fifty-four of these boats reached the Sutlej in the summer of 1845, the other six being lost in transit. These were now provocatively stationed at the Khunda ghat near Ferozepore, only sixty kilometres from the Sikh capital. Although the armed nature of the boats made their purpose clear, Major George Broadfoot, the local political agent at Ferozepore, was confidentially advised prior to their arrival to assure the Sikh authorities that the boats were only required for carrying grain from Ferozepore to Sukker. Once the boats reached Ferozepore, they were moored in a creek about two miles from the city under heavy guard. The crews of the boats were set to training of the building of the bridge. The boats now allowed the British to cross the river at short notice and posed for the Sikh kingdom the serious threat of a surprise attack. Capt. William Humbley of the 9th Royal Lancers, in his account of the eve of the war, wrote:

> Major Broadfoot who was charged with its [the boat bridge] transport aroused the suspicion of the Sikhs and in their opinion virtually acknowledged that hostilities existed between them and the British by manifesting extraordinary vigilance for its safe keeping, placing it under the escort of a strong guard of soldiers and by employing the pontoniers to construct it on the arrival of the boats at Ferozepore.

When hostilities seemed inevitable, and three days prior to the Sikh army crossing the Sutlej, the boats were sunk in a secluded creek of the river, small holes, two inches square, being cut into their hulls allowing for easy repair and for subsequent refloating when required for the crossing.

A year before hostilities, another incident, minor in itself but indicative of a more expansionist British policy, occurred near Ferozepore. A small island in the middle of the Sutlej belonging to Lahore was seized by the British. The conventions of the time made the island Lahore territory beyond doubt as the deeper channel of the Sutlej flowed on the British side. Sikh protests produced little response. Prior to this, in October 1844, the British had appointed Major Broadfoot as the British agent at Ludhiana responsible for the Sutlej area. Broadfoot had an abrasive character unfitted for the delicate position he occupied, and his new position marked a significant downturn in Anglo-Sikh relations. One of his first acts as agent was to declare, without discussion with Lahore, the Sikh estates south of the Sutlej as subject to escheat in favour of the British government should the Lahore dynasty come to an end. Several months later, in March 1845, Broadfoot intervened again and worsened relations. A Sikh magistrate crossing the Sutlej to service the Sikh-controlled area south of the river was prevented from carrying out his duties. Broadfoot had ordered him back across the Sutlej and had fired at the party, an action that caused considerable anger in Lahore. The Sikh troops with the magistrate were stopped from firing back by their commander. Early in November 1845, two villages near Ludhiana belonging to Lahore were seized by Broadfoot for the British. His defence in sequestrating this territory was that there were criminals in the villages that had not been given up to the British authorities. Captain Joseph D. Cunningham, the assistant political agent under Broadfoot, later cited the seizure of this Lahore territory as the spark that led to war.

A more candid view of British intentions relating to the Punjab was let slip by Sir Charles Napier, the conqueror of Sind and future Commander-in-Chief of the British forces in India, in the *Delhi Gazette* shortly before the war. Talking about conditions in Sind to the south of Punjab, he mentioned a war with Lahore as practically decided bar the timing: 'If they [the robber tribes of Sind] were allowed to remain undisturbed while Scinde was quiet, they would become turbulent and troublesome when the British Army was called on to move into the Punjaub.' Napier's indication that a decision to advance into the Punjab had already been made was widely circulated in the Lahore *durbar* and around the villages and cities of the Punjab. This, along with continual British encroachment on Sikh territory, was a source of great anxiety to Lahore and its people. In the minds of the common man and soldier in the Punjab, war was now inevitable. After the war, Napier confirmed this during his conversations with Francois Mouton, a Frenchman under Sikh service: 'Mouton told me that the *Delhi Gazette* made the Sikhs cross the river. It said we were going to attack them. All the Sikhs read it and other papers, and they said, well, as we must fight let us do so on the left bank.'

Alongside the encroachment came the inexorable build-up of British troops on the Sutlej. Ferozepore, the furthest British outpost, had been made a British cantonment in 1838. In 1842 it was made a brigade command. By late 1845, the British garrison comprised eight regiments (one European) of infantry, two regiments of cavalry, two troops of field battery and a reserve company of artillery. In addition, two more native regiments, the 27th and 63rd Native Infantry were also advancing from Moradabad and Sind respectively to bolster the garrison. Ludhiana, further upstream of the Sutlej, had already been a British military post since 1809. There were also reinforcements and munitions for the British positions in Sind to the south of the Punjab, many more than were needed for simply policing the area. Lord Ellenborough summed up the changing British policy towards Lahore: 'Let our policy [towards the Sikhs] be what it may, the contest must come at last, and the intervening time that may be given to us should be employed in unostentatious but vigilant preparation.'

No section of the population was more infuriated by the British build-up across the river than the Sikh army. The Sikh soldiery, confident of their own strength, began talking about a future contest with the British, firstly to protect the Lahore state and secondly to drive the British out of India. The disastrous retreat by the British army from Afghanistan in 1842 seemed to prove to them how overstretched British power was and how easily it could be humbled by a determined foe. Capt. Humbley, in his account of the pre-war period, records the feeling among the Sikh military:

> The Sikh soldiery used to assemble in groups round the tomb of Runjeet Singh, vowing to defend with their lives all that belonged to the commonwealth of Govind – that they would never suffer the kingdom of Lahore to be occupied by the British strangers, but stand ready to march or give the invaders battle on their own ground.

There was a feeling among the soldiers that the army had

been ready for some time to challenge the British, and that the previously adventurous Ranjit Singh had only been prevented from marching on Delhi by his age and increasingly enfeebled state prior to his death. 'The *khalsa* had great ambitions for which it was fully equipped. Their part was to achieve them,' the soldiers were heard to say to the officers. Meanwhile, extracts echoing this view began to be given out in the cantonments and streets of Lahore by *Akali* soldiers enthusiastic for war. Written in them were various prophesies. A more popular one read: 'The army of the Guru shall sit on the throne at Delhi; the fly-whisk shall be waived over its head and it shall have everything according to its desire.'

Despite the hostile intentions of the British, there was little immediate desire for war among either the Sikh army or in the minds of Governor-General Hardinge or Commander-in-Chief Gough. Nor did the British think there was a probability of the Sikh army crossing south of the Sutlej. It was generally thought that the initiative for launching a war could be taken as and when it was deemed that the British army was good and ready for an invasion of the Punjab.

Destruction of an Army

By late 1845, the army *punchayats* at Lahore were too well experienced in exercising power to abandon it of their own accord. The Sikh army of that period is often compared to the Praetorian guard of Ancient Rome or perhaps the Janissaries of the Ottoman Sultan during their worst excesses. The difficulties of the Lahore state ran much deeper, however. While the Praetorians and Janissaries were elite bodyguard units that the head of state could destroy and still retain the affection of the main body of the army with generous rewards, the Sikh army had become a wholly republican force with the generals having only the most nominal control over their troops. It was the common soldiery that elected the *punchayats* and therefore held ultimate power. For the ruling clique to wrest power from the army would mean the wholesale destruction of the common soldiery and nothing less.

Meanwhile the rule of the soldiers continued to weaken the state. Soldiers looted and robbed as they liked, extracting money from the general population. The *kardars*, state officials, were unable to collect tax revenue from anyone who had a relative or friend in the army. Any tax revenue that was collected was stolen from them by roving soldiers. Many soldiers were absenting themselves from their cantonments for lengthy periods while they went on vendettas or carried out looting. Rarely were more than a quarter of soldiers in the barracks and their officers dared not order a roll-call. All around the state, soldiers enrolled their kinsmen for the high salaries now available and the size of the army consequently ballooned beyond control. The only section of the army that had refused to mutiny until now was the *Fauj-i-khas*, the elite brigade of the army stationed at Lahore. Shortly after the murder of Jowahir Singh, the Vizier, the regular army *punchayats*, fearing the still loyal brigade, pressured the generals into ordering the *Fauj-i-khas* to faraway Peshawar so they would have complete sway in the capital. At this stage, the *Fauj-i-khas*, realising the machinations in high places, also broke into open revolt and thus the last vestiges of discipline faded. Eventually Maharani Jindan persuaded them to move away from the capital after offering the troops four months pay in the latter part of November 1845, the soldiers also giving a promise in writing to end their interference in matters of state at the *samadh* (shrine) of Ranjit Singh. Between 23 and 27 November, all the troops situated in the capital – namely the brigades of Sirdar Mehtab Singh, Sirdar Bahadhur Singh, the *Fauj-i-khas* and the irregular cavalry – moved out to the nearby villages of Malikpur, Roar and Dhaori. The promise was short-lived, however, and by 29 November they began to abuse their officers again. The matter of the eighteen *lakhs* of treasure, belonging to Raja Suchet Singh but still held by the British at Ferozepore, was raised. In Dewan Ajudya Parshad's view, the British possession of the treasure was the immediate cause for war.

The Lahore *durbar* for the last few years had been using the dubious method of liberal bribes to keep what little order there was. So much so, in fact, that since the years after Ranjit Singh's death, the monthly pay of a soldier had increased to fourteen rupees, double that of the salary of a British sepoy and beyond the capability of the state to pay indefinitely. By late 1845, the treasury was nearly empty and the army ever more unruly and demanding. The situation was fast coming to a head. In earlier years and with more distinguished leadership, control of the army could have been wrested from the army committees. To the current ruling clique, possessing none of the administrative skills and authority required to retrieve the situation, and with little loyalty to the Sikh state, the safety of British rule now seemed all the more attractive compared to the uncertainties of challenging the demands of the *punchayats*. Their thoughts now turned to how the destruction or dismemberment of the state with British military assistance could benefit them personally. Tej Singh, the Commander-in-Chief, admitted as much to Dr John Honigberger, the east European doctor at Lahore who wrote later that Tej Singh had 'made to me the candid confession that in circumstances like those to which the country was reduced no other remedy was left for its salvation but to surrender it to the English'. Meanwhile, Gulab Singh had already written in March 1845 to the British Governor-General via Broadfoot, the political agent at Ferozepore, suggesting that the Punjab should be invaded. He had promised 50 *lakh* rupees from his own pocket and the assistance of his own army to help in this venture if the British government would confirm him as Maharaja of an independent state carved out of Lahore.

The state could not be surrendered of course until the Sikh army had been destroyed. So sometime in early November 1845, it was decided by the ruling clique that the army would be led to war against the British. Recent aggressive moves by the British ensured the general acceptance and enthusiasm among all sections of Punjab society and Sikh soldiery for war. This would be no war of conquest, however, but one organised specifically to annihilate the recalcitrant Sikh army.

British preparations were as yet incomplete and therefore the Sikh army would be restrained from taking any opportunities that presented themselves. Once the Rubicon of the River Sutlej was crossed, the army would be kept in a defensive posture until the bulk of the British army could make its way in strength from Ambala and Delhi and rendezvous with the various garrisons on the border and other converging reinforcements. In line with this, the British garrisons and cantonments at Ferozepore, Ludhiana, Kasauli and Sabathu, each held with relatively small garrisons and within easy reach of the Sikh army, would not be attacked. The campaign would be waged as passively as circumstances allowed. In any future collisions with the British force, the Sikh army would be kept in a strictly defensive position, refusing any advantages and opportunities that presented themselves during the ebb and flow of battle. Food and ammunition supplies to the army would be delivered as fitfully as possible. In addition, the plans of battle, the locations of Sikh forces, and details of any entrenchments would be communicated to the British. Channels of communication had already been opened with Capt. Peter Nicholson, the assistant political agent stationed at Ferozepore, George Broadfoot, his senior, having gone to Ambala. In short, everything would be done to hamper the Sikh army short of raising the suspicions of the soldiery. It was thought that with as much assistance as the ruling clique dared to give to the British, the Sikh army could be rapidly destroyed and the grateful conquerors, upon being given such vast new territories, would be content to let the collaborators continue to run the state, albeit under British supremacy. And so, on 17 November 1845, war was made certain as troops and supplies began to be readied for a crossing of the Sutlej.

PART ONE
THE CAMPAIGN

I

Crossing of the Sutlej

[The Sikhs were] marching to destruction under the guidance of false and incompetent men.

– Sir Lepel Henry Griffin

Strength of the Sikh Army

The Sikh army had grown rapidly since Ranjit Singh's death and by the close of 1845 amounted to just under 100,000 men. This included 53,756 regular infantry, 6,235 and 16,292 regular and irregular cavalry respectively, and an artillery arm of 10,968 men. Not included in this figure were the tens of thousands of irregulars and levies that the prominent *Sirdars* (court leaders) could bring to battle. Enthusiasm and loyalty from villagers throughout the Punjab for the defence of their state could not be ignored. Numerous volunteers could be counted upon to fight with the army or as skirmishers. In practice, however, only a fraction of the available military resources was utilised. The decision was made to split the army up into seven divisions, one to go to Peshawar to the north-west, one to stay at Lahore and the other five to march against the British. Gulab Singh, the *de facto* ruler of Kashmir, would meanwhile keep his army of some 10,000 men from reinforcing the Sikh force.

Strong contingents of the Sikh army had moved to within three miles of the Sutlej on 9 December 1845. On the following day, more regiments arrived, the Sikhs using the route from Lahore to Khan Kurman with the whole army crossing south on the night of 11 December. The portion of the army under the Vizier Lal Singh crossed at Harike using the fords nearby and the available riverboats. Tej Singh's force used the Nughar ghat further downstream and at Attaree, close to Ferozepore. There a local Jemadar in charge of the British boats at Ferozepore had provided the boats he had for the crossing for which he was well rewarded. At this point, as a demonstration of who carried ultimate authority, the *punchayats* ordered the officers, who ordinarily did not carry firearms, to carry muskets like the foot soldiers thus further reducing any authority they still held.

Accounts vary as to the strength of the army that crossed over the Sutlej. The most reliable source is J. D. Cunningham who estimated 35-40,000 men with 150 guns. However, half of these were irregulars or cavalry with only around 20,000 men being regular infantry soldiers, the backbone of the army. The diary that Capt. Peter Nicholson, the assistant British political agent of Ferozepore, kept before his death at Ferozeshah gives us a valuable insight into the communication between the Sikh commanders and the British agent. Included in these dialogues and letters was information from Lal Singh giving a detailed breakdown of the Sikh army that had either crossed or was still crossing around 18 December. According to Nicholson, twelve battalions of infantry regulars, around 7,200 men, marched to Ferozeshah. With these were 8,000 irregular cavalry and 9,812 other troops, which made a total strength of around 25,000. This included a thousand *Nihangs*. At Ferozepore, Tej Singh commanded a force of twenty-seven battalions comprising around 16,200 men with 2,200 cavalrymen. This would mean a total force of about 43,000 men, assuming a battalion strength of 600 men. But this was not always the case; some battalions had lower numbers. So, Cunningham's figures of 35-40,000 men would seem to be broadly accurate.

Division of the Sikh Army

On the south banks of the Sutlej, the Sikh army was now in close proximity to a number of as yet vulnerable British strongholds. The nearest held British outpost to Harike was Ferozepore, just thirty-five kilometres to the south-west, commanded by Major-General John Littler with 7,000 men and twelve guns. The force consisted of HM 62nd Foot, the 12th, 14th, 27th, 33rd, 54th and 63rd Bengal Native Infantry with the 8th Native Light Cavalry and the 3rd Irregular Cavalry, along with two troops of horse artillery and two light field batteries. Only one of the eight infantry regiments, HM 62nd Foot was European and expected to fight well. The city contained considerable supplies and treasure. Ninety kilometres to the south-west lay Bussean, the main British supply depot readied for the advancing British force. Broadfoot, the British agent at Ludhiana, had procured considerable supplies here in anticipation of the forthcoming campaign against the Punjab. These were also at present poorly guarded due to the unexpected crossing of the Sikh army. In addition to this, other supply depots had also been set up further south at 20-mile intervals. Ninety kilometres to the east of the main Sikh force, Ranjodh Singh already held the Sikh fortress of Phillour opposite Ludhiana, a British garrison town. The British held the city with a small garrison of 5,000 men under Brigadier H. M. Wheeler consisting of HM 50th Foot and the 11th, 26th, 42nd, 48th and 73rd Bengal Native Infantry along with two troops of horse artillery and one regiment of native cavalry. Similar to the Ferozepore garrison, only one of the six regiments, HM 50th, was European.

Neither the Ferozepore nor the Ludhiana garrisons were expected to put up significant resistance against the overwhelmingly strong Sikh force that had now crossed. With the swift capture of Ferozepore, the Sikh army could sweep towards Ambala, destroying Bussean en route. In the east, after the reduction of Ludhiana, Ranjodh Singh could either effect a junction with the main Sikh force or march east to destroy the small British garrisons at Subathu and Kasauli. The destruction or capture of the garrisons at Ferozepore and Ludhiana with a combined strength of 12,000 men would mean Gough, the British Commander-in-Chief who was now at Ambala 250 kilometres to the south-east, would have to rely on the force of around 10,000 men he had with him, assuming Bussean was still in British hands. If the depot was destroyed by the Sikh army, supplies would have to be sent from Meerut and Delhi, meaning further delays and lengthy supply lines for a British advance. Alternatively, he would wait for reinforcements from Meerut and Delhi. This would also entail further delays. Meanwhile, and unopposed, the Sikh army could move southwards, capturing the states under British protection south of the Sutlej.

There were other tangible benefits to moving rapidly against the British outposts. The destruction of the British forces at Ferozepore and Ludhiana would damage British military reputation. British power relied heavily on the fidelity of the vast native sepoy army and the co-operation of native rulers. This fidelity was in turn bolstered by the supposed invincibility of the British military. Thus any significant setbacks or defeats were highly undesirable from a British perspective. Other Indian rulers with ambitions to throw off the foreign yoke would be encouraged to try their luck if early setbacks were encountered by the British. Any advance was a moot point, however. The Sikh army would make very little movement in keeping with the pacifist policy of the Sikh commanders. For the campaign, the army that had crossed would be split into three forces. One contingent led by Tej Singh and consisting of the brigades of Khan Singh Mann, Shumsher Singh, Chutter Singh, Mewa Singh, Rattan Singh Mann – plus artillery and other regiments – was to lay siege to Ferozepore. The main army led by Lal Singh and consisting of the *Fauj-i-khas*, Mehtab Singh and Bhahadhur Singh's brigades, plus the irregular forces and cavalry, would be held at the village of Ferozeshah a short distance from Ferozepore. This force would be further split, with a smaller force to be sent to face the bulk of the British force as it marched towards Ferozepore. A hundred kilometres to the east, the army under Ranjodh Singh at Phillour, opposite Ludhiana, would remain static and not take part in the battles against the main British army near Ferozepore. Thus, by the time of the first meeting of the two armies, the Sikh force would find itself divided into four separate contingents at Mudki, Ferozeshah, Ferozepore and at Phillour.

Immediately after the crossing, Tej Singh had sent word to Nicholson, the political agent at Ferozepore, restating his loyalty to the British and asking for instructions. Nicholson had already sent a message back saying that on no account should Ferozepore be attacked and that the Sikh force should await the arrival of Gough's force. Tej Singh duly moved forward and stationed the army in a wide arc on the north and western side of the British cantonments at Ferozepore by 13 December. As per Nicholson's instructions, there was no attempt to either attack or encircle the British base. The route to the south was left open should Littler, the British commanding officer at Ferozepore, wish to retreat. Meanwhile the main army under Lal Singh moved south to Khool and Sultan Khan Walla before setting up camp at the small village of Ferozeshah to await Gough's main force.

In the British camp, news of the impending crossing of the Sikh army had already reached Littler at Ferozepore prior to 11 December. In addition, Mouton, the Frenchman in Sikh service, had been in the city since September on a spying mission and had successfully evaded capture and recrossed the river. The garrison was put on a high state of alert. Orders were given that no soldier should travel further than a mile away from the cantonments. Moreover, pickets were quadrupled and sixty rounds of ammunition each was supplied to the entire garrison. It is unclear if Littler knew about the Sikh commanders working in unison with Nicholson as after four days of inactivity from Tej Singh, Littler decided to challenge him in spite of the odds. He had but a few guns to oppose the Sikh force and even fewer gunners. Some entrenchments had already been dug around the cantonments prior to the breakout of war but these were incomplete.

Nevertheless, on 15 December, leaving the 27th and 63rd Native Infantry regiments and reserve artillery to guard the city, Littler marched out with his small force, but without any guns. Crossing the large *nullah* near the city and behind the city bazaar, two miles to the south-west of the city and cantonments, he came into view of the Sikh army. Seeing Littler's force, Tej Singh promptly ordered the Sikh line to retreat. At this point, Littler, not wishing to advance further towards Sikh lines that easily outflanked him on both sides, also turned back to the cantonments. Tej Singh's refusal to do battle angered the Sikh soldiers, who were unaware of his real intentions. When questioned by his soldiers as to why they were not destroying the token British force in front of them, Tej Singh is reported to have said that the reduction of such a small force was beneath them and the more glorious prospect of fighting the Governor-General and the main British army should be their aim. The chance to destroy the garrison was not lost, however. Littler would somewhat recklessly advance with his small army for several subsequent days, always failing to draw Tej Singh into a contest. Pte Joseph Hewitt with the 62nd Foot was one of the soldiers in Littler's force; he recorded the daily ritual of the two armies:

> We could plainly see them [Sikh soldiers] although they were the other side of the plain, as there were not any trees of any sort, only low growing shrubs like ether, and about four miles across it, when they saw we were out and marching towards them they turned about and so did we and went back to camp. Several times we had to turn out in the same manner.

Finally, on 16 December, Littler, possibly learning of Tej Singh's working in concert with Nicholson, wrote to Gough saying he had given up all idea of facing the Sikh army and would remain on the defensive. The following day, meanwhile, more Sikh reinforcements crossed over at Nughar ghat.

Bivouac at Ferozeshah

South of the Sutlej, two main thoroughfares ran from the east to west, connecting Ferozepore to the east Cis-Sutlej area of Punjab. These lay almost thirty kilometres apart and yet roughly parallel for much of the way. The northern route from Ropar passed close by the Sutlej, reaching Ludhiana and Dhurmkote before Ferozepore. The southern route moved past Khurur and Latalla, Bussean, Wudnee, and Mudki before turning north-west to join up with the northern route to Ferozepore. The southern route was the most direct route from Ambala and would undoubtedly be the route that would be used by Gough in any advance. The village of Ferozeshah lay a short distance from the route and just twelve kilometres east of Tej Singh's army at Ferozepore. So the main Sikh army established its camp at the village. The *Fauj-i-khas* made their camp to the west of the village with the rest of the army to the south and east of the village. Lal Singh and the officers set up their tents in the centre of the camp. Here the army awaited the arrival of the British force.

The fact that Ferozeshah lay on or near the path of the British route to Ferozepore meant little in itself. With the Sikh army static in its camp, Gough could simply swing a few miles further south from Ferozeshah in order to complete the junction with Littler's force at Ferozepore. In addition, the village itself gave little tactical advantage, situated as it was amid jungle. What Ferozeshah did have was a plentiful supply of water with many large wells in the village whereas the area around the village had none. In the extreme heat of the Punjab plains, this would prove to be of paramount importance.

The British Advance North

The news of the Sikh army crossing south of the Sutlej reached the British camp at Ambala, 250 kilometres from Ferozepore, on the following day. The day after, the Governor-General of India issued his declaration of war against Lahore. Gough had 10,000 troops immediately available at Ambala under Major-General Walter Gilbert. These consisted of the 3rd Light Dragoons, HM 9th, 31st and 80th Foot, the 4th and 5th Light Cavalry, the Governor-General's bodyguard, along with the 16th, 24th, 41st, 45th and 47th Bengal Native Infantry. With the Sikh commanders refraining from attacking the outlying British outposts, Gough could count on HM 29th Foot and 1st Bengal European regiments at Kassauli and Subathu respectively in the foothills of the Himalayas and the 5,000 men stationed at Ludhiana under Brigadier Wheeler.

Therefore the three main contingents of the army at Ferozepore, Ludhiana and Ambala, once unified, would total a combined force of 22,000 with more units joining as the campaign wore on. These extra units were principally the 9,000 men at Meerut, including 9th and 16th Lancers, 3rd Light Cavalry and HM 10th Foot with twenty-six guns and two Ghurkha regiments at Simla and Dehra Dun. In addition, Sir Charles Napier, commanding British forces in Sind to the south of the Punjab, had 15,000 men and eighty-six cannon at his disposal and would shortly march north to join Gough's force.

Despite Tej Singh refraining from an attack on Ferozepore, the possibility of the Sikh troops overriding their commander's wishes could not be discounted and Gough now moved the British force towards the settlement with all possible haste. The daily marches were doubled along with the rations for European and native sepoy troops. Leaving Ambala on 12 December, Gough's force reached

Rajpura, a march of sixteen miles, on the same day. On the 13th, he reached Sirhind, eighteen miles away. On the 14th, Aisru, twenty miles away. On the 15th, the British army reached Latalla, south of Ludhiana, marching thirty miles. On the 16th, they marched through the villages of Bheni, Bission, Riakote, Bussean, Jetpoora, Manuke, Mullah, Rusoolpur, Loop and onto Wudnee, another thirty-mile march. At Bussean, Gough's force was united with the Governor-General bringing forces from Ludhiana. The town was large with a population of around 2,500 and around 500 houses with twenty shops. Camp followers commenced sacking the place as they passed through, despite Bussean being British territory. Gough left all heavy baggage at the town, there being a large depot for commissariat supplies. Broadfoot had accumulated considerable supplies here for the army amounting to 4,300,000 rounds of ball (musketry) cartridges along with round shot, shrapnel, canister and grape.

Wudnee, fifteen miles from Bussean, would be the first meeting point for the two sides. The village was also quite large, around 400 houses with a population of around 2,000 and a fort sitting to its west. A solid brick construction, square in shape, a hundred yards long in each direction with a second rampart before it and encircled by a deep ditch, it was held by a garrison of seventy Sikh soldiers; but it lacked cannon. There could be no possibility of prolonged resistance against the British force. Nevertheless, the garrison refused to surrender. Musket fire was directed at any British soldier who happened to venture close assuming the fort had already fallen into British hands. Count Oriolo, one of the staff of Prince Waldemaar of Prussia, a guest of Hardinge who was accompanying the British advance, nearly fell victim as he approached the fort. The garrison refrained from firing on James Coley, an unarmed army chaplain who had also sauntered close by to the fort. Coley relates the understandably cool reception he received from soldiers and villagers:

> In the course of my wanderings this morning, I passed twice under the fort, and attempted once to enter, but the gate was shut, and a man from inside told me there was no admission. This I did in perfect ignorance of the state of things. The villagers looked sour and surly; nor did I like the appearance of the men with their matchlocks at the

top of the fort. I asked them where the Lord Sahib (name by which the natives call the Governor-General) was; in answer to which they growled something; the only word to which I could comprehend was 'Farungee'. They did not fire at me though I was quite alone; and had it been an hour or two earlier, I might have encountered the same sort of salutation as Count Oriolo and perhaps not have escaped so well.

Furthermore, the villagers refused to sell supplies to the British army. In the event, Gough decided not to expend time and effort reducing the fort but to march on, anxious to reach Ferozepore and join forces with Littler. A rearguard, however, was left behind at Wudnee. The village was also the scene of the first casualty of the conflict. A certain James Brockeman of the 50th Regiment, carelessly assuming the fort had fallen into British hands, was shot by the Wudnee garrison while returning to Ludhiana for his baggage. The fort garrison would only surrender on 30 December after the Battle of Ferozeshah and when all hope of succour from the Sikh army had vanished; the British then seized 5,000 rupees and a few half-starved horses as their prize. Two companies of the 59th Native Infantry would be left to garrison the fort.

By this time, news of Tej Singh's success at restraining the Sikh troops from attacking Ferozepore had reached Gough and the daily march was shortened to rest the army. It was also known that the Sikh army was in the vicinity and a confrontation could soon take place. On 17 December, a march of ten miles to Chirruk near Bhuga Purana was completed. Starting early the following day, the British force commenced their advance towards Mudki, twenty-one miles from Chirruk.

2

Mudki

There, your Excellency, is the Sikh army.
                    – Major George Broadfoot to Sir Hugh Gough

Preliminaries

News of the approach of the British had reached the Sikh camp the previous evening. Rather than moving the whole of the Sikh army forward from Ferozeshah, Lal Singh took the decision to send only a relatively small contingent to face the approaching British. For this force, Lal Singh ordered a regiment out of every division to be used. Artillery and cavalry were also to be sent. The force was too strong for reconnaissance and too weak in infantry and artillery for a proper contest with the main British force. There must have been some disquiet among the troops as to the obvious folly of this decision and Lal Singh's desire for success. Gough's force was not yet strong enough to face the combined strength of the Sikh army. Nevertheless, only the small Sikh force set out for Mudki at around noon and reached Lohaum a short time before the British vanguard there, the cavalry kicking up dust that was visible from the advancing British lines. The Sikh army proceeded to set up the line of battle facing Mudki, five kilometres south-west of Lohaum. A small Sikh advance guard occupied Mudki village itself. The village fort, a small construction which usually held a garrison of 160 troops, was also occupied. As advanced British units began arriving at the village around midday, these pickets and the garrison abandoned the fort, apart from a few men, thus alerting the main Sikh force as to the British arrival. The bulk of the British army began drifting in between 3.00 and 4.00 p.m. British vedettes had also signalled the close proximity of the Sikh army and Gough had ordered the last few miles of marching to be done in battle order.

Mudki was a substantial village composed of around 600 houses with a population of 4,000 people and several substantial *havelis*, private mansions, marking it as a residence of persons with substantial means. The marching in the extreme heat of the day and the heavy sandy terrain had taken a heavy toll on the British soldiers. In addition to this, there was little water to be had from Chirruk to Mudki. As each unit struggled into the village, there was a general stampede towards the village lake as Herbert Edwardes, aide de camp to Sir Hugh Gough, later recalled:

> Beneath the walls of the fort spread a wide clear tank of water; and the reader who has not the memory of that long march of twenty-one miles, with heavy sand underfoot and the air thick with dust, disturbed by fifteen thousand men cannot paint the eagerness with which men and horses rushed to the bank and tried to slake a thirst which seemed unquenchable. In ten minutes the lake was a mass of floating mud, yet fresh regiments kept coming up, and fresh thirsty souls kept squeezing their way in, and thinking it was the sweetest draught they had tasted in their lives.

The rapid advance of the army had meant all commissariat food supplies were trailing many miles behind, and most of the British soldiers had had nothing to eat since marching commenced. The few rations that had reached the advance troops were now eagerly opened. Some of the advance units also began to pitch their tents; the camp encircled the village in a giant square with the bulk of the camp to the west of the village pitched on cultivated land and facing west towards Lohaum.

While the British troops satisfied their thirst, an investigation of the village found the gates of the village fort were closed. Earlier advanced detachments reaching Mudki had been fired upon from the fort ramparts by the small Sikh garrison. Robert Cust (who was the confidential assistant to Major Broadfoot), Major-General

Gilbert and a Captain Mills were deputed to demand the surrender of the fort. However, the garrison had already withdrawn as the advance units of the British army reached the village. As no reply to the demand had been received, a man was tentatively sent over the walls and found the fort unoccupied apart from an elderly shepherd; the bolted gates were then opened for British entry.

Following behind the army, the vast bulk of camp followers had also begun trickling into the village by now and looting had quickly commenced. This had an immediate impact upon the villagers, who closed and secured their shops and houses as best they could. As at Wudnee, the villagers also refused supplies to the British. Cust was given the duty of persuading the local village shopkeepers to reopen their shops so supplies of grain could be bought. In order to encourage co-operation and prevent looting, Cust gave orders placing guards next to the shops whose owners decided to open up their premises. The protection afforded to these shopkeepers had the effect of driving the camp followers to continue their looting around the rest of the village. Controlling the British camp followers – numerically a far bigger force than the frontline soldiers – proved difficult. As thousands more poured into the Mudki, looting created such damage and disorganisation that by 20 December, two days after the battle, Gough gave orders to expel all camp followers from the village. Unable to distinguish camp follower from local, an overzealous officer ordered all people out of the village at the point of the bayonet, effectively leaving the village in a deserted state in which it would remain for several weeks.

First Encounters

A curious conversation involving the Governor-General, Sir Henry Hardinge, took place upon his arrival at the village. Sitting with the Governor-General and some of his staff, Cust records Hardinge asking his staff whether the people of England would consider an actual invasion of the British frontier a sufficient justification of a war. The Governor-General appears to have had doubts over whether he had declared war too hastily. The Sikh army had not ventured into British territory as yet and was still technically in Lahore territory south of the Sutlej. Furthermore, Tej Singh had refused to attack Littler at Ferozepore and the Sikh army had adopted a defensive position at Ferozeshah. The mulling over the rights and wrongs of the campaign was, however, short-lived as news came in of the close proximity of the Sikh army at Lohaum.

What is certain is that with dense jungle and numerous hillocks blocking a clear view of the terrain between Lohaum and Mudki, the two armies never saw each other's positions. Prior to the battle, British vedettes clambered up onto the sandy hillocks near Mudki village and beyond armed with telescopes to get a better view; but they could see no direct evidence of the Sikh army. Yet the huge amount of dust propelled into the air by the cavalry movements of both sides sufficed to give away the location of both armies. Sikh skirmishers had also since clashed with British vedettes moving towards Lohaum.

There are varying accounts of the news reaching the British commander. Sir Henry Havelock's account has Gough, Hardinge and Broadfoot settling down for a meal near the village when news was brought in by an orderly. Upon hearing the news, Broadfoot had commented excitedly, 'The enemy are up us!' Mounting his horse, he had ridden towards Lohaum. On seeing the immense amount of dust spiralling into the air near the Sikh position he rode back and exclaimed to Gough, 'There, your Excellency, is the Sikh army'. Other accounts have Broadfoot already scouting with Christie's horse, the British advance party. Upon seeing Sikh vedettes, he sent a message to Gough informing him that the Sikh army was three miles away from Mudki. Still other accounts tell a different story. A certain Capt. Frederick Haines had been the first to meet the Sikh advance guard. Gough had sent Haines to carry out reconnaissance and he had proceeded to head out west. On the way he had met a Capt. Quinn who had been monitoring the clouds of dust appearing west of Mudki. The message was then sent back to Mudki.

The news of the approach of the Sikh army seems to have caught Gough genuinely by surprise. Spies in the Sikh camp had alerted the British the previous night at Chirruk that a portion of the Sikh army would be moved forward. These reports seem to have been taken lightly by Gough although he had sent cavalry and infantry ahead of his main force as skirmishers and the army now moved in constant readiness. Several sightings of Sikh vedettes had already taken place, although no encounters actually took place before the battle proper. The British troops had neither eaten nor rested sufficiently at this stage. Nevertheless, Gough on the spur of the moment decided on battle despite the fact that night was already fast approaching. As Gough later wrote in his dispatches:

> The troops were in a state of great exhaustion principally from want of water, which was not procurable on the road, when about 3pm, information was received that the Sikh army was advancing, and the troops had scarcely time to get under arms, and move to their positions when the fact was ascertained.

We must assume overconfidence on his part. With the intelligence that only part of the Sikh force was in front of him, his assumption may have been that the battle would be a short one. With Gough anxious to offer battle, there was no time to supply grog to the troops and the British army moved immediately north-west along the Mudki to Lohaum road as and when the units were ready. Such was the amount of the dust in the air caused by the mass movement of British troops and cavalry that eyes could scarcely be kept open and it caused considerable discomfort among the men. Not a few soldiers were sent back to Mudki village for medical treatment.

The Battlefield

The area up to around four kilometres west of Mudki was cultivated with corn fields or loose ploughed ground, the boundaries marked with thorny hedges and large thickets. That was until the fork in the road from which point a dense jungle of *kikkar* (tamarisk) trees and thorny bushes suddenly appeared. This belt of jungle extended around a kilometre in depth – the distance from the fork in the road to Lohaum village – and it covered both of the roads heading west from the fork. At Lohaum and to its west, however, the jungle had been cleared. Corporal Cleveland, fighting in the 31st Regiment on the right of the British line, wrote that 'the enemy had taken up their position in a jungle, by which the open space over which we had to pass was nearly surrounded'. This suggests the belt of jungle pushed eastwards towards Mudki on either side of the Mudki to Lohaum road in a broad semicircle.

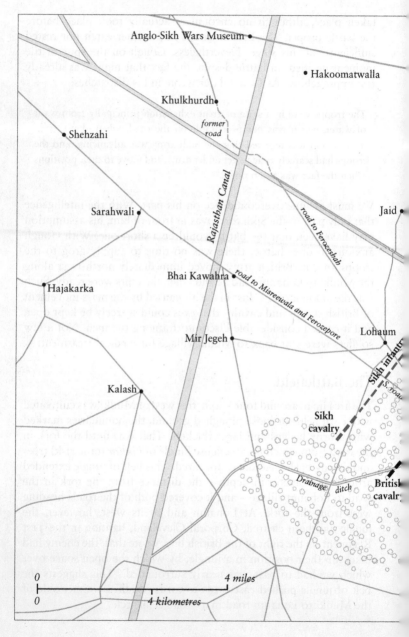

Anglo-Sikh Wars Museum •

• Hakoomatwalla

Khulkhurdh •

former road

• Shehzahi

Rajasthan Canal

Jaid •

road to Ferozeshah

Sarahwali •

road to Misreewala and Ferozepore

Bhai Kawahra •

• Hajakarka

Lohaum •

Mir Jegeh •

Sikh infantry

Kalash •

Sikh cavalry

S. road

Drainage ditch

British cavalry

0   4 miles

0   4 kilometres

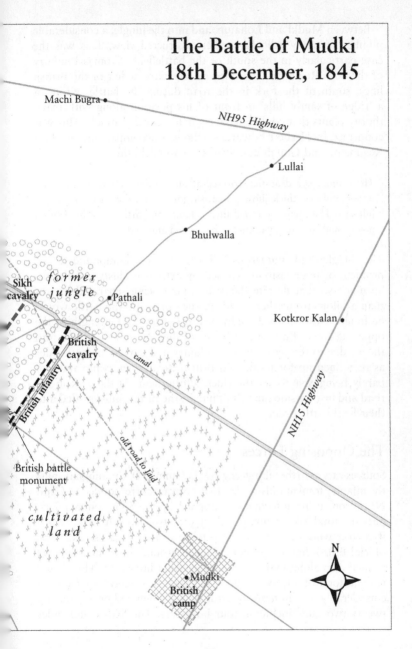

The Battle of Mudki
18th December, 1845

Machi Bugra •

NH95 Highway

• Lullai

• Bhulwalla

former jungle

Sikh cavalry

•Pathali

Kotkror Kalan •

British cavalry

canal

British infantry

NH15 Highway

old road to land

British battle monument

cultivated land

• Mudki

British camp

N

Between Mudki and Lohaum, and into the jungle, a considerable number of sandy hillocks further obstructed view. This was the case particularly in the south of the battlefield. Thomas Bunbury of the 80th Regiment, stationed on the extreme left of the British lines, south of the fork in the road during the battle, wrote of a 'ridge of sandy hills' in front of his position along with many thorny plants that could effectively halt a cavalry attack. This was confirmed by Herbert Edwardes, who was accompanying the 80th Regiment. And Gough described the battlefield thus:

> The country is a dead flat, covered at short intervals with a low, but in some places, thick jhow [tamarisk] jungle and dotted with sandy hillocks. The enemy screened their infantry and artillery, behind this jungle, and such undulations as the ground afforded.

The jungle and numerous hillocks further compounded the problem of poor visibility caused by extremely dusty conditions. So much so that despite the armies now being separated by less than a kilometre neither could see the other, and the battle would be fought with each side oblivious to the size and strength of the opposing force. Enormous plumes of dust continued to rise into the air due to the movement of infantry and cavalry of both sides as they lined up for battle and British cavalrymen complained of barely being able to see the rider before them. At the fork in the road and just outside the belt of jungle, the British units settled into their final battle order.

The Opposing Forces

Sources vary as to the Sikh strength at Lohaum. J. D. Cunningham puts the infantry total at only 2,000. In his private correspondence, Capt. Nicholson, using information supplied by the Sikh commanders, puts the total Sikh army at only 3,500 strong on the day, which if correct would mean a cavalry force around 1,500 strong. The official British figures are much higher: around 3,000 infantry and artillerymen along with 10-12,000 irregular horsemen. This would make a total of 15,000 at most, although it is likely to have been considerably less. In terms of artillery, Lal Singh had brought along twenty-two guns including four howitzers. The Sikh commander kept his force in a defensive position a few hundred metres to the east of Lohaum at the edge of the belt of jungle straddling both the north and south roads and facing towards Mudki. Bahadhur Singh's brigade was placed on the left with elements of the *Fauj-i-khas* situated in the middle and Mehtab Singh's brigade on the right flank. The cannon were dispersed along the line with the infantrymen supporting the artillery. The cavalry, consisting of *Gorchurras* (irregular) and regular units, flanked the line on both sides. Taking their place among the bushes, jungle and hillocks in front of the Sikh line were Sikh snipers awaiting the British attack. Curiously, one of the effects of Lal Singh's *laissez-faire* attitude was that the Sikh army, having only moved the ten kilometres from Ferozeshah, was now decidedly fresher than the British.

The British strength on reaching Mudki was a total of 12,350 men consisting of 3,850 Europeans and 8,500 sepoys along with forty-two guns. Some reports put the total strength at up to 14,000 with forty-eight guns, of which thirty-six were horse artillery. The numerical strengths of both armies was therefore similar prior to the contest. In terms of artillery, though, the British had the clear advantage, outnumbering the Sikh guns by two to one. Gough had decided to use the right flank to lead the attack with the centre and left as holding forces or advancing slightly behind the right. The more dependable European regiments would also bolster up both flanks with the right flank by far the stronger. The middle was left intentionally weaker, composed as it was of only sepoy regiments. In keeping with this tactic, rather than drawing the infantry up in parallel to the Sikh line, the infantry was formed in echelon formation with the right wing advancing first.

The 1st Division on the British right consisted of the 1st Brigade made up of HM 31st Foot plus the 24th and 47th Native Infantry under Brigadier Bolton with HM 50th Foot and 42nd and 48th Native Infantry composing the 2nd Brigade under Wheeler immediately to their left. The whole division was under the command of Lieutenant-General Sir Harry Smith. The centre of the British lines, held by the 2nd Division under Major-General Gilbert, was composed of the 2nd and 45th Native Infantry as the 1st Brigade, while the 2nd Brigade consisted of the 16th Native Infantry immediately to their left. The 3rd Division under Major-General Sir John McCaskill was composed of HM 9th Foot and the 26th and 73rd Native Infantry as the 1st Brigade with the 2nd Brigade comprised of just HM 80th Foot on the extreme left. The 24th Native Foot had been left to guard the baggage at Mudki. In front of the infantry were positioned five troops of horse artillery and two batteries of light field artillery under Lt-Col. Brooke, the acting brigadier. The cavalry was split into three brigades with Brigadier White commanding the 3rd Light Dragoons and one wing of the 4th Bengal Light Cavalry to the right of the British infantry. Brigadier J. B. Gough (no relation to the Commander-in-Chief), commanded a brigade composed of the 5th Bengal Light Cavalry and the Governor-General's bodyguard, stationed initially in the centre. Gough's brigade was moved north to join up with White's, making the right flank very much stronger as was the case with the infantry on the right. On the left, Brigadier Mactier commanded the 9th Bengal Irregular horse with the other wing of the 4th Bengal Light Cavalry.

As with the Sikh lines, those of the British straddled the Mudki to Lohaum road equally on both sides with the right wing of the army approaching but not reaching the road from Mudki to Jaid village to the north, thus stretching just over two kilometres in length prior to the battle. By all accounts, the Sikh line, with its more numerous cavalry, stretched further than the British, which made Gough anxious of a flanking manoeuvre.

The Battle

By a few minutes before 4.00 p.m. the British field artillery and cavalry had moved into position before the infantry had made its way from Mudki and an artillery duel promptly opened up between the Sikh and British guns. The first casualty came with the very first shot of the Sikh cannon: a Major Todd of the British horse artillery had his head severed by the cannon ball. On the Sikh side, there was an early departure, the commander Lal Singh fleeing the battlefield as soon as the cannonade commenced, leaving his army to manage as best they could. He did not join the army at Ferozeshah until early the next day, allegedly spending the night hiding under a bush. Already the December evening was drawing in and darkness fell across the battlefield. Through the jungle the flashes of the cannon of both sides could be seen, alerting gunners to the position of the enemy's guns; it was therefore not long before both sides started to find their mark. The artillery duel continued for approximately an hour with the British calling up two field batteries. The Sikh guns were heavily outnumbered but held their own as the British guns made little impression. Few if any of the captured Sikh cannon examined after the battle would show any signs of damage.

An hour after the cannonade commenced, Gough ordered the British cavalry forward. Of the Sikh contingent sent to fight at Mudki, the Sikh cavalry formed a significant majority. Consisting of regular cavalry and *Gorchurras*, they had formed up on both flanks of the artillery. However, mere numbers could not make up for the loose discipline of the units and the absence of any authority after Lal Singh's departure. Gough ordered both sections of British cavalry to attack simultaneously and the Sikh cavalry fell back under this concerted attack, thereafter playing no further part in the proceedings, but some Sikh cavalrymen chose to dismount to help the infantry rather than retiring. The retreat of the Sikh cavalry tilted the battle heavily in favour of the British. What was left of the Sikh army consisted of 3,000 infantry along with the artillery, leaving them outnumbered by almost five to one. This proved to be a critical time for the Sikh army exposed on their flanks; the British horse artillery could now move round to the north and south of Lohaum for an enfilading attack. Their cavalry was also free to attack the rear of the Sikh line, which they proceeded to do. What prevented a total Sikh disaster was the unsuitability of the jungle for the British cavalry and the steadfastness of the Sikh infantrymen and gunners under danger of encirclement. Sikh snipers quickly began taking a heavy toll on the British cavalry as they manoeuvred to get close through the jungle, forcing them to retire and turning the remainder of the battle into a purely infantry affair.

With the withdrawal of the British cavalry, Gough ordered his infantry line to move forward in echelon formation with the right wing leading the attack, the middle and left following a little further behind. As they proceeded to move into the jungle, Sikh musket men and snipers turned their full attention towards the advancing line and opened up with a hail of fire. There may have also been a move by the remaining Sikh cavalry on the right of the Sikh lines as HM 80th was ordered to form squares for a while.

The case was the same on the British right flank, squares being ordered as a precaution. The threat never materialised and after a while the British lines moved forward again. Once into the jungle, heavy close-quarter fighting ensued. Colonel James Robertson in the 31st Regiment, fighting on the British right flank, wrote a lively account of the contact made between the two armies:

> Just as the line was formed, facing full upon the immense extent of jungle, ping came a bullet just over my company, and an Irishman in front of me exclaimed, 'Holy Jasus! That was a bullet!' Then the word of command was given, 'Quick march', and we advanced straight down on the jungle, which extended right in front of us. When within a few yards, I heard the Colonel call out, 'Level low, men – level low!' but almost before they got their muskets to their shoulders we received a withering volley from the unseen enemy at close quarters, making a terrible number of gaps in the line. Down went the Colonel and his horse and the bugler at this side, all three shot. The men gave a wild Irish yell, and rushed into the jungle, where a desperate hand-to-hand fight took place. Immediately the regiment was entirely broken up in utter confusion.

The Sikh troops were well marshalled and held firm while the jungle of thorny bushes and sand hills through which the British advanced combined to frustrate any attempts to stay in formation. Meanwhile, Sikh snipers and gunners continued to take a steady toll on the advancing line. William Hodson of the 2nd Grenadiers, and part of the Governor-General's escort, described the Sikh fire as the two lines came close:

> We were within twenty, and at time ten yards of three guns blazing grape into us, and worse of all, the bushes with which the whole ground was covered with marksmen who, unseen by us, could pick us off at pleasure.

As they reached the Sikh line, the battle quickly turned into a series of hard-fought skirmishes through the length of the jungle. The bitter fighting amid the confines of the jungle brought about more confusion for the British, and men all along the line found themselves detached from their own companies and were told to simply attach themselves to any superior officer they saw near them. Some, like Col. Robertson, found themselves behind the Sikh lines and in the clearing west of the jungle, as he later recorded:

> Soon I found myself out of the jungle on the other side with one of the men hanging onto my hand, exclaiming: 'Come back Sir – come back! Look where we are!' And sure enough, there we were, right behind one of the enemy's batteries, which was blazing away at our own people. The gunners were too busy to notice us.

As with the other battles of the First Anglo-Sikh War, courage and audacity was shown by soldiers of both sides and few if any prisoners were taken. One of the more memorable examples took place on the Sikh right flank south of Lohaum. As the British advanced, a one-armed *Akali* soldier stepped forward on his own, brandishing his *tulwar* (curved sword) and boldly defying a whole British regiment. A British drill-corporal rising to the challenge rode quickly towards the *Akali* only to be rapidly dispatched by the agile warrior. No other challengers came forward for hand-to-hand combat and a sepoy trumpeter shot the *Akali* with a pistol before his life was finally ended by a British syce. Throughout the battle, Sikh kettle drums could be heard above the din of the combat and the shouts and cries of close-quarter fighting.

Dr Werner Hoffmeister, Physician to Prince Waldemaar of Prussia and present at the battle, wrote one of the few non-British accounts of the battle and described the Sikh infantry charging three times towards the British, although the sheer disparity in numbers brought limited success. Pitched fighting had been continuing along the line for over six hours now and as the battle wore on the pressure of the British numbers gradually began to tell. The last two hours of the battle involved the Sikh army making a slow retreat back to the village. This was accompanied by the most dogged hand-to-hand fighting between Sikh artillerymen and infantry and the British, whose units captured cannon only to have them recaptured by Sikh troops before the British finally captured them again. Sikh and British bodies were later found as much as a mile west of Lohaum, indicating that scattered fighting continued well beyond the village.

The battle ended at around midnight. However, many of the British troops stayed on the battlefield until around 1.00 a.m.

before moving back to Mudki. Most of the Sikh units retired to Ferozeshah though isolated fighting continued to take place. Many Sikh snipers had not left the battlefield with the infantry. Still ensconced in the trees and bushes, they kept up a steady fire on the retreating British units on the battlefield, aiming particularly at the European troops. In the jungle, many British soldiers lost their way and ended up trudging to other nearby settlements only to be fired at by the local Sikh villagers. The vast majority of the British army had returned to Mudki by 2.00 a.m., Gough being one of the last to reach the village.

Casualties

With the cavalry playing little part, the brunt of the Sikh casualties were borne by the artillerymen and infantry. No precise figures exist, but most sources agree that Sikh casualties were no greater than British. Captain Daniel H. Mackinnon of the 16th Lancers, who toured the battlefield the following day, estimated Sikh fatalities at about 300. Many of the casualties were the Sikh gunners who seldom deserted their cannon despite the odds, as Col. Robertson later recalled:

> In this battle as in all others in which the Sikhs were our adversaries, their gunners were conspicuous for their reckless bravery and devotion to their guns. They never left them, but died rather than yield; and there were no white flags and no quarter asked or given by either side, so we just had to fight it out.

Many of the 300 or so Sikh fatalities on the battlefield comprised wounded soldiers showing a preference for dying on the battlefield rather than the ignominy of being taken prisoner. These soldiers invariably refused any offers of help, as Capt. Noel of the 31st Regiment found as he wandered through the field on his way back to Mudki after the battle:

> Today I have almost spent in the field of action, the horror of which I cannot describe; dead heaped on each other, arm and accoutrements soaked in blood, horses dead and dying by dozens, I found four Seikhs alive, severely wounded, they prayed for water, which was close by in

an old artillery bucket. I poured some down one man's throat, which he seemed to enjoy very much, but showed no gratitude, and refused to come into our camp; so there he is with the others to die of starvation and cold. I cannot write all night, as I am fearfully tired tonight and having been on the sand in my cloak the other night, I am almost stupefied with cold. We have suffered fearfully.

Seventeen of the twenty-two Sikh cannon brought to Mudki were captured by the British, fifteen being taken during the battle and two found abandoned later. Thirteen of the cannon were brought into Mudki fort after the battle with four being wheeled in the following day. The gun carriages were destroyed for fear of any attempts to recapture them and several were thrown in the village wells.

The roll-call of the dead and wounded for the British stood at 215 killed and 657 wounded. Like the Sikhs, European soldiers of all ranks had fought with little thought for surrender and among the dead there were some notable casualties. Major-General Sir Robert Sale had his left thigh shattered by grapeshot, a wound from which he would later die. Sale had been one of the commanders of the ill-fated Afghanistan expedition in 1841. Major-General Sir John McCaskill, who commanded the 3rd Division on the left of the British lines, was shot in the chest and died immediately. Brigadier Bolton, leading the 1st Brigade on the right wing, died later of his injuries. Major Herries, the son of a Cabinet minister, was also among the casualties. Brigadiers Mactier and Wheeler and Lt-Col. Byrne and other officers were among the list of wounded.

Aftermath

Early the next day, Sikhs and British mingled with each other on the battlefield looking for their dead. James Coley, the army chaplain to the British forces at the battlefield, commented that: 'The Seekhs have been very quick in carrying off their dead; and we are doing all we can to give our men a decent burial.' Villagers from neighbouring hamlets were seen helping the Sikh wounded or taking them back to their villages. Gough had in the early morning ordered limbers and cattle to the battlefield along with parties of infantry to collect the remaining Sikh cannon and the

British dead and wounded. British soldiers had found there were insufficient *dhoolies* (stretchers), men and elephants to bring back their wounded the previous night hence large numbers of dead and wounded were left to lie on the field to be picked up the next day. Some of the British soldiers resorted to using the *razais* (quilts) of the dead and wounded Sikhs as makeshift stretchers. In the village, meanwhile, two large holes were dug into which were thrown the dead with two large masonry platforms constructed later on top. The officers were buried separately under trees and other quiet spots throughout the camp.

The battle at Mudki, the first between the Sikhs and the British, resolved little and curiously gave confidence to both forces. For the Sikh soldiers, the defiant stand by a relatively small force of their infantry – which comprised but a fraction of the total Sikh strength – against the bulk of the British army boded well for any future contest. Mouton the Frenchman, present with the Sikh army at Ferozeshah, commented after the war that Sikh soldiers were not at all anxious of the result at Mudki and added that the result would have been different had the British not bribed some unnamed commander (i.e. Lal Singh) to desert his post. A Sikh cavalryman captured by the British mirrored this attitude. Conversing with William Macgregor, the surgeon present with the British army, he said: 'If a few thousand Sikhs required the united force of the British to conquer them, how much more difficult it must be to conquer the Khalsa army and how infinitely greater must be the loss.'

For the British, aware of the formidable nature of the Sikh army, the hard-fought victory was welcome. The Sikh army contingent had been driven back and Sikh guns had been captured. Nevertheless, the spirited resistance the Sikh army had shown was an unpleasant surprise. There had been a general impression in British circles that the years of mutiny and an increasingly republican spirit in the Sikh army after Ranjit Singh's death had largely destroyed its effectiveness. As a British soldier wrote later:

So confident were our officers and men that the Sikh army was composed of nothing but a rebel mob, that they did not believe they would hazard an engagement with us – and I heard several officers say (even after the cannonading had commenced), 'O, they will run away before we get up to them – they will not fight us', and several other expressions of a similar kind, showing how very ignorant we were of their real strength and intentions; and in this entire ignorance of the Sikh army, it is wonderful that all were alike involved, even the Governor and Commander-in-Chief, each of whom, it should fairly be supposed ought to have been possessed of correct information on so important a subject.

The Sikh Advance from Ferozeshah

The roar of the guns and muskets at Mudki could be heard loudly at the Sikh camp at Ferozeshah, only ten kilometres away. By this time, word had reached the camp that the whole British force, minus Littler's contingent at Ferozepore, had been engaged at Mudki. Despite this, Lal Singh, who had by this time returned to Ferozeshah, showed little inclination to send out any reinforcements or move the main bulk of the Sikh army forward. Thus the contingent at Mudki was left to cope as best it could while the main force sat at their stations.

One of the few accounts we have of the mood in the Sikh camp during this period comes from a British prisoner at Ferozeshah. Captain George Bidulph, a member of the British 3rd Irregular Cavalry had arrived at Mudki before the British vanguard. Bidulph was attempting to join Littler's force at Ferozepore unaware that an advance guard of *Akali* skirmishers of the Sikh army under Ganda Singh Nihung had occupied the Mudki fort. He was captured by the locals upon entering the village and handed over to Ganda Singh, who held him in the fort for a number of hours before taking him to the Sikh camp at Ferozeshah. He was the first European prisoner of war to be taken during the campaign and as such he aroused much interest in the Sikh camp. Bidulph was taken to Lal Singh's tent. However, the Sikh commander did not converse with him but ordered him to be kept as a prisoner by the Sikh artillery. He was put under the control of Bekani Allie Khan, the commander of the artillery, who had him secured to one of the gun carriages of the Sikh cannon. While there he struck up a good rapport with the men around him. It was a bitterly cold night and ice covered the ground in the morning. Noticing his discomfort, the Sikh artillerymen lit a fire for him and gave him tobacco to smoke and occasionally engaged in conversation with him. Bidulph now had ample time to cast his eye over the camp and gauge the upbeat mood and opinion of the Sikh soldiers regarding the battle.

During the night of 18 December, Bidulph noticed fighting between Sikh and British cavalry had approached very close to the camp, close enough for him to recognise the uniform of the 3rd Light Dragoons. As the cavalry approached, the Sikh artillerymen readied themselves for a contest and lit matches in preparation for firing the cannon but the British cavalrymen declined to approach closer to the Sikh camp. Nor did Lal Singh order the Sikh troops to challenge them. As the night progressed, the mood of the Sikh army consequently grew increasingly frustrated due to the enforced inactivity. Sikh soldiers in the camp believed a success could have been achieved and questions were raised as to why the Sikh force at Mudki had not been supported. A decision must have been pressured on the Sikh commander during the night, for early the next day a Sikh force would march to Mudki.

The strength of the force that Lal Singh sent is unclear, but its sudden appearance on the battlefield early on 19 December caught the British by surprise again. Parties of British soldiers and elephants were scouring for wounded and dead when they were disturbed in their activity. Col. Robertson on the battlefield that morning later recalled the advance of the Sikh force towards the British camp and the call to arms:

> The morning after Moodkee, volunteers were called for to bring in the dead and wounded, and White and I went out with a party of men. We had scarcely got to the field when the Commander-in-Chief ordered us in again, saying that the Sikhs were advancing upon us. I got leave from White to go and look at them, and after riding a little way I saw the camp-followers running like mad; the doolie-bearers dropped their doolies and, making a grab at their lotas and copra bolted. Two or three elephants, loaded with dead, were running as fast as the mahouts, by screaming and kicking, could make them go, and one of our sergeants was hanging on to an elephant's tail, not having had time to get up before the stampede. Presently I saw the Sikh cavalry coming up at a gallop, with Lall Singh at their head. I just took a good look at them, and then cut back as hard as I could. I found the regiment formed in front of the camp and ready to move

forward; but we only stood in the sun all day, and then went into our
tents in the afternoon.

Robertson was mistaken in thinking it was Lal Singh leading the
advance. The Sikh commander was already ordering the return of
the army from Ferozeshah. The prospect of fighting another battle
so soon was taken quite seriously by Gough and an alarm went out
through the camp of the advance of the Sikh army. Robert Cust,
in Mudki village at the time when the alarm was sounded, wrote
later that there seemed to be little intelligence as to the size of the
advancing Sikh force:

> Upon a false alarm of some Sikh horse being in sight our picquets fell
> back and caused some dismay; there was a general depression of spirits
> in the camp and a prevalent idea that a large force was surrounding
> us whose object was to cut off the regiments coming up from behind
> to join our camp.

Gough, under the impression that the whole Sikh army was
approaching, had duly ordered all pickets and troops back and
drew up the British force into a defensive formation round the
Mudki camp. The army was kept in a state of readiness for several
hours after the Sikh army was recalled by Lal Singh.

Ordering an attack on the British camp would have given the
initiative back to the Sikh army. The sequel to the Sikh withdrawal
to Ferozeshah was the arrival of two European regiments, HM
29th Foot and the 1st Bengal European Light Infantry with two
native regiments, the 11th and the 41st along with a division of
heavy guns, principally two eight-inch howitzers in the evening
of December 19, considerably strengthening the British army as
a result. Lal Singh, anxious to show his friendship to the British,
meanwhile released Bidulph who was escorted to the British camp
on December 20. Having been resident in the Sikh camp for a
few days, Bidulph was a good source of information for Gough
regarding the strength of the Sikh army at Ferozeshah.

Leaving aside the time spent awaiting the Sikh attack, the
rest of the day was spent by the British for recuperation and the
retrieval of wounded from the battlefield. Sir Robert Sale, one
of the more notable British casualties, was temporarily buried at

Mudki, saluted by all the pieces of cannon available. His remains would later be moved to Ferozepore cemetery. Men of lower rank were now buried in the field where they had fallen. With the small fort already fully utilised as a hospital for the British sick and wounded, there was no further space for new wounded arrivals: tents were therefore erected in the village and other places, such as the stalls for oxen, were also used.

Hardinge Offers His Services

Also on the evening of 19 December, Sir Henry Hardinge offered his services to Gough as second in command, a request that was accepted by Gough. Hardinge, an experienced soldier, would be an able lieutenant. However, being second in command under Gough, while as Governor-General having civil authority over him, would create an awkward situation several days later at Ferozeshah.

The following day was a period of inactivity for both armies, largely spent resting. In the evening, the British troops were readied for an early departure the following day, and two days of provisions for the troops were readied. With neither Lal Singh nor Tej Singh taking the initiative, the stage was now set for a battle at the Sikh camp at Ferozeshah. Gough, having rested his force, was now prepared to move forward. Orders had been sent to Major-General Littler to move the Ferozepore garrison forward for a junction with the main force. At 4.00 a.m. on December 21, the British force moved off westwards from Mudki leaving two native regiments, the 11th and 41st, with three guns to garrison the village and protect the baggage in addition to the sick and wounded. The path led over the southern section of the field of Mudki. Three days after the battle, some living still lay on the field – a severely wounded Sikh soldier was seen resting on the field by the soldiers of the passing British column. The local Sikh villagers either from Mudki or a neighbouring village had supplied him with firewood with which he had been keeping himself warm during the extreme cold of the nights. British dead were seen littering the field a mile west of Mudki, stripped of clothes and boots by locals looking for trophies. Gough, anxious to join up with Littler's force, forbade the troops from burying these bodies, remarking that 'this was no time for such business'.

3

Ferozeshah

It seemed that we were on the eve of a great misfortune.

– Capt. Robert Napier

Preliminaries

Gough's force marched towards Lohaum before veering further south in a wide arc to avoid a premature clash with the Sikh forces prior to the junction with Littler's contingent. Passing the villages of Kalash (Kullus) and Hajakarka to his north, Gough reached a point south of the village of Shukoor by between 10.00 and 11.00 a.m., less than six kilometres due south of Ferozeshah. It was here that the rendezvous with Littler's column was expected, and the British troops were rested and breakfasted. The seventeen-kilometre march had taken seven hours, the British commander deliberately moving slowly to avoid exhaustion of the troops prior to the battle.

Gough already had intelligence regarding the Sikh army positions at Ferozeshah: Capt. George Bidulph had seen plenty of the Sikh camp when he was previously captured. In addition, Nicholson, the British assistant political agent, through his channels of communications with Lal Singh, had passed information on the position and strength of the Sikh army to Broadfoot, his superior. Broadfoot, in turn had informed the Commander-in-Chief of the weakness of the Sikh entrenchments and, notably, the fact that the northern stretch of the Sikh camp was left undefended by Lal

Singh. Yet Gough, after doing some reconnaissance of his own, decided instead on an attack from the south. There were several reasons for this. Gough was bullish about a positive result for the British despite the prolonged contest at Mudki. He was also a man used to a full frontal assault, typically favouring an outcome decided by the bayonet rather than any fancy manoeuvring on the battlefield. His own soldiers, used to Gough's rather direct tactics, called it the 'Tipperary rush'. So while Broadfoot's suggestion for an attack from the north may arguably have proved easier, it was not Gough's preferred way of going about matters. No doubt another factor in his decision was the dubious loyalty of Tej Singh to the British cause. He was currently encamped at Ferozepore with the second Sikh army. Moving the British army in a broad semicircle around Ferozeshah to enable an attack from the north would take several hours even if Littler should arrive in the near future. This delay would give Tej Singh a chance to join up with the main army at Ferozeshah if he should develop any inclination to help his fellow Sikhs. Certainly the roar of the cannon at Ferozeshah, just fourteen kilometres from Tej Singh's force, would compel him to either attack Ferozepore or come to the aid of Lal Singh's force. The enthusiasm of the Sikh soldiery would make it difficult to keep his army static at Ferozepore. Gough decided a rapid victory at Ferozeshah would eliminate any concerted action by both Sikh armies. If a victory could be achieved at Ferozeshah, then Tej Singh's force could be dealt with separately. So confident was he of success that an immediate attack without Littler's reinforcements was seen as attractive and opportune. Approaching the Governor-General, he declared, 'Sir Henry, if we attack at once, I promise you a splendid victory.'

Hardinge had meanwhile formed a very different opinion of the situation. With the strength of the Sikh army significantly greater at Ferozeshah, he had no wish for another struggle with his force smaller than it need be. The attack would only take place when Littler's contingent had strengthened the British force. Hardinge led Gough away to a clump of trees fifty yards away from the troops to discuss the matter privately with his Commander-in-Chief. A strong expression of unease at an immediate attack did nothing to dissuade Gough, however, who remained enthusiastic about an early advance. This put the Governor-General in an awkward situation. He had elected to be Gough's second in command at Mudki and in military matters had to accept Gough's decision. However, as Governor-General he could override Gough. Convinced that an immediate collision with the Sikh army could only lead to disaster, Hardinge, in his role as Governor-General, now forbade Gough to launch an attack before Littler's reinforcements arrived.

Interestingly, another option seems to have been put forward to Gough by Broadfoot, the political agent. Capt. Robert Napier of the Bengal Engineers would write later of hearing Broadfoot suggesting a march against Tej Singh at Ferozepore. With Lal Singh keeping his army firmly static behind the entrenchments at Ferozeshah, Tej Singh's force could be attacked with impunity. This idea had many merits not least preventing any potential attack on Ferozepore by Tej Singh. Gough, however, dismissed the idea, saying it would be a disgrace to leave European sick and wounded at Mudki. With only a small native guard, they would be vulnerable to a potential attack from Sikh forces at Ferozeshah.

Littler joined up with Gough a little later than expected, between 1.30 and 2.30 p.m., meeting no opposition from Tej Singh after departing from Ferozepore. Having started at 8.00 a.m. and making the twenty-kilometre march himself, Littler and his troops were worn out when they arrived at Shukoor. Littler's force added 5,000 men and two regiments of cavalry and twenty-one field guns to the British force. As Littler's force marched within view, Hardinge nodded to Gough, saying: 'Now the army is at your disposal.' Allowing for the rest required and for reorganising the combined army for the coming battle, it was around 4.00 p.m. with the light already beginning to fade when the British line began moving towards Ferozeshah to the north. The march there took another hour in battle order.

In the Sikh camp, word of the British army's move south of Ferozeshah had arrived from a servant of Bokhan Khan, an officer in the cavalry. This was interpreted initially as a move to the safety of Ferozepore where additional ammunition would be available. Certain sections of the *Fauj-i-khas* had moved westwards to reconnoitre. As it became obvious the British would fight, these contingents returned to Ferozeshah. Bickering broke out as to why units were not being sent to Mudki to sack the now largely undefended British baggage train. According to Dewan Ajudya Parshad, the cavalry was bitter toward Lal Singh and the officers for not ordering an attack at Mudki, and the whole army began to 'plot injury to them' when the British suddenly appeared to the south of the camp.

The Battlefield

The bulk of the Sikh army under Lal Singh had been kept largely motionless at Ferozeshah for the ten days since the crossing of the Sutlej. During this period, with their labours undirected by Lal Singh, Sikh soldiers had used the time to construct a defensive position around the village in the shape of a large quadrilateral, around a mile in length with the shorter sides half a mile in width. The long faces of the quadrilateral pointed north-west towards Ferozepore on one side and southeast towards Mudki on the other. Daniel Mackinnon of the 16th Lancers has left the most detailed description of the camp:

> The entrenchments, which had been thrown forward to cover the village were an irregular quadrangular figure, of upwards of eighteen hundred yards in length, and rather more than half that distance in breadth and consisted of a ditch, about four feet in depth and from six to seven in breadth, the deblai earth from which formed a parapet, protecting the defenders from fire of grape of musketry. Batteries of the enemy's lighter guns were disposed at intervals in rear of the parapets, where the ground was uniformly flat, save in the centre of the position, where it rose gradually into the mound, covered by the mud-houses of the village as before mentioned.

Only at certain places could the earthwork defences be made breast high; other places were lower as they were standard field defences or trenches. In the middle of the camp sat the small village of Ferozeshah on a slight incline. Inside the quadrangle, the tents and bivouac of the army had been set up largely to the south and east of the village. Several sources mention sandy hillocks around ten feet high encircling the village, the hillocks deciding the path, and forming part of, the defensive line. No hillocks are mentioned further from the village, providing an unobstructed view for both

Sikh and British armies up to the perimeter of the jungle. Outside the entrenchment, Sikh troops had prepared the ground before them. All trees and shrubs to a distance of 300 yards had been cut down to give themselves a clear line of fire with mines laid in various positions outside the perimeter of the defences. Beyond this distance, the jungle again closed around the camp and village in a broad circle.

The Opposing Forces

Inside the entrenchment, the 103 guns of the Sikh artillery were dispersed through the western, southern and eastern sides of the defensive line along with both the regular and irregular infantry. Many of the guns were heavy calibre including some sixty-two-pounders. Some of the guns were mounted on platforms within the entrenchments. The bulk of the artillery was situated in the southern half of the entrenchments. Lal Singh had placed relatively few on the long east face of the camp with a long stretch in the middle of the east face being devoid of any guns, thus making this face much less formidable than the south or west faces.

Estimates of the strength of the Sikh army vary wildly between 17,000 to 35,000 men including cavalry and irregulars. The figures given to Nicholson by Tej Singh are probably the most accurate and mention 7,200 regular infantry along with 8,000 cavalry and 9,812 other troops including around 2,000 artillerymen and 1,000 *Nihangs*. This would make a total of just over 25,000. However, the Sikh cavalry stationed both to the north-west and north-east of the camp would not be made use of by the Sikh commander, leaving the 17,000-strong infantry manning the entrenchments to take part in the coming contest.

Fighting within the camp would have attendant problems for the Sikh army. The most obvious was that the initiative now lay entirely with the British, Gough being free to choose to attack whichever portion of the camp he deemed the most promising. The defensive perimeter, a lengthy four kilometres, had also forced the Sikh infantry to spread themselves along the line much more thinly than would have been the case in normal battle order. This did not include the unmanned northern section, which if manned would have further thinned the Sikh ranks. The same argument went for

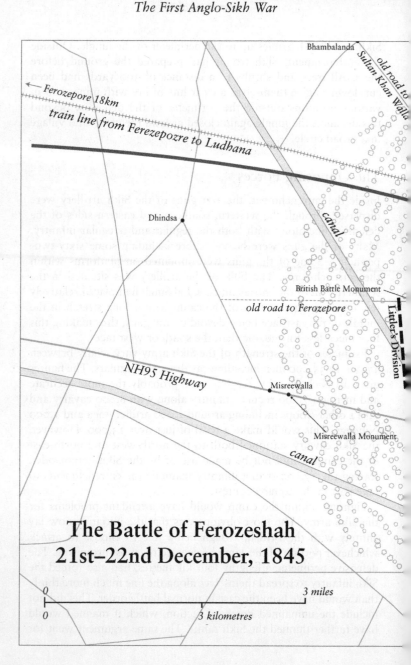

Bhambalanda

old road to Sultan Khan Walla

← Ferozepore 18km

train line from Ferezepozre to Ludhana

canal

Dhindsa

British Battle Monument

old road to Ferozepore

Littler's Division

NH95 Highway

Misreewalla

Misreewalla Monument

canal

The Battle of Ferozeshah
21st–22nd December, 1845

| 0 | | 3 miles |
| 0 | | 3 kilometres |

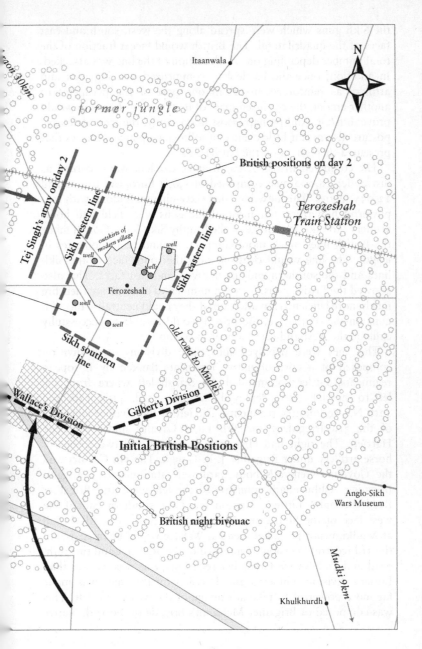

the Sikh guns which were spread along the west, south and east faces of the quadrilateral. The British would face a fraction of the total number depending on which section of the line was attacked. In addition, once the battle had commenced, moving men and artillery as reinforcements from one part of the perimeter to another among the confused mass of tents within the camp would prove difficult. And perhaps most importantly, the strict defensive posture also meant little chance of following up any successes that presented themselves on the battlefield.

The combined British strength at Ferozeshah was recorded as just under 18,000 men composed of 5,674 European troops and 12,053 sepoys. This now included sixty-nine guns along with two powerful howitzers, but most of the guns were field and horse artillery. To take advantage of the lengthy Sikh lines, Gough made the British lines much more compact, around two kilometres in length. The line would confront only the south face of the Sikh lines and the southern ends of the west and east faces. This also allowed the British guns, fewer in number, to concentrate their fire much more efficiently. In addition, if they could neutralise the Sikh guns on the south face, the British would be able to successfully enfilade the west and east faces of the camp.

The lines were deployed into three divisions, each division composed of a core of native regiments flanked by European regiments. Littler commanded the British left where from the left to the right were deployed the 54th, 33rd, 44th, 14th and 12th Native Infantry regiments. The left of the division consisted of the 3rd Irregulars and 8th Light Cavalry under Brigadier Harriett. The right had HM 62nd Regiment and two troops of horse artillery under Brigadier J. B. Gough. The 5th Cavalry and the Governor-General's bodyguard were stationed to the right. Brigadier Ashburnham commanded the left wing and Brigadier Reed the right. Littler's division faced the southern end of the west face of the Sikh camp. The death of Maj.-Gen. McCaskill at Mudki meant Brigadier General Wallace would be in charge of the 3rd (centre) Division. Composed of the 9th Foot and the 26th, 73rd and 2nd Native Grenadier regiments, this was weaker than Littler's division. Gilbert's 2nd Division on the right was made far more powerful to take advantage of the weak Sikh left. This was composed of Brigadier McLaran's brigade of the 16th Native

Grenadiers on the left, the 1st European Light Infantry and the 45th Native Infantry on the right. The extreme right wing was a mix of the 41st Native Infantry, HM 80th and HM 29th. In addition to this, there was Brigadier White's cavalry composed of the 3rd Light Dragoons and the 4th Bengal Lancers. In reserve was kept Sir Harry Smith's 1st Division composed of the 42nd and 48th Native Infantry and HM 50th under Brigadier Ryan and the 47th and 24th Native Infantry and HM 31st under Brigadier Hicks. The horse artillery and other assorted guns were dispersed along the line. At the extreme left were stationed two nine-pounder batteries. Two troops of horse artillery were stationed between Littler's and Wallace's division. Between Wallace's and Gilbert's division were placed a troop of eight-inch howitzers, two nine-pound batteries and two troops of horse artillery. On the extreme right of the British lines was an additional troop of horse artillery.

The Battle: The First Day

Opening Shots

There had been some nominal skirmishing for a short period between Sikh and British cavalry as the British marched forward through the jungle. However, 1,100 yards from the Sikh encampment, the British mortars broke the silence followed quickly by the Sikh cannon. At 800 yards, the British field artillery, followed by the horse artillery, opened up. Leaving aside the confusion of Mudki, this was the first opportunity for the gunners to compete with each other on an open plain, and the Sikh artillerymen quickly established their superiority. Capt. William Humbley, in his *Journal of a Cavalry Officer*, would later comment that 'the Sikh guns were served with extraordinary rapidity and precision'. The Governor-General, a veteran of the Peninsula War, would describe the Sikh cannonade at Ferozeshah on that day as more terrible than the French guns at the Battle of Albuera. It was noted that the Sikh gunners typically fired three shots to every two the British gunners could manage. Many of the Sikh guns were of heavier metal than their British counterparts and could also sustain double charges of grape, powder and round shot. Furthermore, the Sikh gunners' aim was proving far more accurate than that of their

British counterparts. While the British guns made little impression, the Sikh fire progressively took its toll, the result being that most of the British artillery was destroyed or disabled. Col. Robertson, watching the duel of the guns, wrote later:

> We had not a gun left, or if they were, the ammunition was all expended; but most of them were smashed; and dead horses and broken limbers were lying about, having been completely outmatched by the heavier artillery of the Sikhs.

Two hours later, ammunition for the few British guns that remained in working order was also fast coming to an end. With his artillery a spent force, Gough deemed it best to push his divisions forward for an immediate attack, and Littler on the British left was now ordered to advance on the south-west face of the Sikh camp.

Repulse of the British Left

Littler's division began advancing with the sun to their back and silence from the Sikh guns. As the British line advanced to within 150 yards, however, the Sikh gunners and infantry suddenly opened up a terrible fire that tore huge holes in the advancing line. Such was the strength of the cannonade that within a few minutes the whole of the line had effectively been destroyed as a fighting force. The British line initially faltered and slowed to a crawl, and then the regiments began to retreat. Sitaram, a sepoy in Littler's division, recorded the British advance:

> Volleys of musketry were delivered by us at close quarters, and were returned just as steadily by the enemy. In all the previous actions in which I had taken part one or two volleys at short range were as much as the Sirkar's [the British state's] enemies could stand; but these Sikhs gave volley for volley, and never gave way until nearly decimated. They had their infantry placed between and behind their artillery and their fire was terrible, such as no sepoy has ever had to endure. The Sirkar's guns were almost silenced and the ammunition wagons exploded. I saw two or three European regiments driven back by the weight of the artillery fire which rained down on us like a monsoon downpour. They fell into confusion and several sepoy regiments did

the same. One European regiment was annihilated – totally swept away – and I now thought the Sirkar's army would be overpowered.

Only HM 62nd Regiment managed to approach anywhere near the entrenchment before retreating. Robert Haviland, a soldier in the regiment, was advancing to the right of Sitaram's regiment and faced the line of fire from the Sikh infantry behind the guns:

> [We] advanced to within 20 yards when the Sikhs opened such a fire of grape that our men fell like rain in perfect rows on the ground. Why I escaped will always remain a mystery to me.

A few brave individuals reached the Sikh line but in such few numbers it was advisable to retreat rather than face complete annihilation in hand-to-hand fighting. Littler, watching the advance and realising the entire division was in the process of being destroyed, now ordered a general retreat. After pulling back and reforming, the much-thinned ranks of the division were ordered to advance a second time but with the same result. Sikh soldiers along the line let out a huge cheer as the battered remnants of the British left made their final retreat. Losses in the 62nd Regiment alone ran to 281 men killed with eighteen officers killed or wounded. As they retreated back towards the British lines, they were forced onto the defensive themselves by a movement of the Sikh cavalry to their left. The British formed squares, but an attack was never ordered by Lal Singh and the opportunity to effectively destroy the entire British left was missed. Some of the soldiers of the division now joined Brigadier General Wallace's division to their right. The majority of Littler's troops retreated to the village of Misreewalla, three kilometres to the south-west of Ferozeshah, and would play no further part in the battle.

Advance of the British Right

With Littler repulsed, Gough immediately ordered the right wing of the British forces to advance. This attack was to be on the south-eastern corner and weaker east face of the Sikh defences. The right wing had been made the stronger of the two wings of the British force. No less than three European regiments, HM 29th, HM

80th and the 1st European Light Infantry would lead the attack along with the 41st, 45th and the 16th Native Infantry regiments. Working alongside this force would be the 3rd Light Dragoons with the 4th Light Cavalry. Taking advantage of the lesser fire from the Sikh lines, both brigades of the division broke into the camp on this front at the first attempt and fierce hand-to-hand fighting broke out all along the line.

Immediately after the British right had penetrated the Sikh lines, the 3rd Light Dragoons charged further to the north and also managed to penetrate into the Sikh camp. Initial success was hard to maintain, however. The inside of the entrenchments was not ideal territory for cavalry and with their lines broken up, Sikh infantrymen rapidly began picking off the riders as they negotiated their way through the maze of tents and roping. Meanwhile, Sikh snipers in the low doorways of the tents, inaccessible to the horsemen, also began taking a heavy toll. The dragoons withdrew having lost around two thirds of their force; only 250 men remained, six officers had been killed and several more wounded. Despite the heavy fighting, there were cases of chivalry. Daniel Mackinnon of the 16th Lancers relates the story of a Sikh soldier who, on seeing one of the dragoons moving past him through the camp having lost his horse, escorted him towards the British lines (though without his jacket, which was kept as a trophy). As the right flank of the British advanced, so the centre of the British lines was also ordered forward against the south face and the south-western part that Littler's division had attempted to reach. This attack also succeeded, albeit with great casualties. Confused hand-to-hand fighting was now raging along the entire south and east of the Sikh camp among the tents and wagons.

The level of success, then, for the various wings of the British force varied considerably. On the western face, the British attack had been repelled. On the southern face, the British had managed to reach the entrenchments but were facing stiff resistance from the Sikh gunners and infantry. On the eastern face of the entrenchment – the weaker section of the Sikh line – Gilbert's division was having the most success, though not without considerable loss. The 80th Regiment had already lost most of its officers during the advance and early fighting in the Sikh camp. With the British force managing to get a toehold in the Sikh entrenchment, Gough threw in his last reserves commanded by Sir Harry Smith to reinforce Wallace's force in the south of the Sikh line. While Smith's advance undoubtedly helped British success in the short term, it also meant all the British forces had now been fully committed. This could have had dire consequences had the Sikh commander wished to take advantage: the Sikh cavalry stationed to the north of the camp and presently inactive could have been ordered to attack the exposed British rear.

Despite the combined force of Gilbert, Wallace and Smith's divisions, the Sikh line held firm, only being pushed back slowly as evening gave way to night. Only Smith had managed to push his way into the middle of the entrenchment and into the village. By this time the south of the camp, now in British hands, was heavily ablaze, the fire lighting up the battlefield. Ammunition boxes and magazines were exploding amid the camp, inflicting casualties and causing further confusion in the already chaotic fighting within the camp. Several British soldiers were seen to be blown up as they moved past burning ammunition wagons and tumbrils while many more were scorched and burnt. Moreover, many of the tents in the south and where the fighting was taking place had caught fire, making movement difficult for both armies.

The British Retreat

The high-water mark of the British advance came late in the day with the capture of the village and the southern section of the camp, around a third of the entrenchments. However, this came at a high cost. After five hours of hand-to-hand fighting, British soldiers were exceedingly worn out, hungry and thirsty. Largely out of ammunition, they were increasingly resorting to fighting with their bayonets. And fighting in the gloom of the night had also taken its toll in terms of organisation. Few soldiers knew where their officers were and who was giving orders. As the British weakened, the Sikh army staged a significant rally and launched a counterattack all along the line. Although Lal Singh had played little part in the proceedings, the Sikh soldiers had lost none of their morale. Less weary than the British, the Sikh line moved forward and began to progressively recapture the southern area of the Sikh camp.

Aware of the changing fortunes for his army, Gough ordered a general retreat from the camp. Extricating the British troops from the entrenchments in the dark was easier said than done, and it created further confusion and panic among the retreating line. Only some of the troops and officers had heard the order. A British officer as yet oblivious of the order was seen trying to exhort his exhausted troops under him to advance. Their answer was: 'It's no use, it's not in us, Sir. We are done up.' Capt. Robert Napier with the 29th Regiment on that day fighting near the village was also unaware of the order and relates the confusion that had now begun to spread among the ranks as the order came to retreat:

> [Of] this order I was not aware and finding the stream of men hastening in some disorder to the rear, I made repeated attempts to stop them and restore order but in vain. Some said if we had officers we would stop. I said I am an officer, I will form you and I got something like a line formed but some men called out 'he's going to lead us into some b----y battery', and my line began to stream away from each flank and then by degrees moved on to the rear in a flock. They followed instinctively some guns which were retiring and I then thought if I could only stop the guns the men might be restored to some kind of order. I passed Mills with his battery and entreated him to stop, he said go to Geddes, he is in front and commands. I then went to him and found he was returning to the ground which we had occupied this morning. There was no help. Had the enemy known the condition of the troops and attacked them they would have been slaughtered like sheep. We just then reached the rest of Gilbert's division in great confusion. The men were ordered to lie down to avoid the shot which came over us every minute.

Finally managing to extricate themselves from the Sikh entrenchments, albeit in some chaos, the British troops were ordered to move south of the camp for around three to four hundred yards where a defensive camp in the form of a large square was made. An alarm rang out for a cavalry attack by the Sikh army. Not for the first time did this fail to materialise.

The only British units that now continued to hold any of the Sikh camp were the units under Sir Harry Smith in and around the village, mainly the 50th Regiment who had set up their flag over the village. They had assumed defensive squares hoping to hold the village during the night. As the Sikh line now advanced south, Smith found himself under serious threat. Sikh soldiers now commenced attacking the village while advancing on the flanks, threatening to surround the village. Early in the morning, Smith held a short council of war with his remaining officers and retreat was thought extremely advisable. The British column evacuated the village between 2.00 a.m. and 3.00 a.m. with HM 50th leading the retreat. Departing to the west of the village, he joined the broken remnants of Littler's division at Misreewalla. Like Littler's division, his men would play no further part in the battle.

Meanwhile, the advancing Sikh line had now driven out the last remaining British soldiers from the encampment. Given no direction from the Sikh commanders to attack the now rapidly forming British quadrangle to their south, the soldiers stopped their advance once the Sikh entrenchments had been reoccupied by around 1.00 a.m. And here the first day of the battle ended, but the fighting would continue. The positions had been reversed, and the Sikh army now waited for the order to advance while their exhausted counterparts found themselves assuming a defensive formation.

The Night of Ferozeshah

The British position was most critical at the end of the first day's fighting in more ways than one. Although a defensive square had been improvised for a night bivouac, no semblance of order was apparent within the camp with men of all regiments mixed in one large disordered mass. Many of the officers responsible for organising them lay dead on the field. The British camp was filled with the wounded and dying and presented a frightening scene. Order out of this confusion could never be established in the darkness, and Gough did not attempt to try. Soldiers were told to rest where they lay. The best Gough could do was to hold onto a defensive position until daylight when the British order of battle could be re-established.

Much more immediate and overwhelming problems faced the British army during the night. All the supplies and baggage had been left behind at Mudki, fifteen kilometres away. The troops' attempts to get some rest without any greatcoats or tents were proving almost impossible in the intense cold of the December night. Soldiers huddled as close to each other as possible for protection against the elements. Some of the more desperate souls tried to light fires for warmth, a dangerous activity as the light from the fire allowed Sikh snipers and gunners to more easily pick potential targets. For this reason Gough quickly ordered the lighting of fires in the camp to be forbidden.

Along with food, there was also the complete absence of water. Most of the soldiers had had their last drop at Mudki nearly eighteen hours earlier. The only wells in the vicinity were in the Ferozeshah entrenchments now firmly back in the Sikh army's control. The trifling amount brought in by *bheesties* (water carriers) from Misreewalla had long ago been exhausted. Mad with thirst after a day of fighting in the extreme heat, men felt themselves compelled to make the most desperate attempts in order to satisfy their craving. Soldiers could be seen stumbling towards the Sikh camp in the darkness looking for wells with little consideration of being shot or taken prisoner. Others tried to buy some solace, offering huge amounts. Pte Joseph Hewitt of the 62nd Foot in the camp noted that: 'we were now suffering terribly from thirst and dust, not a drop of water to be had for love or money. An officer held up a purse. He said there was 50 rupees in it [six months' salary for a sepoy] and he would give it to anyone for a dram of water. If it had been 500 he could not have got it.' In another part of the camp, an officer of the Bengal artillery, whose account of the battle appeared in *The Times* in May 1846, wrote of bands of men moving round the camp 'with their pockets full of rupees and gold *mohurs* which they offered for a drop of water; but that could not be procured'. The next day provided relief of the most meagre kind. Soldiers could be seen eagerly licking the British guns for the dew appearing on the metal in the early morning.

Ammunition for the British artillery had been all but exhausted. There was little prospect of any being brought up from Mudki or Ferozepore, the other nearest British outpost, before the start of hostilities the next day. Sikh gunners meanwhile pressed home their advantage and continued to pound the British position during the night without reply. In the darkness it was difficult to see the British positions. Sikh soldiers recklessly volunteered to venture as close to the British camp as they could ringing bells or lighting flares to provide an indication of the position of the enemy to the Sikh gunners increasing the discomfort within the British square. Later in the night, Sikh gunners located the area where Hardinge and Gough were bivouacking and heavily pounded the area. Although both escaped, the cannonade killed several staff officers resting close to them. One cannon especially was causing significant damage. With British guns silenced, Gough had to resort to sending large elements of two European regiments, HM 80th and the 1st Europeans to attack the Sikh gunners. In other parts of the British camp, British bugle calls were all that were needed to alert Sikh snipers and gunners to possible targets. To minimise casualties, Hardinge ordered every man to lie down flat and keep quiet. This did not discourage the Sikh musket men who continued to pepper the British camp through the early hours of the night. Every quarter of an hour or so, Sikh gunners also fired a short cannonade at the British camp and sounded their kettle drums to awaken any British soldier who had managed to forget his excruciating thirst and somehow fallen asleep.

The gravity of the situation was lost neither on the British soldiers nor their officers. The mood was one of apprehension as they whiled away the long night in the defensive square. Sitaram, one of the sepoys in the British camp, later commented on this mood:

> [We] dare not light a fire, for fear of the enemy's round shot, there was no water, and we had nothing to eat except the few chapattis some men had put in their haversacks. The sahibs [Europeans] said this was real fighting and the Sikhs were noble enemies but they nevertheless looked anxious and wondered what the morning would bring forth. The weather was bitterly cold and nothing was heard amongst us but the chattering of teeth on empty stomachs. I remember on this night a sahib from a regiment next to mine kept walking up and down singing; he was checked by the other officers but he still continued. The sahib was not drunk but was trying to solace himself for the absence of the officers' mess tent. It was a dreadful night.

During the night, both the Commander-in-Chief and the Governor-General energetically moved through the British camp to bolster morale. Hardinge had lost his left hand at the Battle of Ligny during the Napoleonic wars. As he toured the camp visiting the wounded soldiers, he took care to show his own amputation to raise spirits. The grim night spent on the field of Ferozeshah without food, water and shelter and under constant fire from the Sikh gunners was written about in many emotive accounts by soldiers in the British camp. Lt Bellars, the acting adjutant of the 50th Regiment, wrote in his diary:

> No one can imagine the dreadful uncertainty. A burning camp on one side of the village, mines and ammunition wagons exploding in every direction, the loud orders to extinguish the fires as the sepoys lighted them, the volleys given should the Sikhs venture too near, the booming of the monster guns, the incessant firing of the smaller ones, the continued whistling noise of the shell, grape, and round shot, the bugles sounding, the drums beating, and the yelling of the enemy, together with the intense thirst, fatigue and cold, and not knowing whether the rest of the army were the conquerors or conquered – all contributed to make this night awful in the extreme.

During the night, officers began approaching and appealing to Gough for an immediate withdrawal. Among others, a major and a colonel were seen with Gough during the night urging a retreat. 'Sir, I think it my duty earnestly to recommend our retreating to Ferozepore,' the major was heard to say. Gough, angered by these approaches, replied: 'Never! I'd rather die on the spot. I'll fight them tomorrow and beat them!' The colonel then reiterated the same advice, which was also rejected. The advantages of attempting a move were obvious. Retreating to Mudki or Ferozepore could save the army, and much needed supplies and ammunition would become available. This would not be without risks, however. The exhausted state of the soldiers and the close proximity of the Sikh army would make an orderly retreat difficult and certainly impossible to hide. The retreat could turn into a far worse disaster. Despite Gough's public show of bravado, it is certain he did canvas his officers on the possibility of a retreat to Ferozepore. Capt. Napier of the 29th Regiment recorded a conversation with one of Gough's officers sent out to gather opinion on the practicality of a withdrawal. A Col. Benson approached him during the night to ask if he could lead the troops to Ferozepore. Napier, aware of the severe exhaustion of the troops, replied this would be impossible. Asking what were the alternatives being discussed, he was told by a rather shaken Benson that either terms would be sought or an entrenched camp established.

Gough and Hardinge, too, were not unaware of the weariness of the soldiers around them. But there were also the political ramifications to consider. Pulling back would be an enormous dent to British military prestige in India. The collection of most of the European regiments available in north India at the Sutlej had left the British in a somewhat precarious situation. With only one European regiment remaining between the Punjab and Calcutta – a vast distance of 2,000 kilometres – there would be no loyal troops to quell the uprisings that would undoubtedly occur. Seeking terms or surrender would have similar repercussions for British reputation, though it would avoid inflicting unnecessary casualties on an army now virtually bereft of ammunition. As Hardinge put it to an aide during the night: 'The Commander-in-Chief knows as well as anybody that it will not do for a British army to be foiled.' The result at Ferozeshah would undoubtedly decide the future of the British Empire in India.

If a retreat could not be made and if the implications of surrender were too great to contemplate, the only option left was to continue the contest the next day regardless of the consequences. Gough, after due consideration, declared to Hardinge:

> The thing is impossible. My mind is made up. If we must perish, it is better that our bones should bleach honourably at Ferozeshah than rot at Ferozepore: but they shall do neither the one nor the other.

Hardinge was of a similar opinion and the decision was taken to renew the fighting the next day. However, mindful of the potential result, Hardinge took time out to settle his affairs. During the night word was sent to Frederick Currie, the Governor-General's secretary at the British base at Mudki ordering the burning of all state papers in preparation for a likely defeat. He also ordered the surrender of the garrison there, in his own words, 'to spare the wounded'. At Ferozeshah he began burning his private papers. Crown Prince Waldemaar, the nephew of King Frederick William

IV of Prussia and a guest of the Governor-General, was advised to leave the field of battle and to proceed to Ferozepore. His aide Dr Hoffmeister had already died in the battle. When the prince protested and expressed his desire to remain, Hardinge advised him there was no need for him to lose his life in a cause not of his own, at which point Waldemaar reluctantly agreed. Finally, Sir Henry bid his son Charles Hardinge farewell, presenting him with his sword – which once belonged to Napoleon and which he had been given as a gift by the Duke of Wellington – before sending him away from the field. Following this, the British troops were urged to attempt to get as much rest as they could for what the following morning would bring.

Meanwhile at Mudki, where the sounds of the battle could be clearly heard, the news of the failure of the British attack and the desperate state of the army arrived early in the morning. Along with this came orders for the Mudki force to surrender in the event of a defeat the next day. The grave news was kept confidential from the British sick and wounded in the fort to avoid a fall in morale while the matter was still uncertain.

Retreat of Lal Singh

If Gough and Hardinge had had any inkling of events a few hundred metres away in the Sikh camp, they would have had a far less anxiety-ridden night. As the Sikh guns pounded the British quadrangle during the early part of the night, the camp was full of confidence. The whole entrenchment had been retaken and sunrise would allow the Sikh gunners to clearly see the British position; their heavy guns could destroy the packed defensive square. That the British cannon were now silent did not go unnoticed. In contrast to the dearth of supplies in the British camp, the Sikh army had vast resources of food and munitions and had control of the wells in the village. Mouton, the Frenchman in the Sikh service and present in the entrenchment during that night, would later state that the Sikh soldiers had full confidence that a decisive victory would be theirs the following day, a feeling shared by Mouton himself and the other European soldiers in the Sikh army.

The upbeat feeling would be short-lived, however. The comparative lull in the fighting, although forced on the British, would prove unfortunate for the Sikh army. Even as Sikh snipers and gunners rained shots on a silent British camp, recriminations began to surface between the soldiery and the Sikh commanders. The British had been driven out of the entrenchments but no order was forthcoming to advance. No encirclement of the British defensive square had been ordered. No attempt had also been made to sack the almost undefended British camp and baggage at Mudki with the cavalry. Lal Singh had kept the Sikh cavalry inactive leaving the brunt of the British attack to be faced by the infantry alone. There was also no assistance forthcoming from Tej Singh's force nearby. Either messengers had not been sent to Tej Singh requesting help or if they had been sent, Tej Singh was refusing to advance. He had also declined to ransack Ferozepore and destroy the British garrison.

Within the Sikh soldiery, a deep distrust of the way the Sikh commanders were organising the campaign was growing. Discipline was quickly lost amid the arguments. Frustration led to Lal Singh's tent being ransacked by the *Akali* soldiers. Lal Singh, secretly dreading a victory for the Sikh army the next day, now made excuses for a withdrawal from Ferozeshah. Sometime before daybreak, he withdrew from the entrenchments all the irregular cavalry, an unknown amount of infantry and gunners for sixty pieces of artillery. With this departure, the Sikh guns ceased firing. Both Mehtab Singh's and Lal Singh's divisions retreated behind Lal Singh's cavalry. This left only the *Avitabile* division remaining which would also withdraw before daybreak. While the British army rested in their quadrangle, the majority of the Sikh army had already left and was streaming towards the River Sutlej. The exact time of the retreat is uncertain although it would have been after the time that Sir Harry Smith had been driven out from the village at 3.00 a.m. but well before the British organised their battle order at around 7.00 a.m. for the next day's fighting. Lal Singh's decision to retreat did not take into account the baggage, guns, wagons full of ammunition and other supplies that had been brought to Ferozeshah. These were abandoned to be captured by the British. None of the surviving firsthand accounts suggest that the British had any inkling that the Sikh army was being withdrawn, a move that would have been quite apparent had the artillery, hackeries and wagons been readied for the move.

Not all the men would follow Lal Singh's orders. A small but defiant group would elect to stay behind. The defenders of the entrenchment were now reduced to a small rump several hundred strong. It was quite clear to the garrison remaining that they would have little chance of holding back a British advance the next day. In the few hours they had before sunrise what defence could be arranged was marshalled and steps taken to make a British capture of the camp as costly as possible. Around thirty to forty dead bodies were thrown into each of the wells along with great quantities of gunpowder to deny the water supply to the British. The whole of the entrenchments were mined as effectively as time allowed, and the few gunners left manned several of the cannon. In this state the remaining Sikh troops waited for the morning.

The Battle: The Second Day

The British Move Forward

With daybreak came unexpected help for the British in the form of some camels laden with ammunition from Mudki. As much as these paltry supplies allowed, some of the infantry, around 600 in number, were supplied with sixty rounds of ammunition each. At around 7.00 a.m. Gough ordered the British line to form up. The commissariat supplied some recently arrived grog to the troops. Unaware that the bulk of the Sikh army had already been pulled back, Gough assembled the depleted British line with infantry in the middle and flanked by the horse artillery for a seemingly desperate final attack on the Sikh camp. Gough would lead the right wing of the line and Hardinge the left wing. Conscious of the low amount of musket shot available, orders were sent along the line that only bayonets were to be used unless otherwise commanded. A little after sunrise the British line moved forward in silence, expecting a barrage of fire from Sikh muskets and guns.

What they received was silence. As the surprised British troops entered and negotiated their way through the deserted Sikh entrenchments, they passed unmanned guns and ammunition wagons. Beyond lay rations and supplies of all kinds abandoned with tents full of valuables. It quickly became obvious that the Sikh army had already departed. That not all the Sikh army had gone became equally apparent after the British line ventured a little further into the camp. The few Sikh guns that were manned to the north of the camp opened a defiant fire and the remaining Sikh garrison now opened up a fierce struggle in isolated pockets of the camp. Sikh soldiers were seen ensconced in trees directing the fire of the guns towards the British line. This was accurate enough to force HM 80th Regiment to withdraw two hundred paces, temporarily slowing the British advance. The Sikh artillerymen showed much gallantry, resolutely staying with their cannon to the last. Pte J. W. Baldwin, fighting with HM 9th Regiment, recalled:

> [We] succeeded in expelling the Seikhs from their camp, excepting a few of their artillery-men, most determined fellows, who stood by their gun firing grape at us till the very last, but did not give themselves time to ram well the cartridges so their courageous effort was not very successful; and when our line had nearly closed on them, they absolutely sprang forward sword in hand to meet us, and of course were very soon shot.

One cannon in particular did significant damage, dismantling several of the British guns placed in the centre of the British lines. As well as blowing up the tumbrils, the gunners proceeded to blow up the wagons of the first troop 1st Brigade. In return, the British fired some rockets, the last dregs of the ammunition, having expended the cannon shot. The small garrison was in time brushed aside. The British line progressed from the south and gradually swept northwards until they reached the village. At this point, with most of the Sikh tents to the east of the village, the line turned eastward passing the village on their left before resuming the northwards advance. By 10.00 a.m., around three hours after beginning their advance, the whole camp was in British hands. Upon reaching the north of the camp, Hardinge and Gough were given a large cheer by the British troops.

With the camp captured, a somewhat relieved Hardinge and Gough now retired to the village for a rest, HM 62nd Regiment being used as a garrison and stationed in front of the village as a guard. There was no question of the exhausted troops following the Sikh army northwards. Assuming that the contest had ended, Hardinge gave his men time to rest and recuperate. The men quickly piled up arms outside the village and began to stream in large numbers towards the village wells only to find them effectively sabotaged by Sikh troops. The well buckets had also been removed and consequently it proved difficult getting to the water. The polluted state of the water proved of little concern to British soldiers without water for over a day. Trousers tied to ropes were thrown in to the wells to be wetted, raised up and the water squeezed out into parched mouths. Dense crowds formed round the wells and several men were seen inadvertently pushed or falling in and drowning in the melee. By this time, the forces under Smith and Littler at Misreewalla had made their way to Ferozeshah, thus reuniting the British army.

This lull in the hostilities seemed to have lasted less than two hours when between 11.00 a.m. and noon large plumes of dust along a wide arc to the west of the village could be seen, signalling the advance of Tej Singh's army towards Ferozeshah.

Arrival of Tej Singh's Army

Four days previously, the Sikh soldiery outside Ferozepore could hear the roar of the guns at Mudki until late that night. And the sounds of the much closer battle at Ferozeshah on 21 December had been significantly louder. The left flank of Tej Singh's army stationed at Malwal village, only ten kilometres from Ferozeshah, was still closer to Misreewalla, where the remnants of Smith and Littler's divisions were resting. Nevertheless, Tej Singh had kept his army stationary neither advancing westwards on Ferozepore nor eastwards towards Ferozeshah. The Sikh soldiery, now tiring of his passivity, had eventually goaded Tej Singh into marching to the assistance of the Ferozeshah army. A timely march on the evening of 21 December would have realised Gough's worst fears with the British army fully committed and caught between the two Sikh forces. The Sikh soldiers argued that intervention even at this late stage would still decide the battle in favour of their army. Tej Singh proceeded to lead the advance but had sufficiently stalled it so that the last of the fighting had died down.

And so, late on the morning of 22 December, the Sikh army left the unnecessary vigil outside Ferozepore and marched east to Ferozeshah. Tej Singh's force, including cavalry, horse artillery and regular *Fauj-i-ain* battalions, marched in full battle order as they came within sight of Ferozeshah. Captain Henry Palmer of the 48th Native Infantry witnessed the approach of the Sikh army:

> Two miles off in our front was a sight well worth seeing. A glorious sun at our back played on a truly magnificent advancing line of artillery, infantry and cavalry, a mile in length. Richly dressed Sikh officers, colours and bands all glittering. It was a pretty sight. A Native cavalry regiment from our right made a feint of charging but the enemy must have smiled at them.

In contrast, the British army battle order had already disintegrated with men scouring the camp for food and water while others had commenced looting. No pickets had been stationed west of the village and the sudden appearance of a second Sikh army dismayed Hardinge. Tej Singh had been expected to stay at Ferozepore. The bugle was sounded for the lines to reform. Hardinge could only assume that Tej Singh, having moved his army to Ferozeshah, had shifted his loyalty back to the Sikh cause, in which case he would undoubtedly take advantage of the parlous state of the British army. Readying the troops as best they could, Hardinge and Gough formed a defensive line to the north-west of the village. Close by Hardinge was HM 31st Regiment, which he ordered to form squares in readiness for a likely Sikh cavalry charge. Col. Robertson was among the men in the 31st now marshalled by Hardinge as he rode into the centre of the square:

> The Governor-General addressed us in an affirm voice: 'Thirty-first, I was with you when you saved the Battle of Albuera; behave like men now.' He then took the star off his breast and gave it to his son. He evidently never expected to leave our square alive, and up to that time we had no idea that anything was wrong, but in some unaccountable way the greater part of the army had melted away in the night and Sir Harry Smith's division was left almost alone to face a fresh army, the formed line of which we could see advancing upon us in perfect order, and as this was a war where no quarter was asked or given on either side, and we had to fight it out to the bitter end, things looked very black indeed.

With most troops having no ammunition, Hardinge's message was sent down the British line: 'Recollect, men, you must hold your ground to the last, and trust to your bayonets.' Gough meanwhile proceeded to put the cavalry, principally the 9th and 16th Lancers and the 3rd Light Dragoons and some native cavalry behind bushes some way off from the main camp so that they extended some two miles even though they were few in number compared to the Sikh cavalry.

Retreat by Tej Singh

At around 2.00 p.m. the Sikh army closed to within artillery range and opened up a cannonade. Sources vary considerably as to its length. Capt. Robert Napier recorded the gunfire as lasting around an hour. Lt Alfred Simmons of the 29th recorded the Sikh gunfire as lasting an hour and a half. Pte Baldwin reckoned on the Sikh guns firing for around two hours. Others such as Col. Robertson mention simply that it went on for several hours.

Initially the men in the British line had been told to form squares as a Sikh cavalry attack was suspected. However, the Sikh artillery opened up with great accuracy so that British troops were told to lie down flat on the ground. Yet as the Sikh gunners again found their mark, the British infantry were ordered to be constantly on the move so as to make zeroing in on their position all the more difficult for their opponents.

In response, the few British guns that had any ammunition opened up a nominal fire. Anxious to prevent the guns going silent, Gough ordered the British gunners to fire blanks to give the impression that ammunition was available. Furthermore, British gunners were ordered to rapidly scour the Sikh wagons and hackeries in the camp for cannon shot. Most of the shot, however, was too big for the British guns as the Sikh cannon were of heavier calibre so only fifty rounds of shot were small enough to be used by the British artillery. And these were used up quickly.

Gough ordered a feint by the 3rd Light Dragoons and some native cavalry on the British left. This was the only option available. With the artillery a spent force and the infantry exhausted, a British advance was impossible.

It was at this juncture that Tej Singh astounded both the Sikh soldiery and the British line by ordering a general retreat towards the Sutlej. Unsure of his real motives, the order dismayed the rank and file Sikh soldiers who could not fail to notice the fatigue of their British counterparts. Arguments and accusations surfaced. Tej Singh became the subject of much anger and reproach from his soldiers, as Major George Carmichael Smyth noted:

> [An] old Sikh horseman, a soldier of the times of Runjeet, galloped up to him, and drawing his sword, strove by threats and fierce invectives, to induce the Sirdar to order the advance instead of the retreat of the army. He pointed to the exhausted British forces unable to fire a shot, and asked what was to be feared from them, who, he declared, would not be able to stand a vigorous charge from the fresh troops now opposed to them. The conduct and language of this brave trooper induced Teja Singh with joined hands solemnly to protest and swear by the name of God and his Goroo that he had no other intent in retiring than of saving the troops by preventing their retreat from being cut off by the British. But the old horseman, still convinced of the treachery of the Sirdar, cursed him as a traitor and a coward before the whole army and then quietly returned to his post in the ranks.

The reason for retreat that Tej Singh gave his troops referred to the withdrawal of some British troops towards Ferozepore. A British assistant adjutant general, Captain Lumley, had the night before ordered some cannon back to Ferozepore. This Tej Singh decided to interpret as a flanking move despite the fact that it involved only a few light guns. The years of antagonism and alienation between the soldiery and the officer class now made itself felt. None of the officers who could have grasped the initiative and led an assault did so and none of the common soldiery had the authority to command. Tej Singh's order to withdraw meant a sure victory had been declined for the second time at Ferozeshah by the Sikh commanders after Lal Singh's departure during the night with his army. Dispirited, the Sikh army eventually assented to Tej Singh's orders and began the move north towards Harike and the river.

William Edwardes, Under-Secretary to the British Government, would take time after the war to question the Sikh soldiery regarding Tej Singh's retreat; he was provided with a different reason for the withdrawal:

It was inexplicable at the time to us why this fresh army had failed to advance and reinforce their comrades. Subsequently at Lahore however I was informed that their leaders had restrained the men on the pretext that the day was inauspicious for a battle, it by no means being the intention of the regency that their troops should be successful, but on the contrary, be destroyed by the British, so as to get rid of them forever.

This was quite in keeping with Tej Singh's superstitious nature. It was the explanation Singh later provided to Henry Lawrence – who became Resident at Lahore after the war and who was also curious to understand the Sikh retreat – further adding that it would have been difficult to remove the British from the captured Sikh entrenchments.

The sight of the Sikh army retiring was greeted with some incredulity in the British lines, although in some quarters there were already murmurings of double dealing among the Sikh leadership. Col. Robertson wrote: 'I always believed and I still do that the Sikh General had received an enormous bribe to retire.' William Humbley, meanwhile, suggested that knowledge of Singh's duplicity was commonplace:

> [It] was well known that he was in correspondence with Captain Nicholson; and it is even affirmed, that he had privately furnished an officer with a plan of the intended operations of the Sikh army. It was his object to ingratiate himself with both parties. His position as leader of the army demanded that he should make an attack; while at the same time he foresaw that the British would ultimately triumph in the Punjaub and that it would be for his interest to make friends of them.

It was difficult for Gough to believe his luck. For a second time a Sikh army had retreated at the point of victory. Unable to believe it, he kept the men under arms for around an hour after the Sikh army's withdrawal lest the Sikh commander decide to reverse his decision.

This would not be the end of the fighting for the day. There were three attempts by the small Sikh garrison ejected earlier from the camp to push back the British and fighting continued into the evening. Yet their small numbers failed to trouble the British and by nightfall on the second day all fighting had come to an end.

Aftermath

The copious amounts of food and drink left behind by the Sikh army in the form of wines, beers and brandy helped fuel the celebrations after the battle, and many British soldiers got heavily drunk. Livestock in the form of bullocks, lamb and goats had been left behind along with plentiful amounts of flour and ghee among many other foodstuffs. With utensils also available, British soldiers made their own meals in the afternoon from the available food in the camp, rendering the sourcing of supplies from Mudki unnecessary.

Despite the blaze of battle, which had left some portions of the camp in ruins, vast quantities of bales of silk, valuable cashmere shawls, a collection of fine carpets and other precious merchandise were looted. Several men were severely burnt saving their loot from tents as fires spread through the camp and village. Among the plunder were chests of gold and silver, the looting of which was expressly forbidden to the troops. Dead Sikh soldiers were dispossessed of their valuables. Fingers were cut off to extract gold rings from soldiers killed the previous night, the swollen state of their bodies and hands making them difficult to pull off. And yet, a considerable part of the booty stayed with its new owners for but a short time. The loot, which was being sent back to the Mudki camp using captured Sikh horses and bullocks, was intercepted by the prize agents at the village to be divided up later. Only a few soldiers who had managed to spirit the plunder to Ferozepore on the evening of December 22 managed to keep possession of their gains.

One of the more poignant events during the post-battle looting relates to a Sikh lady who had elected to stay behind after Lal Singh's withdrawal. Baldwin of HM 9th Regiment came across her in a tent where the lady, obviously of high birth or married to a Sikh commander of high rank, was lying on a couch, badly wounded. An elderly woman also lay in the tent, already dead. Baldwin gave the noble lady some water. She was wearing much expensive jewellery: 'a massive gold necklace, bracelets, earrings and an innumerable quantity of finger rings, of gold, set with diamonds, and other precious stones'. Unwilling to kill her for her valuables, Baldwin had left her when the bugle call sounded the arrival of Tej Singh's army. Later in the evening when he ventured into the same tent again, he found she had been murdered and robbed of her jewels by less honourable men. She had been found in a 'magnificent tent lined throughout with silk, the poles of the tent being of solid silver' – a description remarkably similar to that of the tent used by Lal Singh. Other soldiers were attracted to this grand tent for booty, among them Col. Robertson:

> I saw one of my men with an axe in his hand, and asked him what he wanted with that. 'Look here sir,' he said, and taking me into a grand looking tent showed me the tent-pole plated with silver in the most beautiful patterns. We cut it right down on one side with the axe. It was very thick and that ancient tent-pole would have been a prize for the British Museum. Having chopped it (the silver) in two halves, and knocked it into two flat bundles; we had as much solid silver as we could carry. I put my share inside my military cloak, which I had strapped on my back; but the very first day's march I was so tired of my load that I threw it into a ditch.

The last we hear of Lal Singh's tent comes from Thomas Bunbury, commanding HM 80th Regiment as he scoured the camp after the battle:

> A quantity of pomegranates, grapes besides some splendid tents had also been left behind by the enemy. A good deal of Lal Singh's tent was of wrought silk and the tent poles were encased in silver. I sent our Dum-major when I found the tent was being gutted to cut away and bring me a slice of the Persian carpets. It was very splendid and after using it on my way to England, I gave it to the surgeon of the steamer at Suez.

As the looters spread through the camp, they found that it was not entirely empty. Several Sikh soldiers had determined to stay in the camp and sell their life as dearly as possible. Unwary British soldiers met an unexpected end as they entered into certain tents looking for plunder. There were other civilians who were caught in the fighting. Henry Palmer of the 48th Native Infantry wrote of a small Sikh boy on the first day of the battle who had rushed to him for help. The child's younger brother had evidently been badly wounded during the battle. Anxious for help from friend or foe to save his brother's life, the boy had ventured out of his tent and had met Palmer, pleading: '*Aman, aman, mira nicka pura buchow*' (mercy, mercy, save my little brother). Palmer had agreed to help him.

While the Frenchman Mouton had left Ferozeshah for Harike during the night with Lal Singh, there were also several Europeans at Ferozeshah who had decided to stay and fight with the remaining garrison. As would be the case in the other battles of this war, British soldiers showed little mercy to fellow Europeans in the Sikh army. Several of their bodies were seen on the battlefield savagely bayoneted. Joseph Hewitt of HM 62nd Foot, scouring the camp for loot, was told by comrades of the bodies of a European man and woman seen lying dead together in the camp. It was suspected they were French. Several Englishmen in the Sikh army had stayed behind as well. One of them was seen being surrounded by British soldiers. 'Spare me lads! I'm from the old 44th,' he was heard to say. His pleas fell on deaf ears, however, and he was enthusiastically bayoneted by the mob while suffering their abuse.

The Sikh army meanwhile took several British soldiers as prisoners during the battle. Some were taken after the battle as they had got drunk on the brandy found in the camp and had staggered out into the dark. They were treated well by Sikh soldiers. No Sikh prisoners are recorded as having been taken at Ferozeshah.

Mining of the Entrenchments

As the British established a more complete control of the camp, it became apparent that the camp was mined very effectively. Many of the explosions that had taken place during and shortly after the end of the battle had been assumed to be ammunition dumps and hackeries catching fire as various parts of the camp continued to blaze. That this was not the case became obvious a few hours afterwards as casualties mounted in areas of the camp free from fire. In one instance a captured Sikh ammunition wagon being moved out of the camp exploded as it passed over a mine killing all the men and horses in the vicinity. Joseph Hewitt later recalled seeing another mine blow up directly in front of him that evening:

> [The] artillery and cavalry were now retuning to Ferozepore. A cavalry regiment, I believe it was the 3rd Light Dragoons, formed up in line a short distance behind us. I like many more turned round to look at them. Just then a mine exploded with a tremendous noise and blew up several horses and men standing on it. I cannot say if any were killed. If not they must have been seriously hurt. A short time before, two officers had a narrow escape as a mine blew up just as they had passed over it.

Three massive mines were heard to explode during the course of the evening. Many British soldiers decided the risk of looting was too great and moved some distance outside the camp. During the course of the second and subsequent days, it was discovered by the British that around forty Sikh soldiers from the ejected garrison had taken the bold action of infiltrating the British camp and triggering the previously laid mines and hidden ammunition as British soldiers and vehicles passed through the camp. This discovery forced the British to organise armed parties to search the camp. A few of those responsible were caught and these were shot and then hanged from a tree north of the village, supposedly as an example, although it did not seem to have the desired effect. As a further precaution, all unknowns were turned out of the camp in an attempt to curb the saboteurs. Gough also ordered sappers and miners to be sent into the camp to search for unexploded mines. Any found had a guard placed close to them in an effort to prevent more accidental deaths. Nevertheless, mines continued to explode for the next five days. The last British soldier killed by a mine on the battlefield was an officer of HM 80th Regiment on December 24, two days after the battle ended, as he took a dispatch to the Governor-General. Numerous mines remained, however, making the new British garrison's movements hazardous. So much so that Gough had to send back more men on December 28, a week after the battle, to join the sappers and miners working on the mines. Over a hundred mines were found and sprung in the entrenchments.

One of the last fatalities at Ferozeshah was a British sepoy killed by suspicious European soldiers on 23 December. Sepoys in the British army had always held the Sikh soldiers and gunners in high esteem. One of them made the mistake of *salaaming* (saluting) the captured Sikh cannon in the presence of European soldiers. Spotting this, the soldiers formed themselves into a firing squad and executed the sepoy.

Casualties

Various numbers for the Sikh casualties are mooted. Official British sources give a figure as high as 3,000 dead and wounded – several hundred higher than the British numbers. According to Daniel Mackinnon, among others, the Sikh dead did not exceed the British casualties. However, the Sikh casualties were spread over a greater area with soldiers succumbing to their wounds along the way to Harike, which would suggest there were fewer Sikh casualties than the British in the entrenchment. Seventy-three cannon had been abandoned by Lal Singh, including some found in the village wells. Many of these were of heavy calibre. In addition, two guns were also found abandoned at Sultan Khan Walla six kilometres north of Ferozeshah. Some were spiked from the previous day's fighting but most were not. In the entrenched camp, a huge amount of grape, canister and round shot in hackeries and tumbrils had also been left behind. The gunpowder found was estimated to be around 80,000 pounds (between 35 and 40 tons).

British losses totalled 2,415 with 694 killed and 1,721 wounded. In addition, most of the horse artillery and other guns had suffered damage to a large or small degree. One of the more notable casualties was Major George Broadfoot, the abrasive political agent stationed at Ferozepore and one of the architects of the breakdown in relations with Lahore. His body was found by a doctor on 23 December just within the Sikh entrenchments. He had fallen from his horse leaping over a ditch while attempting to attack a Sikh howitzer battery on the south face of the entrenchment and had been shot through the heart and arm. Broadfoot's remains were later laid in Ferozepore cemetery by the side of Sir Robert Sale's and Major Somerset's, with the military honours due to his rank. The Governor-General and his staff attended the funeral. Capt. Peter Nicholson, the assistant political agent under Broadfoot and with whom the Sikh commanders had channels of communication, was also among the dead along with five of the Hardinge's aides-de-camp.

What was never clearly determined were the precise events on the second day of the battle that led to Captain Lumley, the assistant adjutant general, ordering the British artillery back to Ferozepore during the arrival of Tej Singh's army. Lumley was relieved of his position, put under arrest and a court martial ordered due to his unauthorised conduct. A medical certificate was produced declaring the captain to be in an unsound state of mind when he issued the order. However, he had never been known as anything but dependable, and his temporary insanity was treated with a little suspicion in the British press. *The Times* noted that 'the limiting of the period of insanity to the time that he issued the order does not look well certainly; and yet perhaps it may be a solemn truth after all, so we feel ourselves bound to withhold the judgement.' Lumley was later allowed to resign his post and return to England.

News of the battles of Mudki and Ferozeshah would arrive in England on 7 February 1846, seven weeks after the engagements; the reports caused both excitement and anxiety in the press and among the population who remained unaware of how close to a disaster the Battle of Ferozeshah had been for the British. The actual numbers of dead and wounded were kept secret for some time lest it encourage Indian rulers in British territory to reassess their loyalty. The caution over reporting the casualties was such that Sir John Grey's force marching past Ferozeshah two weeks later were never told of the figures and had to resort to estimating the numbers by picking through the battlefield. This inordinate secrecy naturally had the opposite effect; the British public and press correctly assumed the casualties had been high. Nevertheless, a victory had been claimed and the guns at the Tower of London were fired in celebration. Across India, where news was unrestricted and spread by a mail service steamer, word spread rapidly of the near disaster. Crown Prince Waldemaar, the guest of the British government sent away during the night of Ferozeshah, was nonetheless singularly impressed with the conduct of the British army and would later ask the British government for permission to present medals to British officers who had fought at

Mudki and Ferozeshah. He was politely refused as British officers were not allowed to wear foreign medals as a matter of policy.

After the Battle

Gough kept the British army around the location of the Sikh camp for the night of 22 December. With their baggage still at Mudki, full use was made of the Sikh tents and equipment with the troops using looted silk and cashmere cloth and shawls to keep warm during the cold night. The Sikh trenches round the camp served as readymade graves while the Sikh dead were left for the jackals and vultures.

The following day, as mines continued to explode through the camp, the army was moved around two to three hundred yards away from the entrenchments. The job of burying the dead continued and the wounded were transferred to Ferozepore where the barracks were turned into a makeshift hospital. A large pit was dug just outside the fort of Ferozepore for the disposal of the British dead; many of the British wounded had expired on route. The Sikh guns that had not been spiked were now spiked in case the Sikh army should return.

On 24 December, the stench of human and animal corpses and the constant explosion of mines proved too much for Gough, who moved his headquarters to Sultan Khan Walla to the north while the rest of the British army camped at Peer Khan Walla and Khool, seven miles to the west of Ferozeshah. At Sultan Khan Walla, the surplus of Sikh gunpowder that was not required by the British was blown up. The stay at the village was prolonged into the new year.

The withdrawal of both of the Sikh armies had handed a nominal and costly victory to the British. However, a few days later, as the scale of the British losses became more apparent, the battle was declared a victory by the Sikh army. Meanwhile, the close-run nature of the battles so far brought about a realisation in the British camp that the campaign would be much more severe than had been imagined. Robert Haviland of the 62nd Foot wrote during this uncertain period:

> It will give you an idea of how badly we are off for officers. The auctions of the effects of our own poor fellows have been going on

almost every day. Things are selling for a mere song. Nobody will buy in the present state of affairs, not knowing where to put your own things. Brand new regimental – went for 5 shillings which cost at home £7 and everything in the same proportion.

These feelings were not restricted to the lower ranks. Notwithstanding assistance from the Sikh generals, preparations began to be made for a lengthy campaign. Hardinge wrote to Ellenborough, the previous Governor-General of India, from Sultan Khan Walla:

This republican army has more vigour and resolution in it than any with which we have yet had to contend. I have great doubts whether we can cross this season. I cannot tell you the anxiety of watching every movement made for fear of some fatal mistake. It is cruel.

4

Bhudowal

... thousands of bayonets glittering in the morning sun.
— W. Gould, 16th Lancers

Preliminaries

With the British force too crippled after Ferozeshah to advance northwards, Gough would only resume the offensive once his army had been fully rested and new reinforcements and supplies received. Substantial numbers of both were already moving north while the battles of Mudki and Ferozeshah were being fought. From Delhi, a substantial siege train bringing with it five eighteen-pounders, fourteen nine-inch guns, while around 4,000 hackeries and wagons full of supplies and munitions, along with a considerable amount of treasure for the payment of troops, had been organised. This large convoy, stretching sixteen kilometres and protected by a small force of 2,000 sepoys was now moving ponderously towards the Punjab, choking the roads between Ferozepore and Delhi. It was expected to reach Gough's force in early February.

Other reinforcements reached the British force in the early weeks of 1846. On 6 January, Sir John Grey, marching from Meerut, would join the main army at Sabraon with 10,000 men, which included a strong contingent of European regiments. HM 10th Foot and the 9th and 16th Lancers (each 500 strong) were accompanied by the 3rd Bengal Light Cavalry and three other native infantry regiments and a company of sappers. Grey's contingent also included two batteries of artillery (twelve guns), thus considerably strengthening Gough's hand. The artillery included heavy pieces pulled by elephant and bullocks. From Sind, south-west of Punjab, Sir Charles Napier, having received the news of war on 24 December, was marching north with 16,000 troops and sixty guns. With other troops from Delhi, Agra and Meerut being rushed northwards, northern India was to all intents and purposes denuded of British troops.

Thirty kilometres to the north of Gough, the Sikh commanders at their camp at Harike had little intention of assuming the initiative; through late December and January, despite the increasing strength of the enemy, the Sikh army was kept static on the River Sutlej. Ominously, no new reinforcements were being sent from Lahore, and supplies were plummeting. Sikh soldiers would have to watch and wait as British strength steadily grew across the river.

Nevertheless, with both armies immobile a lengthy break in hostilities took place in the Ferozepore theatre of battle. On 17 January, the focus of activities for a time moved ninety kilometres east towards Ludhiana and its vicinity when the Sutlej was crossed by the Sikh army under Ranjodh Singh that had been stationed at Phillour. A not inconsiderable force of 7,000-10,000 infantry and 70 guns, along with some 2,000 irregular cavalry, had been stationed in this location by the Lahore *durbar* both to protect the territories north of the Sutlej and to attack south of the river as the situation demanded. This force had not come in to play since the start of hostilities. As December and January passed, the situation had turned increasingly favourable to Ranjodh Singh as Gough stripped the territory east of Ludhiana of British presence to strengthen his main force. By the middle of January 1846, therefore, a number of inviting targets presented themselves.

Facing Phillour across the Sutlej was the British fort and cantonments of Ludhiana. The transfer of HM 50th Regiment and the 26th, 42nd, 48th and the 73rd Native Infantry regiments to the main force at Sabraon had left the fort garrisoned by a nominal sepoy force consisting of the 5th Native Cavalry plus the 30th Native Infantry reinforced recently by two battalions of Ghurkhas – the Sirmoor and Nusseeree battalions – and four guns of horse artillery under Brigadier Godby. In addition, there was also a force from the Raja of Patiala, ruler of one of the minor states south of the river, anxious to cement his friendship with the British. This Sikh force could not necessarily be relied upon by either the British or Lahore armies. While the soldiers would not fight against their fellow Sikhs, they lacked a commanding officer who would channel their sympathies into a defection to the Lahore army. Ranjodh Singh had more than sufficient strength to destroy the British garrison and capture the city. This was certainly what was expected by the garrison and the population of the city. Large elements of the population of the city were already fleeing. According to a *Delhi Gazette* report, the local merchants were already making provisions for an expected Sikh capture of the city:

> We regret to hear from a most respected party at Loodianah that such has been the feeling at that place regarding the unprotected state of the station, that the mahajuns and cloth merchants generally have deposited their wealth in Phullor, and given large presents to the Sikh force there to protect them in the event of Loodianah being plundered.

Fifty kilometres further to the south-west lay the British depot of Bassian, the main storage centre in the overlong supply chain that connected the main British force with Delhi 400 kilometres to the south. It was important to the British force at Ferozeshah that the town be held if Gough's force were to be supplied. Destruction of the depot's materiel would make Gough's force dependent on the dubious friendship of the Cis-Sutlej states behind him.

The third and much the most attractive target for Ranjodh Singh was the siege train inching its way north into the Punjab. The convoy, escorted by a small contingent of sepoys, was not expected to put up much resistance. Furthermore, a vast sweeping move toward Delhi, its environs now unprotected by any British troops, could be done with ease.

Initially ignoring these opportunities, the Sikh commander had kept his army static at Phillour. There are few descriptions of Ranjodh Singh's character. One that survives dates from after the war and appeared in the *Delhi Gazette* in May 1846 when he was accompanying Hardinge through the Jullunder Doab. The reporter described him as 'about 25 years old, small, rather dull in his expression of countenance and is not a person of ability'. Regardless of his attributes, Ranjodh Singh is generally regarded as loyal to the

Sikh cause, unlike the other Sikh commanders. No direct evidence of treachery on his part has ever surfaced and little is known as to how antagonistic his feelings were towards the mutinous troops. So whether his failings as a commander should be attributed to an indecisive character or to disloyalty is a moot point. Certainly his youth and inexperience would have told against him. Ranjodh Singh would essentially employ the same passive tactics as the Sikh commanders at Ferozeshah, allowing his British counterpart to respond as and when required and with sufficient strength.

Ranjodh Singh had moved closer to the Sutlej possibly a few days earlier than the crossing, thereby destroying any element of surprise; the British Ludhiana garrison was put on alert and his status closely monitored. A reporter for a British Ludhiana newspaper wrote of the Sikh camp on the north bank as 'nearly a mile long with another one smaller several miles down which was pitched yesterday'. Once the river was crossed, Ranjodh Singh's force was joined by a small force of irregulars under Ajeet Singh, the Raja of Ladwa, the only ruler south of the Sutlej to openly join the Sikh cause. With his small army he had partially burned the British cantonments at Ludhiana on 5 January. Without pressing his attack and reducing the British fort, he moved eastwards to join forces with Ranjodh Singh who was now camped at Baran Hara, north-west of Ludhiana. The close proximity of the now enlarged Sikh army to Ludhiana made the settlement an obvious objective for a more effective reduction; yet Ranjodh Singh chose to move in the opposite direction towards Jagraon. The Sikh army encamped at Bhudowal, a small village that was approximately twelve kilometres from Ludhiana and formed part of Ajeet Singh's territories. With no British force either strong or close enough to challenge him, it is difficult to fathom why he chose to dig in here. At just seventeen kilometres south of Phillour, the position was little better than Baran Hara.

While Ranjodh Singh had stayed inactive north of the Sutlej, Gough had largely ignored the threat. However, the Sikh army crossing south required a response and, anxious of an attack on the vulnerable siege train, Gough sent a small force to join up with the exposed garrison at Ludhiana. On 17 January, Lt-Gen. Sir Harry Smith marched eastwards with a contingent consisting mainly of the first brigade of his division: HM 31st Regiment along with the 24th and 47th Native Infantry. Also included were a light field battery and two corps of native cavalry. As more intelligence came in on the strength of the Sikh army, Gough, on 22 January, also sent Brigadier Cureton with the 16th Lancers and two troops of horse artillery as reinforcements for Smith. This effectively totalled one brigade of cavalry and one brigade of infantry, plus eighteen guns.

The village of Dhurmkote fifty kilometres to the east and in the path of Smith's army was held by a small Sikh garrison of around 200 men composed largely of Afghans, Rohillas, Yusufzies and other assorted mercenaries. Dhurmkote was one of the villages south of the river holding grain supplies for the main Sikh army at Sabraon. On arrival, Smith showed little of Ranjodh Singh's indecisiveness at Ludhiana and ordered a cannonade against the village fort. The mercenary garrison, lacking both artillery and a will to fight for the Sikh cause, soon surrendered and were taken prisoners.

While occupied at Dhurmkote, news reached Smith that the Sikh force was encamped at Baran Hara. On 18 January, Smith resumed his march and two days later reached Jagraon, where he was joined by HM 53rd Regiment, which had marched north from Agra and had reached the British base of Bussean the previous day. Smith now sent word to Brigadier Godby, the commanding officer at Ludhiana, to march towards Bhudowal to effect a junction of the British forces. Jagraon was a Sikh town but the sons of the local ruler, Futeh Singh Ahluwalia, allowed the British to occupy the strong fort. Knowing the Sikh army was close, Smith left most of his heavy baggage and four-wheeled transport behind in the fort at Jagraon along with a garrison of two companies of sepoys. On 21 January, between 1.00 and 2.00 a.m., Smith moved out from Jagraon towards Ludhiana. As the chance of an encounter with the Sikh army was strong, Smith ordered his reconnaissance parties to keep a high state of vigilance. In addition, the cavalry and horse artillery were positioned to the front.

The local villagers along Smith's route had been showing open sympathy and support to their fellow Sikhs, doing what they could to indicate the location of the marching British force to the Lahore army. During the night, villagers would set fire to bushes and trees some way off to the British right, visible many miles away. In other areas they passed through, rockets were fired into the night sky. Ranjodh Singh had also sent pickets in the form of two *shutur sowars* (camel riders) to keep any eye on British movements as they slowly marched out of Jagraon. Thus by the time Smith marched out of the settlement, the Sikh army at Bhudowal was ready for battle. Smith knew, thanks to a native informer, that the Sikhs had taken possession of Bhudowal, but the British vedettes had evidently done poor work on reconnaissance because suddenly, at noon, the badly strung-out British force came in sight of the Sikh army only two miles away.

The Battlefield

The village of Bhudowal and its environs had originally been given by the Lahore state as a *jagir* – a gift of territory for an army chief – to Ajeet Singh, Raja of Ladwa. A few years before the war, Ajeet Singh had constructed a small fortified palace for himself in the village. With the onset of hostilities, he gave full support to the Lahore state and had conveyed his family and treasure across the Sutlej for safety. His fort now formed a strong part of the Sikh position. Described by Daniel Mackinnon of the 16th Lancers as a 'solidly built brick building', it now boasted some of Ranjodh Singh's heaviest guns. The village itself was large and possessed a brick wall, ten feet high, which encompassed the fort and made it impossible to scale without ladders. Mackinnon went on to describe the terrain from the west of the village:

> On our front and to the right nearly as far as the eye could reach stretched a sandy plain with scarcely a bush on its surface beyond which lay Ludhiana about 6 miles distant. Our left was flanked by groves of trees and on the left front was the town and fort of Buddewal frowning over the low range of mud houses in its neighbourhood, the whole of which swarmed with the enemy's infantry.

Ranjodh Singh, despite his considerable numerical superiority, had kept his forces in typical defensive order with a considerable number of infantrymen positioned manning the fort walls and village. He had placed a battery of guns in front of the main village gate on a small hill with other guns positioned in or just outside the village. In addition, around the village, he had ordered abattis (tree obstacles) to be prepared and entrenchments dug while some of the lighter guns were placed here, along with some infantry. The defensive line, interspersed with cannon, stretched westwards beyond the village. To the north and west was a largely wooded area both effective for screening troops and making it difficult for the British to see beyond Bhudowal. Ranjodh Singh positioned most of the Sikh cavalry here. Other light guns were placed behind the large banks of sand close to the village, although it is unclear whether these were natural banks of sand or field fortifications. The area around Bhudowal was described by Smith as 'ploughed fields of deep sand'. This was particularly so to the south of the village where the soil was heavily sandy and numerous dunes dominated the landscape, not least a substantial line of sandbanks and dunes a few hundred yards away to the south-west of the village.

The Opposing Forces

Ranjodh Singh's force now numbered between 8,000 and 10,000 men, albeit with a high proportion of irregulars, and forty guns. The British force was comprised of the 16th Lancers, HM 31st and 53rd Foot, and the 24th and 47th Native Infantry, plus a regiment of native cavalry – a total force of around 4,000 men and 18 guns. However, 250 of the men were sick or wounded and incapable of fighting. At this stage, therefore, the well entrenched Sikh force outnumbered the British force by nearly three to one, and they also had a considerable numerical advantage in terms of heavy firepower.

The Battle

With the wood of trees to the north and west of the village hiding most of the Sikh cavalry, it was only the approach of an advance body of Sikh cavalrymen moving towards the British that signalled an imminent engagement, as Mackinnon later described:

> On issuing from the close country upon the plain, a cloud of dust was discerned rising over some trees on our left flank and soon

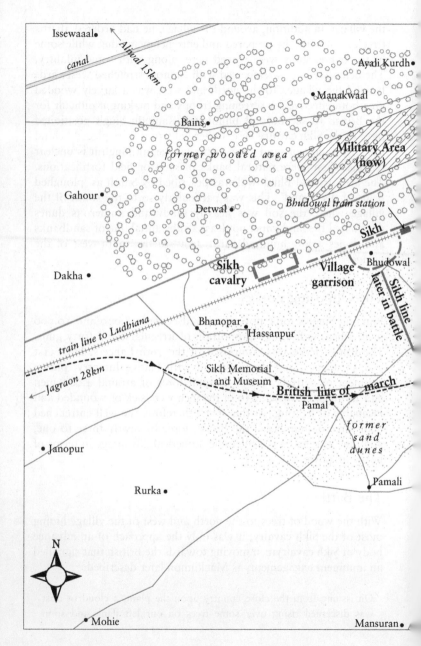

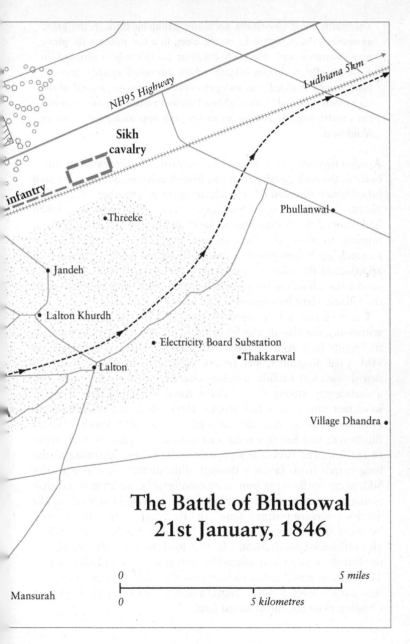

Sikh cavalry

infantry

NH95 Highway

Ludhiana 5km →

•Threeke

Phullanwal•

• Jandeh

• Lalton Khurdh

• Electricity Board Substation

•Thakkarwal

• Lalton

Village Dhandra •

The Battle of Bhudowal
21st January, 1846

0		5 miles
0		5 kilometres

Mansurah

afterwards some Goorchera horsemen galloping through the grove announced the enemy to be on the alert. In a few minutes the grove was swarming with the Sikh irregular cavalry who continued to move parallel with our brigade which advanced steadily into the plain having wheeled into an open column of troops. Several of the Sikh chiefs rode boldly up within a hundred yards of us and watched the cavalry brigade passing in review and approaching the fort of Bhudowal.

Around this time, a distance of 5,000 yards still separated the main body of the Sikh cavalry from the British column, but now the Sikh infantrymen sounded their kettle drums in preparation for combat. Neither side had opened fire despite their close proximity. Smith had stopped the British lines short of Bhudowal for around fifteen minutes to allow the long straggling line of men and baggage to catch up before the march was resumed. Now, as the British approached the village, he ordered a further halt behind the large sand bank affording protection from the Sikh guns south-west of the village. Here he organised and rested his troops.

Carrying out a brief reconnaissance of the Sikh position and witnessing the size of the Sikh force, Smith had little inclination to engage in a trial of strength. Despite being strengthened by HM 53rd Regiment, his orders were to join forces with the British forces at Ludhiana before challenging Ranjodh Singh with a sufficiently strong force. These forces under Godby were to have met him near a hill around three miles east of Bhudowal. However, Godby had not arrived by the time Smith reached Bhudowal, and Smith would now have to get past the Sikh army to reach it. The British troops were quite exhausted owing to the long march from Jagraon through difficult terrain, and with the Sikh army outflanking him quite comfortably, Smith realised that giving battle now would be ruinous. But, bearing in mind Ranjodh Singh's defensive posture, Smith rightly assumed that battle could be avoided by refusing to engage. No doubt his Victorian beliefs also influenced his decision – he was loath to allow the prestige of the British army to be damaged by retreating from an Indian army. Therefore it was decided to veer past the Sikh army position and thus avoid direct combat. Pugh, a member of the 47th Regiment standing close to Smith, stated later:

Sir Harry Smith who had been all through the peninsular war with the Duke of Wellington was a somewhat obstinate old gentleman and thought it would be undignified for him to go out of his way in order to avoid what he called 'some black fellows'; so we marched straight on in open column of companies.

With the Sikh army blocking both the road and the wooded area north of the village, Smith had no choice but to move the British force south of the village thereby passing it on his left. Smith accordingly organised the battle order with the British right in front and the left at the back so that as the line passed Bhudowal with the Sikh army to their left, they could present the normal battle order should Ranjodh Singh order an advance. The cavalry was placed in the front of both flanks to protect the infantry as best it could. The baggage was ordered to stay to the right of the British line. In practice this would be impossible as the baggage train stretched much longer than the British lines so some units formed a small rearguard. This was a token force and it seems Smith had accepted that the baggage needed to be sacrificed in order to get the bulk of the British force to Ludhiana. This was of course assuming that Ranjodh Singh would not be sufficiently adventurous to advance. If he was, the small British force would be annihilated.

British March South

With their battle order established, the British force marched again, veering off to the south but well within range of the Sikh guns, which promptly opened fire with great accuracy and almost brought out the reckless nature of Smith. Pugh of the 47th described the opening of the cannonade from the Sikh artillery:

> We had not gone a couple of miles when bang came a round of shot right into our centre, for the enemy had got the range beautifully. This excited the general and he ordered us to wheel into line, with a view of attacking them in their entrenchments. Only a few yards further a whole shower of grape was poured in upon us. The first round killed a young subaltern of my regiment, Lieut. Rideout. The general, seeing that he had made a mistake as to the strength of the Sikhs, wisely wheeled us back into column.

The Sikh guns were causing casualties but Ranjodh Singh had ordered no advance, and the British force stumbled awkwardly on through the deep sandy stretch to the south of the village. Walking through the dunes was tiring the British infantry rapidly now and Smith ordered frequent stops, especially as it was difficult to stay in formation in those conditions. At various stages, the large sand dunes and ridges sheltered them from the Sikh guns.

At one stage it seemed that Ranjodh Singh would order a cavalry attack as the Sikh cavalrymen formed up ready to be launched. Smith ordered the formation of squares but the British soldiers, desperately tired at this stage, were quite unable to do so. However, the Sikh cavalry advance never materialised. At this time, the British were passing directly south of Bhudowal and the strength of the Sikh army now became much more apparent. As well as the rear, the line of the Sikh army outflanked them east of Bhudowal by around a mile. Sikh soldiers continued to fire on the passing columns with little reply. Smith kept his eighteen guns close to the rear of the cavalry, briefly opening fire for ten minutes in reply.

As the British army columns moved past, the Sikh line to their rear swivelled around to face them from the rear. Around seven battalions of men made a line, with guns in the intervals, and an enfilading attack was commenced on the British column. In order to face this attack, Smith attempted to use HM 31st Regiment as base for a defensive line but failed. Describing the manoeuvre later he would write that 'so deep was the sand and so fatigued were my men, I was compelled to abandon the project'. Soon enough, though, all the British columns had marched past the Sikh line. The British cavalry stayed behind along with some horse artillery for a short duel with the Sikh cannon before retreating and following the infantry towards Ludhiana. The fighting finished three kilometres from Bhudowal when Sikh units ceased firing at the British column that had retreated out of range. With many of the British infantry unable to march the rest of the way to Ludhiana in the intense heat, the British cavalry, principally the 16th Lancers, had to fetch them on horseback. Other men merely clung to the stirrup leathers of the horses or to the horse tails and were dragged along. The British cavalrymen were worn out too, having spent around sixteen hours in the saddle. Around two or three miles from Ludhiana, Smith ordered a stop at a well where the army could rest after the long march.

Capture of the British Baggage

Ranjodh Singh's unwillingness to attack the small column had saved most of the British force, albeit at some expense. Left to their fate were assorted men from various regiments and two *ressalahs* (mounted troops) of irregular horse along with all the camp followers, a considerable number of cattle and the entire baggage train. This rather large and unorganised party was now cut off from the rapidly disappearing British column. Panic quickly spread. Sikh gunners of two light field guns now turned their fire among this contingent, causing a stampede that added to the chaos and confusion. The baggage train became easy prey for the Sikh cavalry who began ransacking it while the British rearguard quickly dispersed in all directions. Some of the units, including elements of the 16th Lancers and HM 53rd Regiment, managed to retreat back to Jagraon while others fled to the south. The thousands of camp followers also dispersed themselves over the countryside as best they could. Many camp followers and soldiers, too exhausted to flee, were seen to lie down in the sand dunes to be taken as prisoners. The British wounded being carried in *dhoolies* had little chance of escape and were captured, the servants having fled. Few of the camels laden with baggage managed to reach Ludhiana although the odd one or two would come straggling in the next day. Smith in his account later stated that some of his own camp followers joined in the plundering of the baggage along with local villagers who had heard of the British predicament.

Given that Ranjodh Singh was disinclined to follow up the skirmish with a concerted attack either on the rear of Smith's fast-disappearing column or the British troops now retreating rapidly back to Jagraon, the battle was effectively over. J. D. Cunningham of the British Engineers attributed the lack of a pursuit to Ranjodh Singh's duplicity, writing that 'the Sikhs did not pursue, for they were without a leader, or without one who wished to see the English beaten'. He also casts some doubt as to whether the Sikh commander was present during the time of the battle.

Meanwhile, detachments from the British Ludhiana garrison,

having heard the sounds of battle, had marched down to join up with Smith. The British force reached Ludhiana around sunset and camped at the partially burnt cantonments, spending an uncomfortable night since all food and shelter had been lost along with hospital supplies for the wounded. During the evening and night, a few stragglers trickled in along with some of the camp followers. Sikh soldiers had released them with the message that they were at war with the British alone.

Casualties

It is unlikely the Sikh army suffered any casualties from the nominal British fire. The British force suffered 69 killed with 68 wounded. In addition, 77 men were missing (most being taken prisoner), although a few of the rearguard drifted in later at Ludhiana and Jagraon. Most of the baggage, including the regimental silver of the 16th Lancers, had been lost along with all the ammunition carts and tumbrils. Two unexpected casualties for the British were self-inflicted, so to speak. Smith suspected that his two Indian guides had deliberately brought his army close to Bhudowal to face the Sikh guns rather than guiding them further south. He personally shot both of them at Ludhiana.

After the Battle

The British force had received a blow but had escaped destruction. Ranjodh Singh's refusal to take the initiative in eliminating the British contingents either at Ludhiana or at Bhudowal now gave the British forces the opportunity to merge. Along with reinforcements, they would meet the Sikh army again at Aliwal. While the battle had little overall effect in the campaign, this latest British setback, albeit small, along with the substantial casualties taken at Ferozeshah and Mudki, was having a bigger effect further south in the towns and villages of British India. It seemed to the populace that the Sikh army, ill-led though it was, might yet destroy the power of the foreigners.

The shift in the general mood north of Delhi was witnessed and recorded by Herbert Edwardes, an aide-de-camp to Sir Hugh Gough. Accompanying the siege train from Delhi, Edwardes had the chance to meet the local people as he progressed northwards. News regarding Mudki and Ferozeshah had already started filtering in before his departure from Agra. Edwardes had learned from a cloth-merchant that a letter he had received from a friend at Delhi mentioned that 'there had been a great expenditure of white cloth on the Sutlej, and that the supply was supposed to be nearly exhausted', white cloth being a euphemism for Europeans. It was also reported that the Governor-General and Commander-in-Chief had also been killed, the British army destroyed, and that the Sikh army was marching towards Delhi. It had only been on 28 December 1845 that reliable information was received of the inconclusive battles. Joining the siege train under the command of Major-General Ekhart and passing through various territories, Edwardes wrote of the increasingly 'silent and sullen' attitude of the local people, who were sympathetic to the Sikh cause and conscious of the British setbacks.

It was at Pehowa in modern Haryana and less than thirty miles away from Patiala that the train halted. A man was sent as far as Malerkotla, around eighty kilometres away, to investigate the situation. At the town he met with six British camp followers who had fled from Bhudowal. These men were brought back and supplied information on the capture of the British baggage train and the numbers of Europeans dead or missing. This had the effect of halting the siege train. Eckhart ordered the troops escorting the cannon to make an entrenchment. The fear of a Sikh attack on the siege train was very real and expected. This was merely a cautionary move as the single native sepoy regiment would have fared badly against a force the size of Ranjodh Singh's army. As another British officer commented, 'It impressed on our mind how easily a more enterprising enemy might have swooped down on our unwieldy line, and captured the whole train.' Eckhart, as commander, also took the precaution of keeping the camp followers in his tent before having them escorted far out of the British camp without the opportunity to fraternise with the sepoys escorting the siege train lest the damaging news be spread.

Nevertheless the news from Bhudowal did spread. It was at this sensitive time that Edwardes was told to leave the siege train and travel to the state of Patiala by the Governor-General. Patiala, a Sikh state south of the Sutlej, had accepted British suzerainty in 1808. Karam Singh, the Maharaja of Patiala, had died on 23 December 1845. Showing little loyalty to his fellow Sikhs, the Maharaja had remained a firm supporter of the British. There were rumours that he may have been poisoned by courtiers wishing Patiala to make a united stand with Lahore against the British. The state of Patiala lay close to the British supply lines for Gough's army and a change in Patiala's allegiance would therefore make it impossible for the British to maintain their position on the Sutlej. To ensure loyalty, Edwardes was ordered to take costly gifts to Karam Singh's successor, Narinder Singh, who was alleged to be wavering in his support. There was already a strong anti-British feeling at the court and the inconclusive nature of the campaign was helping to tilt the sympathies of the Patiala court towards Lahore. This stretched to the ordinary population of the state. Edwardes writes of the 'unfriendly' attitude of the locals as he travelled to see the new ruler. In fact, an escort had to be arranged for fear he would be attacked. Locals hurled abuse at Edwardes, taunting him that the Europeans were 'flying to Calcutta to their ships' while Muslims called the foreigners '*kaffirs*' (infidels) as they passed by. It seemed at one stage that it would be difficult to actually reach Patiala. However, it was reached and upon arrival Edwardes also recorded the 'sullen and reserved demeanour' of the *sirdars* and other notables in the court towards himself. The next day, prior to the new Raja's investiture, the guns at Aliwal could clearly be heard at Patiala. Following his crowning later that day, the Raja told Edwardes how the *sirdars* in the court were for forgetting old animosities with their fellow Sikhs and wanted to fight alongside the Lahore *durbar*. This may have been a play for getting concessions or a genuine statement of their thinking. Edwardes, realising the new Raja was anxious to maintain his position, reminded him that if the Sikh troops were successful they would incorporate the Patiala state into the Sikh Empire whereas the British would preserve it. In addition, the Raja would be given some of the captured Lahore territory at the conclusion of the war should the British be successful. This, along with a promise to increase the number of guns used for the royal salute for the Raja, was enough to swing his loyalty firmly behind the British. Any thought of Sikh unity was suppressed. During the rest of the campaign, the Raja would help the British with utmost effort.

5

Aliwal

There was no dust, for the country round about was green and grassy,
and the January sun shone with almost unclouded brilliance.
                    – Nathaniel Bancroft, *From Recruit to Staff Sergeant*

All India was at gaze and ready for anything.

                                        – Sir Harry Smith

Preliminaries

Bhudowal changed little for both sides and had the effect of
maintaining Ranjodh Singh's advantage. The situation now
resembled the period at Mudki, except that the British forces were
now fragmented while the Sikh army was as one force. Twelve
kilometres to the east of Ranjodh Singh lay the British troops
under Smith at Ludhiana. The small force now included a high
proportion of convalescing troops. Nevertheless, there was a good
chance that Smith, allowing for his reckless streak, would accept
a contest should Ranjodh Singh have the inclination to attack the
city. Thirty kilometres to his west, Jagraon, with its token British
sepoy garrison (along with the remnants of Smith's rearguard
that had retreated from Bhudowal) presented a still weaker force.
In addition, the targets that were vulnerable prior to Bhudowal
still remained so. To his south, around thirty kilometres as the
crow flies lay Bussean, the main British supply base. The town lay
undefended; most of the force stationed here had joined Smith's

force at Jagraon. And of course the siege train, moving north and now only sixty kilometres south of the Sikh army, was closer than ever before.

Ranjodh Singh would ignore these opportunities, however. Upon news reaching the Sikh camp of reinforcements on the north bank, he instead chose to march northwards towards the river ostensibly to cover their crossing of the Sutlej. Thus, at a most critical time, the chance to turn the war decisively in favour of Lahore was given away. Critiquing Ranjodh Singh's tactics, Smith later wrote:

> He should have attacked me with the vigour his French tutors would have displayed and destroyed me, for his force compared to me was overwhelming; then turned about upon the troops at Ludhiana and beaten them and sacked and burned the city – when the gaze I speak of in India would have been one general blaze of revolt.

Early on 23 January 1846, Ranjodh Singh moved the Sikh army north-west from Bhudowal towards the small village of Aliwal, close to the banks of the Sutlej. The exact route is uncertain. Mackinnon mentions the Sikh army having moved to 'the heights of Valore which flank the direct road between Loodiana and Ferozepore and extend to the waters of the Sutlej'. He was almost definitely making a reference to the village of Gahore, just five kilometres north-west of Bhudowal and directly on Ranjodh Singh's route to Porein and Aliwal. On reaching Aliwal later that day, the Sikh army set up camp adjacent to the river, around three kilometres north-west of the village itself. A few hundred metres south of the river ran a large but shallow *nullah* whose north bank was utilised as part of the defensive perimeter round the camp. Prior to reaching Aliwal, Ranjodh Singh had ordered all boats in the location and from Phillour to assemble at Tulwan ford near Aliwal. Around fifty boats had been collected and subsequently used to ferry the new reinforcements that had arrived on the north bank on the night of 27 January. These reinforcements totalled 4,000 regular or *Fauj-i-ain* troops including the crack troops of the Avitabile regiment along with twelve guns and a contingent of cavalry. Crossing the river, the regulars set up their bivouac adjacent and to the west of the main army along the river that night. These appear to have been the only regular troops that

Ranjodh Singh would have and would play an important part in the coming battle.

Meanwhile, in the British camp at Ludhiana, 22 and 23 January had been given over to rest for the troops by Smith. With no commissariat and rations available, British troops and officers alike were obliged to trek the eight kilometres to the bazaars of the city for food, despite the close proximity of the Sikh army. News had reached Smith by now that a fraction of the baggage and rearguard of the British column at Bhudowal had in fact escaped back to Jagraon.

British native irregulars at this stage were being used to infiltrate the Sikh camp after Bhudowal and were now sending back intelligence regarding the movements of Ranjodh Singh's force. On 22 January, word reached Smith that the Sikh army was readying itself for an attack on Ludhiana. The British force adopted a defensive posture on the plain north of the city. Vedettes and advance units were placed at a considerable distance forward of the British line. On 23 January at 11.00 a.m., news sent by spies reached Smith of the Sikh army's move north towards Aliwal. Possibly sceptical of these reports, Smith and his staff and some cavalry nevertheless rode westwards that day the fifteen kilometres towards Aliwal to investigate before returning having convinced themselves.

The news of Ranjodh Singh's move north meant Smith could now move back to Bhudowal and reunite with the portion of his army that had retreated to Jagraon. In addition, Gough had sent additional reinforcements in the form of Wheeler's brigade. Wheeler, who had by now recovered from his injuries at Mudki, left Sabraon with two regiments of native cavalry and four guns. On the evening of 22 January, he reached Dhurmkote. On the 23rd, learning of Ranjodh Singh's presence ten kilometres to his east, blocking his direct path to Ludhiana, he halted at Sidhma Bet (Sidham) returning the twenty-five kilometres back to Dhurmkote before travelling in a semicircular fashion to the south thus avoiding a collision. Passing through Jagraon and then to Ludhiana, he would effect a junction with Smith on 26 January at Bhudowal. Smith's move west for a junction with the forces of Wheeler and the Jagraon contingent would mean a strong combined British force for the first time and would end Ranjodh Singh's opportunity to attack the various British-held towns with relative impunity.

Sacking of Bhudowal

Early on 24 January, Smith forbade leave for troops to go to Ludhiana as a move forward was imminent. At 5.00 p.m. on the same day, the British commenced moving westwards to Bhudowal. Upon their arrival at the village, the British troops bivouacked in the abandoned Sikh village and fort. At this point, one of the more unsavoury incidents of the war took place. Many of the local inhabitants had sided with their fellow Sikhs at the time of the retreat of the British rearguard during the earlier battle; they helped the Sikh army capture British soldiers and camp followers while simultaneously relieving them of baggage and valuables. Angry at the reverse they had suffered, British soldiers and camp followers now fanned out that evening, burning and looting the nearby villages and killing locals suspected of helping the Sikh military. Smith disapproved of this indiscipline but in the event did little to stop the destruction. While at Bhudowal, camp followers and commissariat who had fled during the previous battle now began to reappear from the surrounding villages and Jagraon. The sacking of Bhudowal and its fort yielded little as the Sikh army had taken care to leave nothing of value.

Smith was now reinforced by the Shekhawattee Brigade, increasing his force by a thousand. He was also joined on 25 January by the 2nd Brigade of his division under Brigadier Wheeler. Two additional eight-inch howitzers from the fort of Ludhiana, each requiring twenty large bullocks, were also added to the force that day. January 27 was used as a rest day for the reinforcements under Wheeler that had joined the previous day. The time was also used to bury the British dead littering the sand dunes in the vicinity. Preparations were made for battle the next day.

Just before sunrise on 28 January, the camp was levelled and the British marched from Bhudowal, leaving a few native troops in the village fort guarding the baggage. Smith kept his army in close columns of companies ready for deployment. The cavalry formed the vanguard, followed by the infantry and artillery in the centre, and more units of cavalry bringing up the rear. British advance pickets reached Porein, around five kilometres away from the Sikh army at 8.00 a.m. with the main British force arriving around 9.00 a.m. By all accounts the day was beautiful. The sun shone and there was not a cloud in the sky. No dust rose into the air, giving both armies a clear view of each other and the field separating them.

The Battlefield

The battlefield, an open plain that lay between the two armies was markedly different from the jungles of Mudki and Ferozeshah, or the sands of Bhudowal. The Sutlej, as it wends its way west past Aliwal, finds itself in a huge but shallow valley that it carved in the distant past when the river was a more substantial affair. To the south, the plain is bounded by a substantial ridge in places around fifty feet high, which in former times was the ancient Sutlej bank. The villages of Porein, along with Kotlee (Kotli) and Bhutha Dua (Bultatoa), sit on the edge of this plateau south of the valley. The plateau is uneven in its direction. East of the battlefield, it juts northwards at the villages of Bhutha Dua and Hambran from whence it travels south-west to Porein for around three kilometres. Just south of Porein, the ridge moves north-west to Bhundri around five kilometres away.

Below this ridge was an almost perfect plain running towards the villages of Aliwal and Bhundri with the exception of a gentle ridge running between Aliwal towards the south-west and the village of Gorahoor on the ridge. Daniel Mackinnon left the best description of the battlefield viewed from the village of Porein on the ridge:

> Soon after sunrise, having marched about 8 miles, we reached the verge of a sandy ridge, beneath which lay a hard, level plain, nearly two miles in breadth, and about one in length, flanked on our right by the Sutlej and on the left by trees through which an open country could be discerned to a considerable distance.
>
> To our right front lay the fortified village of Aliwal and to our left front that of Boondree, amidst a thin grove of trees. Along the ridge connecting these villages were thrown up light field entrenchments (then invisible to us) from whence a gradual slope towards the ridge where we stood gave the position a resemblance to the glacis of a low fort, and rendered it peculiarly suited for defensive purposes.

From Mackinnon's description, it appears the ridge or elevation

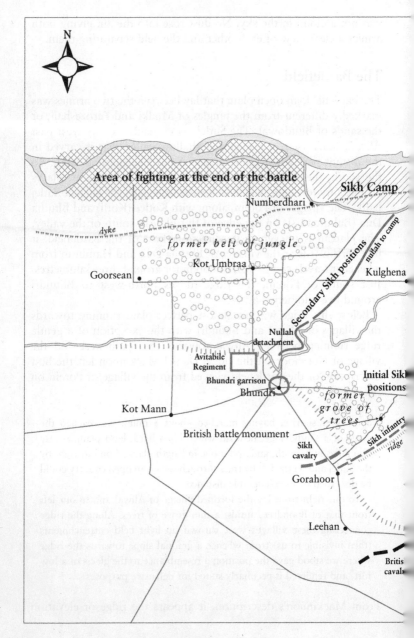

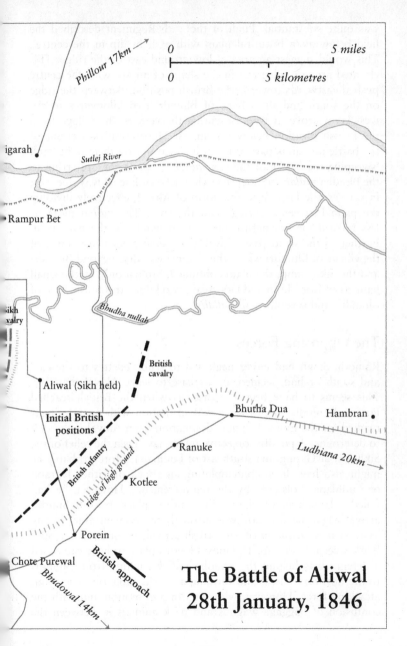

Phillour 17km

0   5 miles
0   5 kilometres

Sutlej River

igarah

• Rampur Bet

Bhudha nullah

Sikh
cavalry

British
cavalry

• Aliwal (Sikh held)

**Initial British
positions**

• Bhutha Dua   Hambran •

British infantry

ridge of high ground

• Ranuke

Ludhiana 20km →

• Kotlee

• Porein

British approach

Chote Purewal

Bhudowal 14km →

The Battle of Aliwal
28th January, 1846

was quite substantial. Pugh of the 47th Regiment described the field below as 'a beautiful plain with a slight dip in the centre'. This would suggest an area of low ground east of the ridge. This elevated area or ridge ran in the shape of an arc with the centre pushed eastwards towards the British position. Between the ridge on the south and the village of Bhundri two kilometres to the west lay a grove of trees obscuring the view of the village from the British position below Porein. Sir Harry Smith's account of the battle mentions part of the British cavalry on their right flank 'sweeping the banks of the wet *nullah* on my right' referring to the Bhudha *nullah*, a Sutlej river channel wending its way due west in very erratic fashion to the north of Aliwal, effectively dividing the plain between the ridge and the river. The *nullah* more or less formed the northern edge of what would be the battlefield. Further to the west, past Aliwal, the *nullah* passed just north of the village of Bhundri where the channel was dry. Beyond Bhundri and the Sikh camp, the plain continued, broken only by the small hamlets of Kot Mann and Goorsean, two kilometres to the west of Bhundri, and several small *nullahs*.

The Opposing Forces

Ranjodh Singh had either neglected to send vedettes to the east and south or had decided in any case to leave Aliwal that day. This seems to have been the case, as when the British reached Porein, Ranjodh Singh's force was in motion with pack animals readied for the move. His new destination from Aliwal is difficult to determine. A possible objective might have been the relief of the Sikh fort at Goongrana southeast of Ludhiana. More probably he might also have been contemplating an attack on either Jagraon or Ludhiana, bolstered by the reinforcements. However, he had failed to launch an attack on either of these places prior to Smith's arrival when the situation was distinctly more favourable. In any case, as news came in of the British arrival, he ordered the Sikh battle lines to form up. The most obvious place to have organised a defence was behind the Bhudha *nullah* running from Bhundri to the north of Aliwal and forming a considerable obstacle to an attacking force. However, with the camp in motion and with the confusion of baggage wagons and pack animals in between the camp and Bhundri, by far the quickest way of readying a defensive line was to push the fighting units eastwards to establish a line along the natural ridge from Aliwal towards Gorahoor. Ranjodh Singh therefore established the Sikh line along the ridge with the left flank of the Sikh army resting on the bank of the Budha *nullah* that ran less than a kilometre north of Aliwal. From this position, the line ran over 2.5 km in a south-westerly direction to the village of Gorahoor.

The strength of the Sikh army by this time was between 14,000 and 18,000 men. This included the 4,000 *Fauj-i-ain* regular troops, the remainder largely being irregulars or mercenaries. The battle order was established as follows. On the right flank, near Gorahoor on the Porein ridge, was placed half of the Sikh cavalry. To the left of this was placed the Avitabile regiment followed by more regular units. The entire left was held by the irregular troops and mercenaries. Just behind the left flank was the other half of the Sikh cavalry. In addition to this, a small garrison held the village of Aliwal a few hundred metres in advance of the Sikh line with two guns. Ranjodh Singh had also ordered some breastworks to be dug on the ridge in as much as time allowed prior to battle commencing, and he had placed most of his artillery along the defensive line. Between thirteen and nineteen guns were left in the fortified encampment and would have little role to play in the coming battle. This left up to fifty-two cannon of varying calibre, including mortars and howitzers, which were dispersed along the line.

Smith had meanwhile paused at the village of Porein, taking time to ascend to the highest house in the village for a view of the Sikh lines. He described the Sikh line as follows:

> From the tops of the houses of the village of Porein, I had a distant view of the enemy. He was in motion and appeared directly opposite my front on a ridge, of which the village of Aliwal may be regarded as the centre. His left appeared still to occupy its ground in the circular entrenchment; his right was brought forward and occupied the ridge. I immediately deployed the cavalry into line, and moved on. As I neared the enemy, the ground became most favourable for the troops to manoeuvre, being open and hard grass land.

Bearing in mind Ranjodh Singh's reticence to take the initiative at Bhudowal, Smith correctly assumed the Sikh army would be kept in a defensive posture and organised his tactics accordingly. He had noticed the weaker Sikh left flank. Singh had also neglected to put a sufficient garrison in the village of Aliwal. While the village did not form part of the Sikh lines proper, its position on the extreme left flank, if it was captured, would allow the British artillery to enfilade most of the southern part of the Sikh lines quite comfortably. After an examination of the Sikh lines, therefore, the capture of the lightly guarded village was made the initial target. Smith advanced his men forward down the ridge where they formed into line.

The British force was 10-12,000 strong. Of this, about 3,000 were cavalry and 7,000 infantry. Accompanying the men was a total of thirty-two guns, of which twenty-two were horse artillery.

Brigadier Godby commanded a brigade composed of the Gurkha Nusseeree battalion and the 36th Native Infantry on the right. On his left was Hick's brigade made up of HM 31st Foot and the 47th and 24th Native Infantry. On the British left was Wilson's brigade composed of HM 53rd Foot, the 30th and 56th Shekhawatee Native Infantry with Wheeler on his right with HM 50th, the 48th Native Infantry and the Gurkha Sirmoor battalion. Most of the artillery – twenty guns including two eight-inch howitzers – were placed in the middle of the line to the left and front of Hick's brigade. The remaining twelve guns were place on the left in front of Wilson's brigade and opposite the Sikh regulars.

The cavalry on the right was composed of the 1st and 5th Light Cavalry, the Governor-General's bodyguard and the Shekhawatee cavalry regiment along with the 4th Irregulars. On the left was placed the 16th Lancers and the 3rd Light Cavalry.

Eight of the eleven regiments and three out of the six cavalry regiments would attack the weaker Sikh middle and left. This left Wheeler's brigade and McDowell's cavalry on the British left. Thus the British right would deliver a powerful and overwhelming attack while the British left would engage with the Sikh regulars. With the line formed, Smith found the Sikh left flank extended further than his right. HM 31st Regiment on the extreme right of the British line was then ordered to move further northwards.

The Battle

At ten minutes to 10.00 a.m., Smith ordered forward the British skirmishers. As they went forward, the first cannon fire ensued from the Sikh guns. The skirmishers were promptly ordered back and the British horse artillery pushed forward accompanied by the 16th Lancers to within 700 yards of the Sikh lines for a duel with the Sikh guns. The cannonade continued for more than half an hour and, though keenly fought, was not marked by any notable successes for either side. Accordingly, Smith ordered the British right to advance with Godby and Hick's brigades directed against the village. It was captured quite easily with HM 31st Regiment doing much of the work. The troops that Ranjodh Singh had stationed there, Dogra hill men irregulars and assorted mercenaries, had little heart or desire for a struggle. Upon firing a volley and seeing the British brigades moving towards them, they rapidly melted away. A Sikh general commanding the left, on seeing the irregulars streaming away from their lines, gallantly charged the British line on his own, hoping to rally the men. Pugh of the 47th Regiment, fighting in Hick's brigade to the south of the village, wrote the following:

> As we came tolerably near, the greater portion of their infantry bolted. I remember a Raja, one of their leaders who, when he saw his men bolting, rode fiercely down upon the 31st Foot on our right; but before he had ridden half the distance, he fell riddled with bullets. The Sikh gunners also bolted and we took possession of their guns. Having secured them we swept through the village of Aliwal which gave the name to this fight.

Robertson of the 31st, fighting on the right, also recalled the lone horseman riding towards the British line:

> Just then a mounted man rode right at us all alone, and I ran out to meet him; but before we met both he and the horse rolled over dead, shot by my own men behind. He fell right at my feet, and I picked up his sword.

This display of courage did not have the desired effect on the retreating soldiers, however. The short struggle left the village in British hands along with the two guns the irregulars had abandoned. Ranjodh Singh, upon seeing the loss of the village, moved forward his cavalry on the Sikh left to try and recapture the town. The British attack was too strong and well-supported though. There are no records as to the size of the Sikh cavalry. Mackinnon suggests a relatively small number, writing later that 'a small band of Sikh horsemen, many of them richly attired, suddenly rode forth from behind the batteries'. They were quickly overwhelmed by the advancing British line. Smith now sent Brigadier Cureton's cavalry brigade on his right flank to help in the possession of the village, the British cavalry driving away any remaining Sikh cavalry without too much effort.

By this time, the various irregulars on the left also began streaming away under the advance of the British infantry. Nevertheless, a few brave individuals attempted to make a desperate stand. A British soldier's account, later appearing *The Times*, ran as follows:

> One very fine fellow came down at me whilst I was leading the troop on. I shouted to him to lay down his arms and he should not be killed but he waved his sword over his head and with great courage came right at me. He tried to get on the near side of my little horse when I suppose he thought he could do as he liked; but this of course I would not allow and kept him on my sword side. All the sergeants of the troop were shouting out to me to take care – 'Take care sir; for God's sake, take care, sir, he will be using his matchlock!' but he contented himself with his sword and whilst he was trying to cut at me one of the men rode at him and gave him a fearful blow over his head.

The British line was not delayed for long and the dissolving of the entire Sikh left had changed the nature of the battle within minutes. With the irregulars and mercenaries rushing towards the river, only the veteran regulars around 4,000 strong on the right, and some units in the Sikh middle, were left holding the line. From a position of numerical superiority, the remaining Sikh army now found itself not only outnumbered but in grave danger of being outflanked on the left. According to J. D. Cunningham, at this stage Ranjodh Singh also fled the field, leaving the remaining Sikh forces on the field to fend for themselves. With no one to manage the Sikh line, there was little chance of recovering from the disaster on the left. British units were already wheeling to their left to attack the remaining Sikh units. The regular units of the Sikh army, however, were made of much sterner material and, as at Mudki, they showed little inclination for a withdrawal. They now dug in for a fight as the British lines opposite them and to their left advanced.

British Attack on the Sikh Right

With the Sikh lines forming an arc with the middle closest to the British lines, the two lines first met in hand-to-hand fighting in that middle. Daniel Mackinnon recorded the fighting there:

> The two squadrons moved forward in compact and beautiful order, charged home and captured every gun under a storm of fire from the Sikh artillerymen, and musketeers stood their ground and fought with desperate bravery and resolution. Venting their unconquerable hatred in savage yells of abuse, the swarthy warriors cast away their discharged muskets and rushed sword in hand to meet their abhorred opponents preferring death to retreat.

On the Sikh right, the fighting was still more intense. The Sikh guns caused chaos among the advancing British lines, firing grapeshot and chain with great rapidity. One of the Sikh shells burst directly over Smith, the fragments cutting his telescope in two and nearly hospitalising him. As the firing from the Sikh line became too severe, the advancing British units were ordered to lie down to escape the worst of it. After several minutes, they were ordered to rise and move forward forty to fifty yards. This manoeuvre had to be repeated several times until the line managed to get close enough. Once close enough, the line charged forward with bayonets and fighting began at close quarters.

Further on the Sikh right, the Sikh *Gorchurra* horsemen came under attack from the British 3rd Light Cavalry but drove them off. The 16th Lancers were ordered in as reinforcements for the light cavalry, which turned the balance of the fight towards the British, the *Gorchurras* retreating. Now heavily outnumbered, it became impossible for the Sikh army to maintain its present line and the decision was made to withdraw to a more defensible area further back. This manoeuvre meant the whole Sikh line swinging back using the right flank almost as a pivot with the left flank moving from Aliwal to the southern edge of the Sikh camp 2.5 km away while the right flank moved a shorter distance of around a kilometre to the village of Bhundri. Although perhaps simple on paper, in reality this entailed covering quite a distance while under fire from the British line. Nevertheless, the Sikh right flank moved back through the grove of trees while the middle moved back, setting up a new defensive line at the Bhudha *nullah*. With the absence of a Sikh commander, it is unclear who now gave the orders. Even so, the retreat was orderly and well-executed.

The Battle at Bhundri

Sikh troops occupied the village of Bhundri, and the Avitabile regiment now took up position to their right, while a strong unit took up position north-east of Bhundri using the Bhudha *nullah* as a makeshift trench. Smith ordered the 16th Lancers and the 3rd Light Cavalry to charge the Avitabile regiment. As the charge closed, the regiment formed a square. The defensive square was successful with the British cavalry charging through it making little impact. Finding themselves behind the Sikh lines, the 16th Lancers charged again but from behind. Unable to break the formation, they charged for a third time. Also under increasing fire from twelve British horse artillery guns 300 yards away, and lacking no guns with which to answer, the Avitabile regiment gradually retreated, putting up dogged resistance as they moved the three-kilometre distance towards the river. Mackinnon of the 16th Lancers was involved in the desperate fighting against the regiment and recorded their slow and stubborn retreat from Bhundri towards the river:

> [When] driven at every point from their well chosen position, the Aeen battalions fell doggedly back, but never condescended to fly, though plied with musketry and shrapnel. They retreated, maintaining the character they had earned, and facing about at intervals to check their pursuers by a retreating fire. Those troops, the pupils of Avitabile, did credit that day to themselves and their master; and however

we may abhor their treachery and thirst for blood, displayed in the revolutionary annals of the Punjab since the death of the old lion of Lahore, we must at least bear witness to their resolute courage and soldier-like bearing.

British units now moved in to capture the village. HM 53rd and the 30th Native Infantry cleared Bhundri and proceeded to swing northwards to where remnants of the Sikh regulars were making a stand. The last of the heavy fighting took place around the Bhudha *nullah*. Mistakenly called a 'ravine' by Sir Harry Smith in his account, the river bed was the same that flowed to the right of the British right prior to the battle. In the riverbed, around a thousand Sikh infantry men were making a desperate stand, holding up the British advance in the centre. By this time, the 30th Native Infantry had circled behind Bhundri and were threatening to attack the regiment from the rear. In addition, British horse artillery guns had been brought to the village and were now firing into the Sikh troops in the *nullah* without reply. The position was becoming undefendable and the retreat now became general.

Retreat to the River

The spirited rearguard action of the Avitabile and *Fauj-i-ain* troops near Bhundri had prevented the Sikh collapse on the left turning into disaster. With the British force occupied at Bhundri, the interval had by this time allowed large numbers of Sikh troops to commence a retreat across the river. Following the capture of Bhundri, the British right had moved forward, capturing the Sikh camp and reaching the banks of the Sutlej. Meanwhile, on the British left, a general sweep in clockwise fashion through Bhundri and the villages of Goorsean and Kot Umbraa to the west and north of Bhundri and on to the river was executed. A last ditch attempt was made by Sikh troops at the river's edge. Nine cannon were unlimbered and readied to be fired, and the Sikh gunners managed to get off one volley before they were overwhelmed by the advancing British line.

The Crossing of the River

The disadvantage of forming a defensive line with the river at the rear now became apparent. Considerable numbers remaining on the banks of the Sutlej were attempting to swim across to the north bank, becoming easy targets for the British horse artillery and musketry arrayed along the south bank. To the east of the camp the Tulwan ford allowed some of the Sikh troops to cross. The ford had also allowed the removal of several pieces of artillery. Two of these now became stuck in the river mud and had to be abandoned; they were subsequently captured by the British. A third sank in quicksand. There were some attempts to rescue these but the British musket and cannon fire from the south bank of the river was too great now to allow isolated units to successfully rescue the guns. Two cannon were successfully dragged to the other side and unlimbered but were abandoned in the face of furious fire from the British artillery on the other bank. The cannon were spiked by British troops crossing the river. By 2.00 p.m. the battle was over and the whole Sikh camp and the river's south bank were in British hands, although gunfire across the river would continue until around 3.30 p.m.

Casualties

British records estimate the Sikh casualty figure to be as high as 3,000 dead and wounded although it was certainly no more than several hundred. Intelligence reports relating to Ranjodh Singh's army received later by the British put his strength at no lower than prior to the battle. Most of the casualties came during the retreat across the Sutlej with British artillery and musket fire killing hundreds of soldiers as they swam to the other side. This was confirmed downstream at Sabraon by Sikh soldiers where many bodies were seen floating down the river a few days later. In other places like Bhundri village, the scene of heavy fighting, the number of dead and dying of both sides suggested a much closer and keener contest. Capt. J. D. Cunningham, present at the battle, observed that 'the ground was more thickly strewn with the bodies of victorious horsemen than of beaten infantry'.

Like the British soldiers, Sikh soldiers preferred death on the battlefield to surrender. Even after the end of hostilities, wounded Sikh soldiers lying on the battlefield chose to fight and die rather than be taken prisoners, as William Gould of the 16th Lancers recorded as he toured the battlefield later that evening:

> Riding back in the dark we could plainly hear the groans of the wounded and dying Sikhs; we could not help them, and even if we attempted, they have been known, even when almost dead, stretching out their hand and stabbing a Sepoy or one of our own, who may have been near them. However, all of ours were collected.

The Avitabile regiment, forming the rearguard, survived the battle intact despite getting much attention from the British, managing – it was later reported – to cross with their baggage intact. Gulab Singh, the Raja of Jammu would distribute 9,000 rupees among its troops for their gallant stand. Much more damaging than the human casualties to the Sikh army was the loss of the artillery. Sixty-seven cannon of various calibre, including mortars and howitzers, were captured by the British along with forty swivel guns that would prove difficult to replace. As at Ferozeshah, several British fought on the Sikh side and while the Sikh soldiers rarely asked for mercy, some of the Europeans did. This provoked a mixed response as before. One of these was an Englishman by the name of Brown. Born in Maidstone and working for the East India Company artillery regiment, he had decided to desert eighteen years earlier and join the Sikh army. He held the rank of colonel in the Sikh artillery by the time of the battle. Name changes were common among deserters in order to make themselves untraceable, and Brown had changed his name to Potter. British soldiers vied to shoot him, but he was spared by an officer because of the intelligence he could provide on the Sikh army.

The British losses amounted to 151 killed with 422 wounded and 25 missing, making a total of 598 casualties. A total of 245 of the casualties were cavalrymen. Most of the casualties had been on the left where Wheeler and McDowell's brigades had been positioned along with the 16th Lancers, who on their own suffered a quarter of the total casualties fighting against Sikh regulars.

Sacking of the Camp

The Sikh camp was sacked in the afternoon. Among the valuables carried away were numerous shawls, bangles of gold and other jewellery including magnificently made shields gilded with gold. One consequence of the collapse of the Sikh left wing was that the British troops nearer the Sutlej had the opportunity to enter the Sikh camp far earlier than the soldiers on the British left, who had a greater distance to the river and faced much fiercer resistance. This resulted in a rather uneven distribution of loot causing considerable disquiet. Many of the British units complained of the native Shekawattee cavalry carrying away much of the loot before the rest of the British army could engage in the plundering. Hundreds of camels of the Sikh army loaded with tents were claimed by new owners.

After the Battle

Ranjodh Singh, meanwhile, retreated to Phillour around twenty kilometres east of Aliwal. According to intelligence reports gathered by Frederick Mackeson, superintendant of the Cis-Sutlej territories after the war, his force faced much taunting by the *banniahs* (shopkeepers) and locals for their failure. In any case the troops were anxious to recross the Sutlej or to join up with the main force at Sabraon. Ranjodh Singh wrote back to Lahore blaming the Aloowala troops of the Kapurthala Raja, a vassal of Lahore, for the defeat at Aliwal.

Following the battle, Ranjodh Singh still had 14,000 men remaining under arms. This was not far short of the total he had prior to the battle. However, the loss of equipment and baggage told a different story. The irregulars in his army, having lost considerable possessions that had been left in the camp, had insufficient means to re-equip themselves. As compensation, Ranjodh Singh distributed ten rupees per horseman. The loss of guns meant, however, that he was now virtually bereft of artillery apart from some old cannon in the Phillour fort.

Looking around for other sources, the son of Illahee Baksh, the commander of the Sikh artillery, was sent to Kapurthala, requesting the ruler Nihal Singh to give all the artillery he had.

Nihal Singh refused, so Ranjodh Singh also attempted to extract some guns from the local Sikh chieftains, managing to obtain two guns in this fashion. With the seven guns from the fort of Phillour, along with the nine the army still had, this only gave the army a total of eighteen guns. He also attempted to procure materials to make new guns. However, the Battle of Sabraon and the end of the campaign would occur before any concerted action to replace the guns could gather momentum.

The loss at Aliwal meant the Sikh army having to abandon the minor forts still in their possession on the south bank of the Sutlej. Bhudowal fort was lost along with Noorpur, just east of Aliwal and thirty kilometres due south of the Sutlej. The Sikh garrison in the fort of Goongrana was also evacuated to avoid being cut off.

The British meanwhile spent the evening of the battle tending to their dead and wounded. The fighting had stretched a considerable distance from Porein to Aliwal and through the villages of Goorsean and Kot Umbraa to the banks of the Sutlej nine kilometres away; the collection of the casualties would therefore take longer than expected. Gould of the 16th Lancers, one of the men assigned to gather the dead and wounded, would later recall the bloody scene:

> We had five miles to go over to collect the wounded, and bury the dead. The carnage was fearful; horses, dead and mutilated most fearfully, as they plunge very much when wounded. Several were trying to get about on three legs; we killed these outright. Where the fighting was close, as in square, men's bodies were thickest; wounded in all conceivable ways; jaws shot away; often heads; some disembowelled.

Most were dispatched to Porein village where a field hospital had been set up. Other units buried British dead where they lay on the field. Those with less severe wounds were sent to Ludhiana. Smith set up the British camp that night close to the former Sikh camp, despite the numerous corpses of man and beast littering the place.

A considerable amount of ammunition in the form of cannon shot, shell, grape and ball cartridges in the Sikh camp had fallen into British hands, along with shot found in the limbers of cannon and loaded wagons. Smith reserved six large hackeries of gunpowder to destroy the nearby forts in the coming days. The remaining shells were thrown in the river while the shot was kept for British army use. The rest of the ammunition was destined for destruction. The cartridges had been packed in large wooden cases. During the night of 28 January, whether due to fire in the camp or for other reasons, the cases exploded through the night. In another part of the captured camp, British soldiers with orders to destroy the ammunition blew up a large amount. The resulting loud explosion unsettled horses and camels in the camp and hundreds broke loose and proceeded to stampede through the camp causing chaos before order was re-established.

On 29 January, with their baggage having arrived from Bhudowal, the British moved camp close to Aliwal village. The captured cannon were all brought into the encampment by the horse artillery. The disposal of the British dead on the field continued. However, it was found that the bodies that still lay on the plain had already been stripped and plundered quite efficiently, only those whose wounds had marred their clothing having been spared. Who had done this was difficult to ascertain; all the surrounding villages were still deserted from the previous day. The majority of the British camp followers, who had quite effectively plundered Mudki, were still safely ensconced in Bhudowal twenty kilometres away. It was thought the advance guard of the camp followers, who had reached Aliwal the same day of the battle, were the culprits.

The rest of the day was assigned for rest while some units were ordered to continue disposal of the captured munitions. The cannon shot and shells were thrown into the deeper parts of the Sutlej. However, the disposal of this large cache of artillery munitions came to the notice of some of the Sikh soldiers on the north bank. A number of intrepid souls recovered some of the ammunition by swimming the Sutlej and bringing away the shot, although British soldiers opened fire at the swimmers from the south bank and managed to kill some.

On the afternoon of 29 January, many of the British dead were buried on the ridge close to Porein. The officers were buried in the evening. On the same day, news of Smith's victory was also received at Sabraon where Gough ordered the whole of the army into line and a salute was fired to mark the victory. The following day, disposal of the ammunition continued and the men rested. Some of the ammunition was taken to the deserted Sikh forts in the immediate vicinity for destruction. The forts of Bhudowal and Noorpur, among others, were blown up.

On 1 February, the rest of the British wounded were sent to Ludhiana along with most of the captured artillery, forty-seven in number. The five most splendid pieces, said to be palace guns, were readied to be taken to the main camp. Smith wrote later that they were 'the most beautiful guns imaginable, which will, I believe, be placed in St James's Park, London'.

Smith had considered the option of crossing the Sutlej, but he neither had the authority nor the supplies or commissariat required for a strike north. Instead he now rejoined the main army, reaching Sabraon on 8 February and leaving Wheeler's brigade at Ludhiana to watch the Sutlej fords for an unlikely move by the Sikh force north of the river. Smith's force halted a mile before Sabraon with a delighted Gough personally coming out to greet and salute them for their victory at Aliwal.

The victory had provoked a mixed response toward Sir Harry Smith. It cemented his profile in England where the success was reported with much relief after the heavy casualties and uncertainties of the previous battles. It perhaps flattered him more than he deserved; his arrogance and recklessness at Bhudowal were less easily forgotten by the soldiers and fellow officers. Lord Dalhousie, Governor-General of India during the Second Anglo-Sikh War, wrote:

> But here Sir H. Smith is treated with ridicule or worse. His entire suppression of the facts of the affair of Buddiwal just before Aliwal, where he was shamefully surprised – lost all his baggage, many of his sick and followers, and was saved from utter rout only by the cavalry under Cureton, who personally extricated him – is regarded with great contempt, and that circumstance perhaps leads to his getting less personal credit for managing Aliwal than he does at home, and possibly less than he deserves. In short, while all admit him to be a gallant, dashing soldier, he has no military reputation in India. There his apotheosis in England created unmitigated disgust.

Aliwal, like Bhudowal, was of considerably less importance than the main battles that occurred further west. Nevertheless, a clear British victory here had an important psychological effect on the minor states nearby. The optimism among the local Sikh population generated by Mudki, Ferozeshah and the British setback at Bhudowal was negated by the Sikh defeat at Aliwal. This was especially so for the local petty rulers who now rushed to offer help to the British. With Ranjodh Singh's army a spent force and Smith moving back to join Gough, the focus of the war moved permanently back to Sabraon.

6

Sabraon

*You destroy a whole army, which, whatever its faults and crimes may
have been, has always been ready to obey the orders of the state and
its officers.*

— Sikh soldiers to Tej Singh, Sabraon

Preliminaries

The abandonment of the guns and stores of supplies and munitions
at Ferozeshah by Lal Singh would have a telling effect on the
capabilities of the Sikh army through the month of January
1846. For the first time in the war, the Sikh artillery, dominant
at Ferozeshah, was now weaker than its British counterpart.
A disproportionate number of Sikh artillerymen had also been
among the fatalities in the previous battles, victim to the Sikh
commander's policy of withholding the Sikh cavalry from the
contest. Still, many heavy pieces remained, as the British would
note after the Battle of Sabraon; most of the Sikh guns used
in the fight were heavy artillery rather than the lighter horse
artillery. The problem of supplies should not have hampered the
Sikh army under normal circumstances. Compared to the British
supply lines stretching to Delhi and Meerut, the Sikh army's routes
were much shorter. Lahore was less than eighty kilometres away.
However, the authorities at Lahore were also taking the precaution
of sending supplies on a very fitful basis to further weaken the
army in line with their own goals. As food stocks dwindled, the

soldiers resorted to sending deputations back to Lahore to beg for assistance. Alexander Gardner, an American soldier at the court of Lahore, was a witness to one of the parties sent to the Lahore court to meet Maharani Jindan. The men, he recorded, complained that they were resorting to eating grain and raw carrots at Sabraon:

> I was standing close to the Rani, and could see gesticulations and movements of the deputation. In answer to the urgent and loud complaints of the sacrifice to which the army was exposed, she said that Gulab Singh had forwarded vast supplies. 'No he has not,' roared the deputation; 'We know the old fox: He has not sent breakfast for a bird (*chiria-ki-haziri*).' Further parley ensued, the tempers of both parties waxing wrath. At last the deputation said, 'Give us powder and shot.' At this I saw some movement behind the purdah (the little Dalip was seated in front of it). I could detect that the Rani was shifting her petticoat; I could see that she stepped out of it, and then rolling it up rapidly into a ball, flung it over the screen at the heads of the angry envoys, crying out, 'Wear that, you cowards! I'll go in trousers and fight myself!' The effect was electric. After a moment's pause, during which the deputation seemed stunned, a unanimous shout arose, 'Dulip Singh Maharaj, we will go and die for the kingdom and the Khalsaji!' And breaking up tumultuously and highly excited, this dangerous deputation dispersed and rejoined the army.

Gulab Singh, the ruler of Jammu and a vassal of the Sikh state was as antagonistic towards the Sikh army as the Sikh commanders and hoped to engineer an independent state of his own under British supremacy if the Lahore army could be destroyed. As Gulab Singh was unreliable, the *punchayats* came to Lahore on 1 February to escort him to the Sabraon camp. They were offered 300 rupees each to return to the camp by the court, anxious to get rid of the armed men. This was refused along with a further offer of 500 rupees. Gulab Singh would never come to the front despite the clamour for help. In order to show his allegiance to the army, however, he is alleged to have organised a novel way of supplying the army. Small amounts of supplies were sent a horse at a time in long lines to make his aid look larger than it actually was.

A more reliable source for the army during the early part of

January had been the Lahore *jagirs* (landholdings) on the north bank of the Sutlej. The fort of Dhurmkote held plentiful supplies of grain which were ferried over. Smith's capture of the fort on 18 January ended this supply line. Despite the calls for help to Lahore, rations would never come in the quantities required. The lack of supplies extended to forage for the cavalry horses, forcing Sikh parties to make raids across the river and engage in the dangerous activity of gathering forage in the no man's land between the two armies on the south bank. Perhaps more ominously, of the meagre munitions being received from Lahore, significant portions were being found to be deliberately sabotaged. Many of the Sikh shells would be seen to explode in midair in the coming battle. In addition, of the few sacks of gunpowder that were arriving, many were found to be full of sand.

The only welcome piece of news for the Sikh soldiers was the arrival of General Sham Singh Attariwalla at Sabraon. Sham Singh was one of the old guard, having spent years campaigning with Ranjit Singh's armies against the Afghans in the north-west, Multan and Kashmir. Unlike the other commanders, his loyalty to the troops was assured. He had resigned from the army as the troubles after Ranjit Singh's death engulfed the state. Although at first in the village of Kaonke Kalan south of the river when the war commenced, he had no wish to be in British territory while the Sikh state was at war with foreigners, and he promptly returned to his ancestral village of Attaree. When the news reached Lahore on 25 December 1845 of the army's retreat from Ferozeshah, Maharani Jindan had sent a troop of horsemen to persuade him to join the army, a request he readily accepted. Sham Singh had always counselled against war with the British, particularly in the confused and unprepared condition in which the state found itself. However, once hostilities had broken out and his country needed him, the old general was ready to join the troops; he reached the Sikh army camp at Sabraon on 28 December. Prior to leaving, and knowing he would not be returning to his village, Sham had settled all his accounts. On his arrival at Sabraon, Tej Singh kept overall command of the army, assigning only the defence of the Sikh left flank on the south bank to the veteran general.

Despite the enforced inactivity of the Sikh army and the lack of supplies, discipline and morale stayed high, and the Sikh soldiers

1. Tej Singh, the commander of the Sikh army. Tej Singh, along with the Vizier Lal Singh, would maintain a friendship with the British via secret correspondence before and during the campaign. (*National Army Museum*)

2. Dhuleep Singh, the young Maharaja of the Punjab during the time of the First Anglo-Sikh War. He had succeeded to the throne after a period of uncertainty following the death of Ranjit Singh. (*National Army Museum*)

3. Lal Singh, posing for a sketch by Charles Hardinge (son of Sir Henry Hardinge) a few weeks after the end of the war. 'I then asked Raja Lal Singh, the Ranee's favourite, to let me sketch him, and he appeared to be pleased with the proposal as he took the trouble of putting on a suit of armour and, stroking his beard, seated himself in what he fancied was a most picturesque attitude.' (*National Army Museum*)

4. Gulab Singh, ruler of Jammu and a nominal vassal of Lahore. He had aspirations to become the ruler of Kashmir following a war with the British. Sketch by Charles Hardinge. (*National Army Museum*)

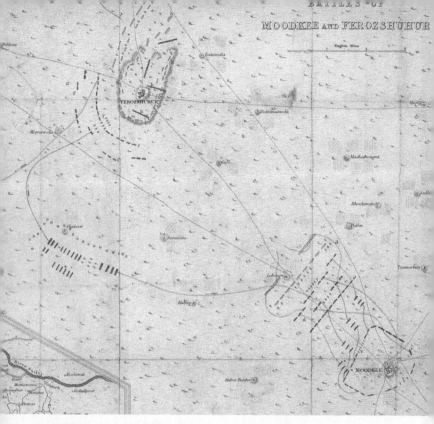

5. Detail of a contemporary map, showing the order of battle at Mudki and Ferozeshah. The Mudki section to the bottom right shows the village of Lohaum behind the Sikh lines, a detail missing in most maps of the battle. However, the fork in the road on the Mudki battlefield is shown erroneously to the immediate north of Lohaum. The north road from the fork, the direct road from Ferozeshah to the Sikh position at Lohaum is shown and still survives in large parts. The south road leads to Ferozepore to the south of the Sikh position. On the day of the Battle of Ferozeshah, rather than using either road, Sir Hugh Gough, the British Commander-in-Chief, veered west before advancing north to effect a junction with Sir John Littler's forces. (*British Library*)

6. The field of Ferozeshah on the second day. The area shown is most likely to the east of the village. Sketch by Charles Hardinge. (*National Army Museum*)

*Tree under which
Simmons & mols
were buried after the fight –
at Ferozeshah – A marks their grave*

7. Sketch among the papers of Lt Alfred Angelo Simmons, HM 29th Regiment, showing the battlefield north of Ferozeshah village. British soldiers bury their dead below the large tree after the battle. Notice the distant line of trees ringing the field. Sikh soldiers had felled most trees to a distance of 300 yards around the camp and village. The writing beneath the tree reads: 'Tree under which Simmons [& mols?] were buried after the fight at Ferozeshaw – *A* marks their graves'. (*National Army Museum*)

8. A sketch by the same unknown hand of the view north of Ferozeshah village. The tree on the left shaded the burial plot of a British soldier, while the tree on the right was used to hang a Sikh saboteur, one of many who had infiltrated the British camp to set off mines. The writing beneath the tree reads: 'This tree was the one the Sikh was hung under the morning after the Battle, he was caught firing a mine'. (*National Army Museum*)

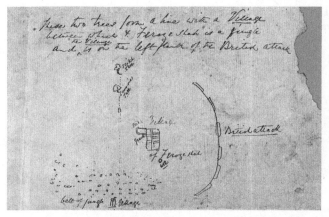

9. Contemporary sketch of Ferozeshah, then a small village of around ten dwellings with a dense belt of jungle separating it from Misreewalla to the west, the direction in which Major-General John Littler retreated and from which Tej Singh's army arrived. The sketch also shows a British grave dug immediately adjacent to the village. The writing at the top reads: 'These two trees form a line with a village between which and Ferozeshah is a jungle and the village is on the left flank of the British attack'. (*National Army Museum*)

10. The field of Ferozeshah after the battle. This picture, by Julius Moxon of the Madras army, is possibly the only image that shows the wrecked village in any detail. (*Royal Geographical Society*)

11. Detail of a contemporary map, showing the order of battle at Aliwal. (*British Library*)

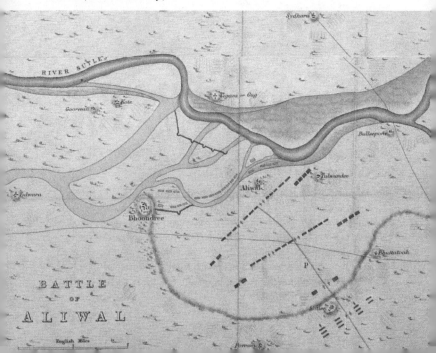

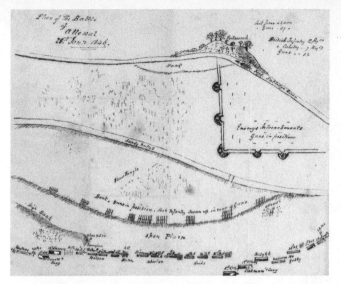

12. Map drawn by Charles Reid, Adjutant of the Sirmoor Gurkha Battalion, of the Sikh encampment opposite Tughara on the banks of the Sutlej. Notice the *jhow* (tamarisk) jungle west of the camp and the Sikh line. (*National Army Museum*)

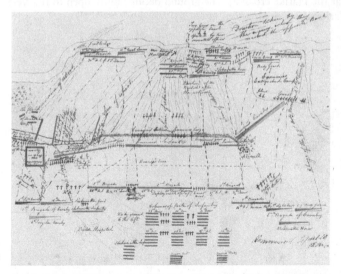

13. A more detailed diagram of the Battle of Aliwal, showing the Sikh encampment to the right and the square formed by the Avitabile regiment to the right of Bhundri village. (*National Army Museum*)

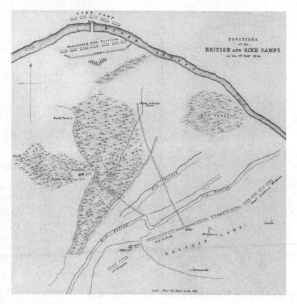

14. Sketch by W. W. W. Humbley of the area separating the two armies at Sabraon. The British line was protected by a large dry *nullah* beyond which stretched some elephant grass. The high grass was also present near the Harike crossing. The ground became more open to the west. (*National Army Museum*)

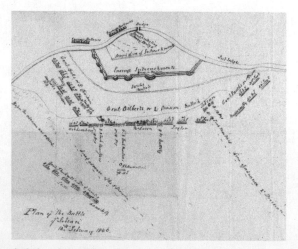

15. Detailed sketch by Harry Lumsden, 59th Bengal Native Infantry, of the Sikh entrenchment and British positions prior to the battle. (*National Army Museum*)

16. Detail of a contemporary map, showing the order of battle at Sabraon. (*British Library*)

17. British outpost at the small village of Rhodewalla. Sketch by Charles Hardinge. (*National Army Museum*)

18. High-prow ferry boats on the Sutlej, typical of the time and used for the construction of the Sikh army's bridge. (*Royal Geographical Society*)

19. Photograph of the Sutlej, *c.* 1900, most probably taken near Harike and Sabraon. The north bank here becomes considerably higher than the south and formed the location of the Sikh encampment north of the river. The breadth of the river here was substantial, but several fords between Harike and Ferozepore allowed cavalry to cross without too much trouble. (*Royal Geographical Society*)

Above: 20. Entry into Lahore of Dhuleep Singh, escorted by British troops, following the end of the war. Sketch by Charles Hardinge. (*National Army Museum*)

Below: 21. Sikh soldiers being paid and disbanded at Lahore fort as a part of the reduction of the Sikh army after the war. Sketch by Charles Hardinge. (*National Army Museum*)

22. Early photograph, *c.* 1849, after the end of the Second Anglo-Sikh War, of British troops standing guard at the fort and palace of Lahore. The fort was occupied at the end of the First Anglo-Sikh War and, with the Treaty of Bhyrowal (Appendix C), the British presence became permanent. (*National Army Museum*)

23. Theatrical poster from 1846. The hard-fought battles against the Sikh army, and the subsequent reduction of the last independent state in India, generated considerable interest among the general public in England.

24. Earliest known photo, *c.* 1870, of the Mudki battlefield. Looking east from Lohaum, it shows the area still covered with brush and tamarisk trees. The recently erected British monument can be seen in the middle of the picture in the distance. (*National Army Museum*)

25. Middle of Mudki battlefield looking south-east toward the monument and where the initial British lines were formed.

26. Hillocks, such as these, formerly occupied Mudki battlefield in great numbers. In addition to the jungle that has now disappeared, they significantly reduced visibility so that both sides were oblivious to the opposing force's position and strength.

27. The line of trees along the canal in the distance marks the north of Mudki battlefield and the location of clashes between Sikh and British cavalry.

28. British monument at Mudki, soon after its construction in 1870, twenty-five years after the battle. (*National Army Museum*)

29. British monument at Mudki in the present day. The original commemorative plaques no longer exist. Inferior replacements have recently been put in place.

30. Remnants of an old *haveli* at Mudki. The village had a substantial population with several large properties.

31. Exposed sections of the second floor of Mudki fort, revealing decorative work and construction.

32. View south-west from Ferozeshah village Gurdwara. The Sikh line during the battle passed just a few metres from where the Gurdwara now stands. Sir Henry Hardinge, commanding the central British division, would have advanced from the distance.

33. Early photograph, *c.* 1870, of the Ferozeshah battlefield from the east of the village. The newly built British monument can be seen in the distance on the left of the picture (south of the village). (*National Army Museum*)

34. British monument at Ferozeshah, the most elegant of the four obelisks built by the British, pictured a year or so after its construction in 1869. 'Ferozeshah' is inscribed in large letters in English, Punjabi and Persian on its three sides. (*National Army Museum*)

35. British monument at Ferozeshah in the present day. The structure remains in good condition, although the plaques that originally decorated it have disappeared.

36. An arch built as a memorial to the Battle of Ferozeshah stands at the junction with the NH95 highway. Ahead and to the left, a power substation and various village shops now mar the initial position of the British army and its bivouac during the night of 21 December 1845.

37. The Anglo-Sikh War Museum, opened in 1976 and a short distance from Ferozeshah, contains large paintings depicting scenes from the First Anglo-Sikh War and has a collection of contemporary weapons on display. Outside the museum stand two horse artillery cannon of the period.

38. Battlefield south-west of Bhudowal, close to Pamal village. Sir Harry Smith and the British force took this route rather than the direct road to Ludhiana in an attempt to avoid Ranjodh Singh's force. Cultivated fields now occupy what was a heavily sandy area in the mid-nineteenth century.

39. Museum near Pamal village where the fighting commenced, around three kilometres south-west of Bhudowal. It is the work of a retired army officer, Capt. Amarjit Singh Sekhon, who lives nearby. Adjacent to the museum is a small monument in memory of the Sikh soldiers who died in the war.

Above and below: 40 and 41. Phillour fort, opposite Ludhiana, on the north bank of the Sutlej. The fort was a Sikh stronghold and the location from which Ranjodh Singh crossed south of the river.

42. Southern section of Aliwal battlefield looking towards Porein. The view is from the location of the Sikh line where much of the fighting took place.

43. Porein ridge, from the middle of the plain of Aliwal. The initial British line was formed under the ridge.

44. Bhudha *nullah*, the dry river bed adjacent to the village of Bhundri and the scene of fierce fighting during the Battle of Aliwal. Sikh regulars used the riverbed for a last desperate stand before retreating to the river.

45. River Sutlej, north of Bhundri village, where the last of the fighting took place along the banks, moving westwards for approximately four kilometres.

46. British monument at Aliwal, not long after its construction, *c.* 1870. It is situated on the former Sikh line. Note the hard flat ground in the distance, characteristic of the battlefield. (*National Army Museum*)

47. The Aliwal monument in the present day. It has lost both its original base and tapering column. The remainder of the monument is heavily altered, suggesting it was at some point rebuilt.

48. Looking east towards the position of the British lines at Sabraon from the extreme east of the Sikh line at its junction with the Sutlej River. The right wing of the British army, led by Sir Harry Smith, approached the Sikh line adjacent to the river (on the right of the picture). Several Sikh cannon were placed on the north bank (on the left), which enfiladed the British attack.

49. Harike ford, two kilometres east of the Sikh line at Sabraon. The ford was used by Sikh cavalry for crossing the river from the right bank for daily skirmishing with their British counterparts. On the day of the battle, Brigadier-General Charles Cureton's force of the 16th Lancers, with the 3rd, 4th, and 5th Light Cavalry, were stationed on the left bank in the foreground.

50. Less than two kilometres separated the Sikh outpost of Sabraon (mid-picture to the right) from Rhodewalla village, where the British advance outpost was situated and from where this photograph was taken. Artillery fire and sniping between the pickets of both sides was frequent.

51. The sizeable south *nullah* ran in front of the centre of the Sikh lines that formed on its left bank at the Battle of Sabraon. The British centre division approached and crossed from the bank on the right. The *nullah* was dry on the day of the battle, although there were pools of deep water in several places.

52. The extreme left of the Sikh flank at Sabraon ran parallel to the east *nullah* that can be seen rejoining the river in the foreground. Unlike the rest of the entrenchment area, only cowherds and their animals now frequent this marshy, uneven area.

53. The location of the Sikh bridge of boats and scene of the tragic last act of the campaign. Under intense fire from British soldiers lined up on the left bank, and braving the swollen fast-flowing river, thousands of Sikh troops drowned attempting to cross to the north.

Above: 54. British Sabraon monument, pictured a couple of years after its construction in 1868, located south of Rhodewalla village. (*National Army Museum*)

Right: 55. Sabraon monument in present day. A short, four-sided obelisk made of burnt brick, it is now in need of repair and attention.

Left: 56. Grave of British political agent Major George Broadfoot in Ferozepore cemetery. Broadfoot had a large part to play in the deterioration of relations between the British and the Lahore state. Killed at Ferozeshah, he had fallen from his horse and been shot through the heart.

Below: 57. Grave of Major-General Sir Robert Sale, who died from the wound he sustained at Mudki. His left thigh had been shattered by grapeshot.

made sure their soldierly rituals continued as Mackinnon of the 16th Lancers, employed as a scout at the time, recorded:

> From the ramparts of a small village on the right flank of our position, we could observe the Sikh battalions turning out every evening for parade and exercise, and their artillery practice was almost unremitting. The fire of cannon and musketry, which was constantly heard even after nightfall, made us frequently conjecture that some point of our position had been attacked, but it proved that the enemy were only amusing themselves.

Charles Hardinge, son of the Governor-General, riding out close to the river commented that the Sikh soldiers could be seen on the other side of the river 'apparently very much at ease'. A British spy returning from the Sikh camp on 15 January told a similar story: the men were confident and talked of reaching Calcutta, the capital of British India, if only ammunition and supplies were forthcoming.

The army was still strong enough to challenge the British if the commanders had wished. A crossing south of the river for an immediate battle during January was the obvious option as the British were still awaiting reinforcements and supplies themselves. This was actively discussed by the Sikh soldiers and it was generally agreed that this course of action would be taken as soon as reinforcements from Gulab Singh arrived. Another possibility for the Sikh army would have been to oppose a crossing of the river by the British at Ferozepore where the full strength of the army could have been deployed. The British boats and the position of the British army could be easily monitored and a crossing in the face of such a force would have been hazardous and not without heavy casualties. Instead, a fatally flawed position was adopted by the Sikh commanders, deliberately designed to destroy its remaining strength. Approximately half the Sikh army would be moved south of the river and positioned in a defensive entrenchment. The other half of the army would be kept stationed on the north bank of the river thus ensuring the British would do battle, as at Mudki and Ferozeshah, with only a portion of the Sikh army.

The duplicity and indifference shown by their generals was not lost on the ordinary Sikh soldiery. When Lal Singh ordered contingents of the army to the vulnerable position on the south bank, Sikh soldiers manhandled him over the bridge despite his desire to stay in safety on the north bank. They would also walk into his tent and abuse him as and when they desired. Major George Carmichael Smyth recorded the nature of the harangues directed towards the commanders by their troops:

> "We know that you have leagued with the court to send us against the British and to pen us up here [in the entrenchment] like sheep for them to come and slaughter us at their convenience; but remember, that in thus acting, you play the part not only of traitors to your country, but of ruthless butchers and murderers. You destroy a whole army, which, whatever its faults and crimes may have been, has always been ready to obey the orders of the state and its officers. We might even now punish you as you deserve, but we will leave you to answer to your Gooroo and your God while we, deserted and betrayed as we are, will do what we can to preserve the independence of our country."

The soldiers had alienated the officer class over the years with their ambition for power and truculence, but the unseating of the present leadership was beyond their powers of organisation and none had the authority or experience to step forward as a credible alternative. In any case, the court at Lahore fully backed Lal Singh as Vizier and Tej Singh as Commander-in-Chief of the army. The gulf between the soldiers and the commanders became increasingly public and vocal, the *Delhi Gazette* reporting on 6 January 1846 that:

> [It] is ascertained that the Sikh soldiers in the camp have become very insubordinate and will not heed the orders of Sirdar Tej Singh. They accuse him and others of being in league with the British.

While the long pause between hostilities was damaging to the Sikh army, it provided a welcome break for the British, allowing new stores of ammunition to reach the army. During late December and January, the roads leading from Ambala to Sabraon were full with supplies heading north towards the latter settlement. Nevertheless, the level of munitions was still at such a critical level during the first half of January that Gough contemplated reusing as much ammunition as he could find. On 5 January, Robert Cust was sent back to Ferozeshah to offer the villagers in the vicinity a bounty of eight *annas* (half a rupee) for every cannonball they brought in from the battlefield. How successful this operation was is not recorded. The lull in hostilities also allowed for the many wounded to be treated. Substantial numbers of British soldiers were suffering severe dysentery after Ferozeshah due to their manic drinking of water contaminated with gunpowder from the village wells. It took more than a week of rest before most of the men had recovered from the ill-effects.

By 25 December, the British baggage from Mudki had begun drifting in at Sultan Khan Walla. On the same day, the Governor-General, in an attempt to encourage desertion from the Sikh ranks, declared that Sikh soldiers' present and future pensions would be secure if they came over to the British side. In addition, any lawsuits the deserters may have in British provinces would be dealt with immediately.

Realising that a prolonged period of recuperation after the bloody battle of Ferozeshah would be interpreted as a sign of weakness across the country, both Gough and Hardinge were anxious to move north. This was a gamble, and should a concerted attack by the Sikh army materialise, Gough was prepared to retreat. On 7 January, the British camp moved northwards to Arufkee village (Hurruf) with an advanced contingent under Smith moving to Malowal village, twelve kilometres short of the Sikh army position north of the Sutlej. Malowal contained a strong fort that was garrisoned. The route was a circuitous one, the British army keeping a distance of around five kilometres from the river. On 12 January, Gough moved his headquarters to the village of Bootewalla, around eight kilometres south of the Sikh encampment, where the army encamped in battle order. Malowal, however, remained the headquarters for the British cavalry. Both armies now lay in sight of each other on opposite banks of the Sutlej.

Emissaries from Lal Singh

Hardinge had left the British force on 24 December, moving to Ferozepore after his baggage had arrived to continue the civil business of British government. While there, the Sikh commanders sent him messengers headed by Chuni Lal, a prominent Lahore newswriter, reconfirming their allegiance to the British (their normal channel of communication with the British, the political agent Peter Nicholson, had died at Ferozeshah). William Edwardes, Under-Secretary to the British Government and present with the Governor General at the meeting with the messengers, wrote that 'while there, emissaries from Rajah Lal Singh arrived, and gave us valuable information respecting the enemy's position. From the intelligence thus received it was determined to attack the entrenchment on its extreme right, where Lal Singh reported the defences to be low and weak'. Gough, meanwhile, had also taken the precaution of obtaining intelligence from his spies in the Sikh camp. One of the spies, a young boy, confirmed Lal Singh's information. He also confirmed that the Sikh right flank did not end at the riverbank. Tej Singh, the commander in the entrenchment, had taken care to leave a significant gap between the end of the Sikh line and the river guarded by an insignificant number of Sikh cavalry. Breaking through this area and the weak Sikh right would take British forces behind the main Sikh lines and into the heart of the camp. There seems to have been an ongoing communication between the Sikh commanders and the British at Sabraon as well. Daniel Mackinnon mentions in his account that 'on more than one occasion, Sikh officers visited and returned from the British camp'. On 8 February, two days before the battle, *vakeels* (ambassadors) from Lahore came to visit the British camp at Sabraon again but were turned away by Hardinge who had determined to leave any further communication until after the battle.

The Battlefield

For a course of around 100 kilometres or so as it leaves the foothills of the Himalayas, the River Sutlej follows a westerly course through the plains of the Punjab. On reaching the area north of Jagraon it changes course, following a gentle curve north-westwards towards the confluence with the Beas River near Harike. Eight kilometres downstream from Harike, as it passes the vicinity of the village of Sabraon to its north, the river reaches its most northerly point since leaving the mountains. Downstream from the village, the river changes course definitively assuming a south-westerly direction on its way to join the Indus. The southern banks of the substantial curve in the river at this point would define the battlefield of Sabraon. The Sutlej was a considerable body of water during the nineteenth century. Travellers passing through the Harike area reckoned on the river having a width ranging from 500 to 900 yards. William Barr, who travelled through Harike in 1839, estimated the width of the river when in flood to be as much as a mile and a half to two miles. As the river nears Sabraon, however, its course becomes much more defined and narrower, especially on the north bank which is steeper in most places by as much as forty feet. On the south bank, there are no high riverbanks round the entire Sabraon curve, leaving the river to expand southwards when swollen. In addition, various large and normally dry *nullahs* to the south take much of the river waters from the main stream during times of flood. Gough, in his letters to the Duke of Wellington, reckoned the width of the river at the Sabraon bend to be 350 yards at the time of the battle.

Despite this the river was shallow at various points, the nearest being the Harike ford immediately to the east of the Sikh position. Here a large area of high ground in the path of the river cut the flow into two streams shallow enough to allow cavalry at least to cross, the high ground effectively forming a large island midstream. The area near Attaree twenty-five kilometres south-west of the battlefield was the other fordable point close to Sabraon. Near to Ferozepore was another ford at Khoonda ghat or Gunda Singh Walla. There were known to be other fordable points in addition to these. The ferrymen at Harike were known to be quite secretive about the shallow areas of the Sutlej, greater public awareness of these crossing points being against their interests. These were known to the Sikh army, however, and Sikh horsemen would cross the river in the days before the battle at locations both above and below the Sikh army camp for skirmishing with the British. Upstream from Harike ford was located Harike village, the main crossing point for general and commercial traffic. Ferry boats from Harike transported travellers and goods across to the other side of the river north of Makhu on the south bank.

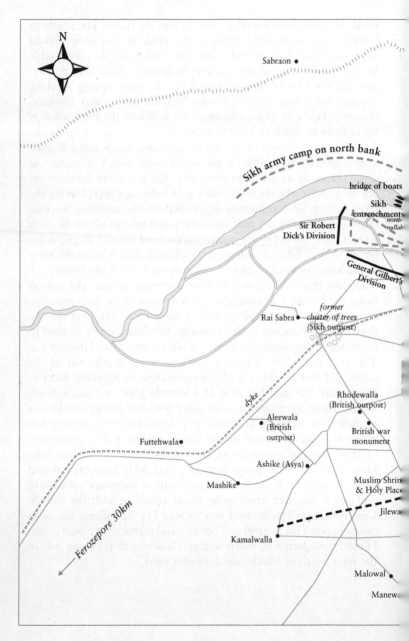

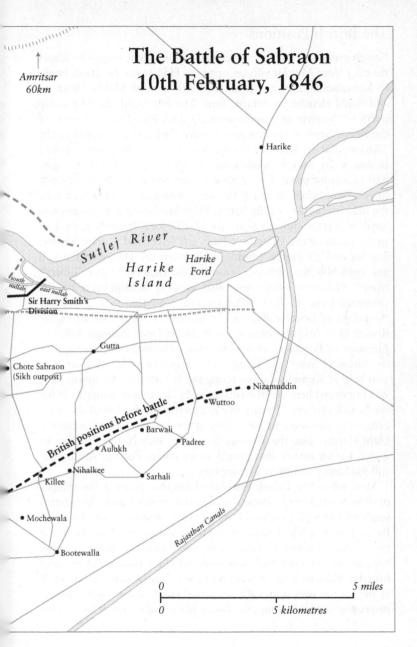

The Battle of Sabraon
10th February, 1846

↑
Amritsar
60km

Harike

Sutlej River

Harike Island

Harike Ford

south nullah
east nullah

Sir Harry Smith's Division

Gutta

Chote Sabraon
(Sikh outpost)

Nizamuddin

Wuttoo

British positions before battle

Barwali

Padree

Aulukh

Nihalkee

Sarhali

Killee

Mochewala

Rajasthan Canals

Bootewalla

| 0 | | 5 miles |
| 0 | | 5 kilometres |

The British Positions

Gough organised the British position along a long string of villages running from Makhu village, opposite Harike on the north bank, to Kamalwalla, eleven kilometres south-west of Makhu, with an additional element at Attaree ford. The line faced the Sikh camp north of the river in a north-westerly direction. The right wing of the British army stationed near Harike ford was the closest to the Sikh camp at around four kilometres' distance. The position rested behind a dry *nullah* running just north of the string of villages, part of a substantial dry riverbed further to the south. The British forces bivouacked in much the same formation that would take the field on the day of the battle. Brigadier Cureton was stationed north of Nizamuddin to guard the Harike ford. From Nizamuddin to the north of the villages of Pudree (Puttee) and nearby Wuttoo was located Sir Harry Smith's force. From the village of Barwali and onto Nihalkee were stationed Major-General Walter Gilbert's troops. Nihalkee village was also used as headquarters by the Governor-General. Two kilometres due south of Nihalkee lay the village of Bootewalla, used by Gough as his headquarters. Sir Robert Dick held the British line from Nihalkee through Killee to Jileewala (Tilleewala). From Jileewala to Kumalwala were spread the forces of Scott and Campbell's cavalry brigades. A force was also held at Kumalwala protecting the British left. A cannon park was organised between the villages of Nihalkee and Bootewalla for the British artillery. Twenty five kilometres south-west of the main camp was stationed Sir John Grey at the Attaree ford with the 8th Light Cavalry and the 41st, 45th and the 68th Native Infantry to watch for an attack that would never come. Further south-west still sat Littler's force at Ferozepore.

Meanwhile, the British established advance posts at the villages of Rhodewalla and Aleewala, situated around four kilometres south of the Sikh position. Both of these positions were fortified. By 20 January, Rhodewalla was garrisoned by one European and two native regiments along with two twelve-pounder cannon. Sappers and miners had been used to build entrenchments and breastworks round the perimeter of the village. A watchtower built at the village was frequently used by Gough and his generals for inspecting the Sikh camp, the tower being high enough to see into the Sikh entrenchments. The watchtower would also serve as a vantage point for the Governor-General and Commander-in-Chief on the day of the battle during the opening cannonade. The other outpost at Aleewala, two kilometres due west of Rhodewalla, commanded the area along the western part of the bend in the river. It was occupied on 12 January and a tower was built on the same day and garrisoned by a brigade with guns and light infantry, while sappers were employed to construct defensive works. A garrison was kept at the village of Chote Sabraon during the early days of January, but the village was captured by Sikh forces. There was also a tower close to the Sutlej and inside the area that would form the Sikh entrenchment south of the river; it was manned by a small garrison. This was abandoned when the Sikh army crossed to the south. In addition to this, there was a house opposite the entrenchments belonging to a local *zamindar* that had been commandeered by the British and from which British officers continually watched the Sikh lines with telescopes.

British Bridge of Boats

At Ferozepore, meanwhile, British preparations were already being made for the crossing of the Sutlej. Military boats had been brought up from Bombay for a bridge across the river prior to the war. Sunk prior to the war in one of the creeks of the river near the Khunda ghat, they were now refloated during 2 January and readied for their intended purpose. The Sutlej at this time was around 1-2,000 feet across near Ferozepore. Around six kilometres from the city and just above the Khoonda ghat, the river divides itself into three branches, two of them fordable, the third only around 600 feet in width. This stream was spanned by the bridge. Twenty one of some sixty boats were used for the bridge, and a single roadway was prepared with tamarisk brushwood and earth; it would be ready by 12 February. In addition, fourteen rafts (Pasley pontoons) stored at Ferozepore were made ready and a few local ferry boats commandeered. Conscious of the Sikh army's ability to prevent a crossing, Brigadier Edward Smith, Chief Engineer of the British army at the Sutlej had recommended to Gough on 7 January the use of twelve to sixteen of the captured Sikh heavy guns as part of the defence for any *tete-de-pont* on the right bank of the Sutlej. In the event, the absence of any Sikh opposition to the British crossing meant they were never used. On the evening of 14 February, four days after the battle, a second bridge would be constructed with the remaining boats twenty yards downstream from the first bridge to facilitate British supplies across the river.

For the bulk of the troops of both sides there was little to do except watch and wait during the month of January. As with the Sikh troops, British troops carried out their frequent drills and exercises, the rest of the days being spent amusing themselves by playing cards while reinforcements gradually trickled in. Meanwhile, Sikh preparations for the forthcoming battle were monitored by the British. The building of defensive entrenchments south of the river was little danger to the British themselves until they were ready to take the field. Without new stocks of ammunition, Gough made no attempt to stop the entrenchments being built for fear of prematurely precipitating a major battle. In addition, Smith had taken a significant portion of the army eastwards to Ludhiana. Gough would wait for both the siege train and Smith's contingent to return. It was also sound reasoning to attack what would only be a portion of the Sikh army, albeit behind entrenchments, rather than face the hazards of attempting a crossing of the river opposed by the entire Sikh army.

During most of the month of January, therefore, Gough's policy was the destruction of any boats on the south bank of the river to stop them falling into Sikh army hands, thus delaying a possible contest. British vedettes and pickets were told to keep an eye out for boats both upstream and downstream of the bend in the river. Most of the boats in the vicinity had already fallen into Sikh hands but as late as 22 January the British sank six boats.

In early February, however, the British attitude changed. On 6 February Gough had already received considerable reinforcements with the arrival of Sir John Grey with 10,000 men, including HM 9th and 16th Lancers, HM 10th Foot, two native cavalry regiments and three regiments of native infantry as well as a company of sappers. With the now imminent arrival of the siege train and Smith's return from Aliwal along with other reinforcements, the British were ready to advance. The preparations of the Sikh army on the south bank therefore went largely unchallenged. On 7 February, the siege train finally arrived, lifting British anxieties concerning the lack of ammunition. Furthermore, twelve ten-inch howitzers increased British firepower still further. The following day, Smith returned with his force from Aliwal, giving Gough the full resources he required for the coming battle. By the time of the battle, a full thirty-one battalions of infantry were assembled, including nine European regiments along with nine regiments of cavalry and numerous irregulars – by far the most powerful army the British had ever assembled in India. In addition to this, Sir Charles Napier was marching north from Sind with additional reinforcements of 16,000 troops and sixty guns.

The prolonged stay at Sabraon began to prove problematic for the British during February. Sanitary conditions dropped alarmingly and there were fears of an epidemic in the camp. On his return from Aliwal on 7 February, Sir Harry Smith had noted the filthy state of the camp but moved his division to the position requested by Gough. The conditions proved too much, however, and he requested permission to change location the next day, which was granted. The arrival of the siege train was a welcome sign, therefore, providing the opportunity to commence hostilities and abandon the camp.

Sikh Camp North of the River

The Sikh camp north of the river encompassed most of the area adjacent to the river between the Harike ford and past the northernmost part of the bend in the river, a distance of around four kilometres. The higher banks on the northern side of the river gave the Sikh army a good view of any British movements and gave British reconnaissance parties a good view of the sea of tents reaching around the north bank. James Gilling of the 9th Lancers, stationed on the extreme right of the British lines on outpost duty, left a description of the Sikh camp:

> As we debouched over a rising ground, the whole of the Sikh camp suddenly developed itself to us on the opposite side of the river. Myriads of tents of various shapes and colours extended along the sandy bed of the river. Almost as far as the eye could reach from right to left; while drawn up in front to defend this fairy-like city were the turbaned and long-bearded Sikhs, the whole presenting a strikingly picturesque scene. As we approached the river the enemy opened a

desultory fire on us, and as we still neared them, gun after gun belched forth its angry missiles, until the whole opposite bank seemed one continuous line of smoke and fire.

On another reconnaissance trip close to the Sutlej, he noted one tent amid the others as particularly eye-catching:

> In the midst of the cluster of tents opposite to us, was one more conspicuous than the rest, from being of a brilliant crimson. This was the field tent of Lall Sing, since so notorious in Sikh history from his connection and secret intriguing with the Ranee Chunder, the dowager queen of Runjeet Sing.

The Bridge of Boats

The only transports available on the river in any quantity were the ferry boats or *chappus*. These long, slim boats were commonly used at Harike and other ferry areas along the Sutlej. The *chappus* were typically flat and shallow, square at the bow, and with a high pointed end at the stern, giving them a long triangular shape. Across shallower parts of the river, bargepoles were used to navigate these boats across the water. Other ferry craft were typically bigger, again triangular in shape with a high prow and around 45 feet long and 18 feet wide at one end.

The bridge of boats connecting the Sikh camp in the north to the south bank was completed sometime in the first week of January 1846, meaning that the requisitioning of *chappus* and other boats for construction of the bridge must have commenced sometime in late December, less than a week after the battle of Ferozeshah on 21 December. This would suggest that the decision to commit the army to fighting on the south bank of the river was taken by the Sikh commanders only a few days after the retreat from Ferozeshah.

Sir Hugh Gough, in his letters to the Duke of Wellington, notes the bridge to be almost fully constructed by 2 January, all but two boats missing on the south side for its completion. Capt. Daniel Mackinnon mentions the bridge having been completed minus four boats, the Sikh army leaving it in this state for several days before completing it and constructing field defences on the south bank. There was also a rumour prevalent in the British camp that the bridge had been mined by the Sikh army to prevent its use by the British. The earliest mention of a completed bridge is recorded by Orfeur Cavenagh of the 4th Irregular Cavalry on 7 January during a reconnaissance mission into the bend of the river.

The bridge, along with the fords, was initially used purely for reconnaissance and by Sikh skirmishers engaging in daily contests with their British counterparts south of the river. No Sikh troops were permanently stationed on the south bank, protection of the bridge being provided by the array of guns on the north bank. The absence of Sikh troops on the south bank during the early part of January meant British patrols could venture quite close to the banks of the river. A hillock or raised area of ground on the southern bank where the bridge was attached is mentioned in various sources; it obscured the bridge from British view and artillery. The bridge, although made of ferry boats, was evidently strongly built and would withstand much punishment from both British cannon during the battle and sappers after it.

As late as 22 January, Sikh soldiers continued to commandeer any available boats from the southern side despite the bridge of boats having been completed nearly three weeks earlier. This may have been to facilitate the movements of troops across the river or perhaps the building of a second bridge may have been mooted.

The northern banks of the Sutlej are higher than the sandy stretches marking the south of the water's edge around most of the length of the bend in the river; this made the building of a bridge difficult. One exception to this height differential was an area a few hundred metres downstream of where the north *nullah* leaves the Sutlej. Here a large sandy stretch marks the place where an ancient and large *nullah* flowed into the Sutlej. This sandbank provided a good location for a bridge to the south. Interestingly, the various sketches that survive tend to show the bridge crossing the river in diagonal fashion with the southern end of the bridge slightly further upstream than the north end. It is possible that the southern bank directly opposite the sandbank was not suitable for a bridge.

The Sikh Camp in the South

Three *nullahs*, two of them sizeable, would play an important part in defining the nature of the battlefield on the south bank of the

Sutlej. In the present work, these are referred to as the north, south and east *nullahs* after their positions relative to the Sikh camp. The south *nullah* leaves the Sutlej near Harike ford curving north before turning south-west to join the Sutlej west of the bend in the river. The *nullah* is approximately 50-70 metres wide and around two metres deep near where the Sikh camp was located south of the river. Part of this dry riverbed merges with the north *nullah* described later. As the *nullah* moves west of the Sikh camp, it becomes progressively shallower and wider. The small east *nullah* branches off from the south *nullah* shortly after it leaves the Sutlej, curving northwards again and rejoining the river a kilometre away. The north *nullah* leaves the Sutlej 2.5 km downstream of the south *nullah*. Executing a number of twists and turns, it then heads west to join up with the south *nullah* and the Sutlej after the bend in the river. It is less wide than the south *nullah* near the Sikh lines at 20-30 metres but deeper at 2-3 metres in most places. Like the south *nullah*, the north *nullah* becomes much shallower and wider downstream.

With the bridge allowing a sure route of getting sufficient supplies to a force on the south bank, organised construction of the entrenchment could now start. Initially a company from every brigade crossed over to build a bridgehead. Soon British outposts and reconnaissance parties began to report significant numbers of men working during both day and night. The perimeter of the Sikh army camp south of the river lay largely in the tract of land in the middle of the north, south and east *nullahs* with the *nullah* banks being utilised as the defensive line. Both ends of the defensive line met the Sutlej. To the southeast, the Sikh outer line ran along the left bank of the east *nullah* where it approached the Sutlej. This stretch of the line was around 200 metres long. Leaving the *nullah* bank as it curved away, the line crossed a stretch of land approximately half a kilometre long between the east *nullah* and the south *nullah*. Upon reaching the south *nullah*, the line ran along its north bank for a further kilometre. At this point the south *nullah* branched into two streams with one stream merging with the north *nullah* while the main stream continued westwards. The defensive line followed the main stream for a few hundred metres before veering northwards towards the north *nullah*. Across the *nullah*, the line continued just west of the junction between the north *nullah* and the branch of the south *nullah* until it reached the banks of the river, around 250 metres away. By following this course, the entrenchment assumed the rough shape of a half ellipse with a slight concave in the middle, the defensive entrenchments being around three kilometres in length. Bancroft put the length of the defensive line at 3,500 yards, very close to the actual figure. The distance where the right met the river was two kilometres downstream from the left with the furthest distance from the middle of the entrenchment to the river being around 550 metres. Thus, the total area within this entrenchment was just over one square kilometre.

The area was not completely barren, some parts being already under cultivation, as James Gilling noted:

> The bed of the river, to the extent of three or four hundred yards from the stream, was at this time dry and sandy, then a perpendicular bank abruptly rises to an undulated plain, intersected with both dry and wet *nullahs* and covered – except here and there where the peasant has cultivated small patches – with long elephant grass and stunted underwood.

Thick reeds and undergrowth were particularly apparent opposite Harike, where Sikh snipers frequently lay in wait and shot over-inquisitive British vedettes. The jungle here was burnt by the British in early January.

Despite the river being swollen with floodwater, none of the surviving accounts describe any of the *nullahs* as being wet on the day of the battle. Thus the *nullah* banks formed an obstruction but did not act as a serious impediment at any point, although some accounts describe certain areas of the southern *nullah* along which the Sikh line ran as having small deep areas of stagnant water. Robert Cust specifically states that the *nullahs* surrounding the Sikh camp were dry on the day of the battle.

The building of the outer line could be considered to have started from 13 January onwards. The first account we have of British pickets noticing the construction work was on 14 January when James Gilling, part of a reconnaissance party, mentions the appearance of the fortifications being put up. Capt. William Humbley also mentions venturing close to the bridge on the same day. From his account it seems the Sikh army had still not crossed and made a camp on the south side, although it is likely a bridgehead or first defensive lines had been made. Sikh soldiers were stationed on the south side lest British parties attempt to destroy the bridge. On 16 January, Robert Cust recorded his comments on the Sikh camp in the south:

> The western bank of the Satluj from Harike Ke Patan downwards is much loftier than the eastern. On this high bank commanding the ford and ferry of Sabraon which lay before us, were the hosts of the enemy who had formed a bridge connecting the two banks and a tete-de-pont on the Eastern side. Through a telescope from the watchtower all this was visible and we could see the Sikh soldiers swarming about like ants on an anthill. We kept up a brisk interchange of shots with some of their sharp shooters. The embrasure of their guns was distinctly visible in their entrenchment.

That gun embrasures could be seen on the outside line would indicate that much of the outside line had been readied by this time. It would have been impossible to create a defensive line three kilometres long with wooden ramparts for the whole length. Instead only some of the areas in the south and the east were made formidable. In the north, the defences constructed were much more nominal. Various descriptions of the nature of the defences at different points survive, allowing a separate appraisal of the eastern, southern and the northern defences.

The Eastern Section

From the banks of the east *nullah* to the point where the defences met the south *nullah*, the ramparts were reported to be as high as a man if not higher at various places. Earth and planks were used along with fascines, redoubts and epaulements. These along with the height of the banks of the southern *nullah* made for a good defence. Significantly, the defences in this area were marshalled by Sham Singh Attariwalla. Col. Robertson with HM 31st Regiment, stationed opposite this section of the line and adjacent to the Sutlej, describes the line here as 'protected all round by a rampart nine or ten feet high with portholes constructed of wood on a level with the ground outside, which could therefore be swept with grapeshot'. Whether Robertson was including the bank of the *nullah* in the height of the ramparts is unclear. The top of the rampart was high enough that only the heads and shoulders of the defenders would be visible. Pte Hewitt of HM 62nd Foot also records that 'the embrasures where the guns were pointed through the breastwork, had timber laid across the top, and earth piles on that as a protection for the gunners'. Furthermore, the defences here were well-manned. Additional men would be deployed with the Sikh infantry for reloading rifles while they fired a second. Thomas Bunbury of the 80th Regiment, also facing this section of the line, mentions 'a vast number of wall pieces, called *tambjors*, mounted on swivels placed on top of the parapet.

There's little mention of the east *nullah* as an obstruction, the dry stream along which the extreme south end of the Sikh line ran. This *nullah*, which has disappeared completely in present times, may already have been quite nominal during the nineteenth century.

The Southern Section

The southern section of the Sikh line that followed the north bank of the south *nullah* was around 1.4 kilometres in length. The section adjacent to the eastern section had similarly strong defences as the eastern section. In some areas, opposite where the Bengal European Regiment would be stationed, in the middle of the Sikh lines, the defences were too high to scale without ladders during the battle. There was also a large bank or mound of earth on the south side of the *nullah* between where the 1st European Regiment and the entrenchment lay, which obscured the formidable defences at this point.

However, as the line moved north-westwards towards the north *nullah* around a half kilometre further on, the *nullah* banks become almost nominal, providing little advantage to the defenders. Here the barricades vanished to be replaced with simple breastworks and trenches. Joseph Hewitt of HM 62nd foot was stationed on the extreme left of Gilbert's division, which faced this section of the Sikh lines, and described the position as having only breastworks and no fixed defences of any kind that would pose a barrier to an attacking force. From across the south *nullah*, the British position was also higher than the defenders, enabling them to see into the Sikh camp. Daniel Mackinnon of the 16th Lancers, stationed behind HM 31st at Harike ford, commented on the differences between the eastern and southern sections:

> On the left of the enemy's works, a high parapet had been thrown up, and part of this front was protected by a *nullah*, with a steep bank acting as a counterscarp, and the bed of this watercourse was filled, in some places, by deep pools of stagnant water, which extended along the centre. On the right flank, the track of the *nullah* was but faintly marked; and in this quarter, the works had not been completed and were not formidable than the trenches at Ferozeshahr before described.

The defensive line was also not continuous with gaps wide enough for Sikh cavalry to ride through. However, the gaps could also allow British cavalry to enter the camp more easily in the coming battle.

The Northern Defences

In the northern sector of the entrenchment, where the defensive line left the southern *nullah* and curved round towards the Sutlej, the state of the defences was in a still weaker state. Here the south *nullah* forks with one stream joining the north *nullah*, the other main stream curving south-westwards to join the Sutlej beyond the bend in the river. The defensive line followed the north banks of the main stream for a few hundred metres before curving northwards to cross the north *nullah*. After crossing the north *nullah*, the line continued for 250 metres or so without reaching the Sutlej. A significant gap had been left between the defensive line and the river – to be defended only by a small force of cavalry. The most logical line of defence would have been to follow the bank of the stream joining the north *nullah* and use the high east bank of the north *nullah* as the line in the north. However, Lal Singh had extended the lines, making the whole northern part much less defendable. The soil was reportedly even sandier than in the south, which precluded constructed defences of any kind. Instead, only minimal trench works and foxholes were dug. None of the Sikh artillery would be placed in this sector by the Sikh commanders.

In addition, irregular troops, rather than the regular *Fauj-i-ain* troops, were placed here. It seems this section of the line was also grossly undermanned. William Edwardes mentions that Sir Robert Dick's division, which faced the Sikh right on the day of the battle, found the defences there to be 'weak and easily surmountable' and that the British soldiers attacking this section found hardly any defenders present. HM 10th Regiment marched in totally unopposed 'with their firelocks at their shoulders'. The soldiers had asked Tej Singh to place the *Gorchurras* here, along with howitzers and other guns, but this was not done. Dewan Ajudya Parshad, present at Sabraon, blames the weakness of this section on the soldiers. Each brigade had been asked to send detachments to man this section, but not wishing to reduce their strength, they had continually postponed sending troops to the north.

The Inner Lines

The defences are usually described as having triple or quadruple lines but the inner lines were much more nominal, being composed of trenches and pits. Crucially, Tej Singh had ordered these lines to run parallel to the south *nullah* so they did not face the weak northern sector. With a British attack on the Sikh right, these trenches facing south would be of little use. The innermost line was formerly the bridgehead, protecting the immediate area close to the bridge of boats. The first line was around 700 metres long, running from the northern *nullah* to a distance less than half the length of the entrenchments. The second and third lines were longer than the first, and were placed in between the first line and the outer line. As with the inner line, these never touched the riverbanks at either end to form an enclosed space.

In addition to the trenches, the *Akalis* in the Sikh army had dug large pits within the entrenchment. These had the dual benefit of providing shelter from the forthcoming British artillery barrage and of breaking up any enemy cavalry movements within the camp. These were evidently quite large. Thomas Bunbury described how he had seen fifty to sixty dead Sikh soldiers in many of the pits. Colonel Row of the 33rd Native Infantry records 'several square places in the interior surrounded by ditches having been apparently occupied by the enemy in dense masses'. In addition to this, Tej

Singh had placed some heavy guns on a raised platform close to the bridge, where they would play little role in the coming battle.

Some descriptions survive of living conditions within the camp. With up to 20,000 men in the camp, large areas would have been taken up with material for bivouac. Robert Cust, in his description of the Sikh camp, mentions wicker huts being used by the Sikh soldiers. The more usual canvas tents prevailed in other places. Daniel Mackinnon's account confirms this, adding that the wickerwork huts were predominantly on the southern end of the entrenchment behind the parapets. Shelters directly behind the strongest part of the defensive line made eminent sense as protection from British artillery, and would allow Sikh soldiers to quickly man the barricades in the event of an attack.

Cannon on the North Bank

Lal Singh had kept thirty-six guns on the north bank with some on both flanks of the southern camp. These were positioned there ostensibly to enfilade any British attack on the Sikh flanks. During the time of the battle, most of these would never be fired as they were too far from the action. On 9 February, the eve of the battle, British vedettes counted six guns on the north bank of the Harike ford, opposite to the southern end of the entrenchment. Robert Cust mentions that entrenchments for eleven guns had been dug on this bank although only seven were in place for the battle the next day. If a similar quantity of guns is assumed as being in place in the north, it would mean that around twenty guns were stationed near the bridge or along the bank.

Weaknesses of the Entrenchment

For the Sikh forces, the perils of fighting with the Sutlej to their back were obvious, but the disorganised construction of the defences by Tej Singh made the situation even worse. J. D. Cunningham of the British Engineers perhaps best sums up its nature and flaws:

> The entrenchment likewise showed a fatal want of unity of command and of design; and at Sabraon, as in the other battles of the campaign, the soldiers did everything and the leaders nothing. Hearts to dare

and hands to execute were numerous, but there was no mind to guide
and animate the whole:– each inferior commander defended his front
according to his own skill and his means, and the centre and left,
where the disciplined battalions were mainly stationed, had batteries
and salient points as high as the stature of a man, and ditches which
an armed soldier could not leap without exertion; but a considerable
part of the line exhibited at intervals the petty obstacles of a succession
of such banks and trenches as would shelter a crouching marksman
or help him to sleep in security when no longer a watcher. This was
especially a case on the right flank, where the looseness of the river sand
rendered it impossible to throw up parapets without art and labour,
and where irregular troops, the least able to remedy such disadvantages,
had been allowed or compelled to take up their position. The flank in
question was mainly guarded by a line of two hundred 'zumbooruks' or
falconets; but it derived some support from a salient battery and from
the heavy guns retained on the opposite bank of the river.

The state of the defences, Cunningham goes on to say, 'showed no
trace whatever of scientific skill or unity of design'. In addition to
the weaknesses of the defensive line, the sandy nature of the soil
on the south bank of the river would destroy the effectiveness of
the Sikh artillery all along the line, the Sikh guns being moved and
positioned with great difficulty. Thomas Bunbury would examine
the stronger part of the defences in the south after the battle:

> The soil was sandy and from this cause, in bringing the guns to bear
> upon the men advancing along the line of the entrenchments and those
> who had already entered, the wheels of the gun carriages sunk so deep
> that the muzzles could not be sufficiently depressed to occasion much
> mischief. Still the Sikhs did not abandon their guns.

Further to the north, where the line was much weaker and the
defences more dependent on the artillery, a similar problem
hampered the Sikh gunners. Sgt Pearman with the 3rd Light
Dragoons faced this section of the entrenchment and quotes
Major-General Sir Joseph Thackwell's comments on the problems
the Sikh gunners were having against the advancing British lines:

> It was a miracle we were not properly riddled, but from the constant

fire the trails of the guns had so sunk in the sand that the gunners could not depress the muzzles sufficiently and therefore most of the grape went over our heads.

Perhaps the greatest problem caused by the decision to fight on the south bank in a defensive position was the inability of the whole Sikh army to be deployed in the battle. Many infantry units and the entire cavalry would remain on the north bank, unable to help the garrison in the south, along with much of the artillery.

Meanwhile, Tej Singh, the commander in the entrenchment, continued to show indifference to the flaws in the Sikh position. He did, however, spend time ordering the construction of a small circular tower for his personal protection close to the bridge. A superstitious man, he had taken the precaution of asking a Brahmin astrologer for assistance. The tower was built according to the specifications given him by the astrologer, who was paid the large sum of 500 rupees for his supernatural knowledge on defensive structures. Despite its small size, it was triple-walled. The walls of this fort were as instructed by the astrologer, made a thickness equal to the length of 333 long grains of rice (3.75 yards). An inner circular chamber, the diameter of which was made 13.5 spans of Tej Singh's measurement, was also included. He could retire to this tower in perfect safety from British guns during the battle, so the astrologer said. In the event, the structure was little used; Tej Singh crossed the bridge and fled to the north bank shortly after the battle commenced.

The Sikh Outposts

The Sikh army had established two outposts two kilometres south of the main position. The village of Chote Sabraon was the main outpost held by a small garrison. Sikh soldiers had constructed a watchtower at the settlement. The village had originally been in British possession, being used by British soldiers for targeting Sikh grass-cutters and syces when they ventured within musket range. This went on for several days until the village was seized by the Sikh army.

In the otherwise treeless plain between the Sikh entrenchment and the British camp, a solitary clump of two or three trees stood around two kilometres due west of the village of Chote Sabraon and north of Rhodewalla. These were used as a second outpost by the Sikh soldiers who constructed platforms on the upper branches of the trees. Around the trees, trench works were constructed that could be occupied by a small garrison. Crucially, Lal Singh only had both outposts garrisoned during the day.

The Skirmishing

During the six-week interval between the battles of Ferozeshah and Sabraon, the close proximity of the two forces inevitably led to frequent skirmishing between advance contingents and parties of vedettes with as much as a quarter of Sikh irregular cavalry crossing south of the river every day. This was particularly so in the plain west of the two forces near the Sutlej and away from the range of the big guns and the outposts. With the Sikh outpost at Sabraon being less than two kilometres from the British at Rhodewalla, sniper fire also became common. Occasionally, Sikh soldiers would train their guns at British soldiers climbing the watch tower at Rhodewalla and vice versa. The British Commander-in-Chief was a favourite target, the large entourage around him signalling his presence to Sikh skirmishers and gunners who would duly fire off a few musket balls and camel swivels at the huddle of officers. Taking this into account, sentries were ordered to remind senior British officers to show as little of themselves as they could when on the tower. Gough, never taking much precaution, was reminded himself many times by a sentry until he wearily reminded him, 'Sure my good man, aren't I the Commander-in-Chief and can't I do what I like?'

The following is a chronological account of the various events and encounters that unfolded during January and early February 1846.

Ninth January

From 10.00 a.m. onwards, the Sikh army, still on the right bank of the river, commenced artillery practice. The sound of the big guns, heard clearly in the British camp, caused Gough to send out British pickets to ascertain the cause.

Tenth January

This day is recorded as being exceptionally cold, a fierce westerly wind blowing across the camps. The dust billowing up in consequence reduced visibility considerably and little movement was made by skirmishers of either side.

Eleventh January

At 2.00 p.m. on this day, a Sunday, British pickets signalled an alarm and the British army was readied for battle. It was a false alarm.

Twelfth January

The prolonged stay at Sabraon was already having an effect on living conditions in the British camp and various units were ordered to change positions, their previous positions considered to be too unhealthy.

Thirteenth January

At 2.00 p.m. Gough ordered the whole British force to assemble in battle order having heard that the Sikh army had crossed the Sutlej and was approaching. The British line moved three miles northwards close to the banks of the river, giving the British and Sikh artillery men the opportunity to try their luck against each other. As Hope Grant, commander of the 9th Lancers describes, the Sikh gunners usually had the better of the exchanges:

> On 13th January 1846 we were suddenly turned out by a report that the enemy were advancing against us, and Sir Hugh Gough ordered a large force of infantry, cavalry and artillery with 12-pounders and a rocket train to take up a position with a view of destroying the bridge of boats. When the guns opened fire, the enemy replied with such accuracy that it was found necessary to move us farther out of range. Our own round shot and rockets seemed to produce no effect whatsoever and we were ordered back to camp as the enemy had apparently changed their minds and had no intention of troubling us further.

In fact, only a strong Sikh reconnaissance party had crossed. Gough, short on ammunition, did not wish to turn the cannonade into a battle and neither did Tej Singh have any inclination to move forward. The duel was memorable due to one of the biggest of the British cannon, an iron eighteen-pounder, bursting during the contest and severely wounding one of the British artillerymen, which brought the contest to an abrupt end. The encounter also allowed the British to try out rockets against the Sikh entrenchment for the first time. Both sides fell back around 6.00 p.m. During the night, a British artilleryman was killed and a sepoy wounded very close to the bridge.

Fourteenth January

British outposts sounded another false alarm. This led to similar results as the previous day with Sikh and British forces engaging in a four-hour cannonade. Sikh troops had brought some light guns with them. The British had two eight-inch howitzers along with a twenty-four-pounder cannon, which burst after only a few rounds were fired and nearly killed Sir Robert Dick, the British second in command. The Sikh troops withdrew around 4.00 p.m. as the daylight began to vanish. British forces had been told to stay in a state of readiness from 8.00 a.m. to 1.00 p.m. that day. The increasing tension and increasing false alarms may have been due to large numbers of Sikh soldiers crossing the river to build entrenchments.

Twentieth January

By 20 January, after further skirmishing and false alarms, the British outpost at Rhodewalla had been considerably strengthened by the addition of entrenchments. On the north bank, the Sikh army had positioned around 5,000 men to guard the Harike ford in case of an attempted British crossing.

Twenty-first January

The Sikh artillerymen engaged in artillery practice this day, many of the heavy guns being fired. A British party of twenty men were sent to scour the nearby riverbank and to attempt to destroy any ferry boats being used by Sikh skirmishers to cross the river. Some boats were destroyed but it had little impact on the Sikh skirmishers, who had been collecting boats since their arrival at Sabraon.

Twenty-third January

There was another false alarm with the British army turning out from noon before retiring around 4.00 p.m. The alarm had been caused by the Sikh army practising manoeuvres on the north bank due to which large clouds of dust drifted south towards the British camp. Sniping continued in the area between the camps and there was some minor action close to the British outposts. Major-General Sir Joseph Thackwell recorded it as 'a good deal of firing at the outposts today – the enemy showing a good many sowars!'

Twenty-fourth January

The following day, Sikh irregular cavalry, the *Gorchurras*, attacked the British outposts and fought against the British irregular cavalry.

Twenty-sixth January

Two days later, cavalry from both sides had another contest in the open ground between the two camps. The skirmishing was frequently continued after sunset. Daniel Mackinnon records a party of Sikhs crossing over and surprising a British patrol of irregular cavalry, killing three or four men in the dark.

Twenty-seventh January

Sikh infantry occupied the watch tower at Chote Sabraon village accompanied by a strong cavalry force. This force pushed the British cavalry back to Rhodewalla amid heavy skirmishing on this day.

Twenty-eighth January

Cannon fire from the Battle of Aliwal, over forty miles away, could be heard clearly at Sabraon from around 10.00 a.m. An organised assault by Sikh cavalry and infantry, a total of around 1,000 men, attacked and captured Aleewala village, the most westerly of the British outposts, and burnt it. Substantial British reinforcements were sent by Gough, including units from the 3rd Light Dragoons who managed to recapture the village. Four hundred Sikh *sowars* with camel swivels bombarded the village.

Twenty-ninth January

News reached the British camp of the success at Aliwal. The whole British army turned out and a twenty-one gun salute to the victory was fired. The British received several hundred hackeries worth of ammunition and supplies this day along with more reinforcements. A prolonged skirmish lasting an hour and half developed on this day. Sir Joseph Thackwell recorded that there was considerable activity and dust swirling into the air from the direction of the Sikh camp although he was unable to ascertain whether this was due to building work on the entrenchments or troop movements.

Thirtieth January

Significant amounts of Sikh cavalry crossed onto the south bank on this day. Around noon, the British again moved closer to the Sutlej to attack them near the bridge of boats. By this time, the British were fully aware of the Sikh commander's tactic of a defensive posture with a portion of the Sikh army south of the river, the entrenchments being too extensive to be temporary. An increasing amount of work was being done on the Sikh entrenchments.

Thirty-first January

For the first and last time, British and Sikh soldiers were seen fraternising on the open plains between the camps.

Second February

The substantial number of cavalry of both sides required much forage for the horses. Syces and grass-cutters from both sides could be seen wandering around collecting forage in the vicinities of the outposts. One of the less hostile encounters occurred on this day. Five grass-cutters from the Sikh camp happened to approach too close to the British forces. They were captured but shortly released with a warning. Some days prior to the battle, two junior British officers were seen walking towards the Sikh entrenchment and were stopped by Sikh soldiers rounding up cattle and camels that were grazing on the land in front of the camp. The officers said they were under the influence of wine and had lost their way. They were sent back, although it was suspected that they were spying on the defences.

Seventh February

The skirmishing largely ended on 7 February, three days before the battle. Gough forbade anyone from British lines moving towards Sikh lines. This was both to stop Sikh spies entering the British camp and to prevent British soldiers being taken prisoner and thus alerting the Sikh camp of British preparations. Pickets and vedettes were told to fire upon any British soldier, grass-cutter or anyone else who happened to be moving towards the Sikh lines. The last person seen crossing the lines was a sepoy of the 42nd Native Infantry collecting firewood, who was promptly ordered back. The long-awaited British siege train had also arrived. With Sir Harry Smith returning with his contingent from the Battle of Aliwal on 8 February, Gough now had all the forces he required.

Both sides had mixed fortunes during these daily encounters with Sikh horse artillery proving superior to their British counterparts in the open field. Lt Reynell Taylor recorded a typical encounter between artillery of both sides coming across each other by chance:

> A troop of our horse artillery was taken out to reconnoitre the other day and came within range of their artillery also on the move. Both parties unlimbered and began blazing at one another. The Sikhs' range was exact and in a few minutes our troop had to retire with a loss of

several horses, more men, a couple of tumbrels blown up and a gun injured. This was told me by the artillery officers of the troop.

As far as cavalry was concerned, British units generally proved superior and more disciplined. The skirmishing was not limited to the day; night patrols from both sides frequently passed close to each other and exchanged fire. The Sikh army had marked the Harike ford with flares allowing for night crossings by horsemen. Occasionally, hostilities seemed to end for sport; this area around the Sutlej was full of game. Major-General Gilbert, a well-known pig-sticker, could be seen chasing boars for his daily sport. Sikh infantrymen sportingly refrained from shooting at his hunting party during these times.

The Opposing Forces

The total number of Sikh soldiers present at Sabraon according to most British sources was around 35,000. Gough estimated the force to be 42,626 in number. This, however, included the army on the north bank and the Sikh cavalry. Cunningham, present at the battle, calculated the garrison on the south bank that would take part in the contest at less than 20,000, not all being regular troops. Other sources put the garrison as low as 12,000 men. The logistical problem of supplying a large force by a narrow bridge precludes a number much larger than this. Certainly, the single pathway could never have supplied enough daily supplies for the whole army along with forage for 20,000 cavalry horses.

Although the garrison was almost exclusively composed of infantry battalions there is known to have been a small amount of cavalry. Sixty-seven cannon of varying calibre were placed in the entrenchment. The exact positioning of the artillery is lost to us, but we do know that under the instructions of Tej Singh there were no guns placed in the northern, weaker part of the entrenchments close to the north *nullah*. Instead, the bulk of the *zambarooks* or camel guns, around 200 in number, were placed there. The only units in the north capable of assisting the garrison were the gunners manning the Sikh batteries on the riverbanks to either side of the entrenchment. Command of the left of the entrenchment was given to Sham Singh, the middle to Mehtab Singh Majithia, along with troops led by Kahn

Singh Mann and Gulab Singh Povindia. The Avitabile troops were stationed here in the centre left. On the weak right, Attar Singh Kalianwala and Mouton, the Frenchman, were the commanders.

British strength for the battle was not wholly dissimilar to the Sikhs, amounting to around 20,000 men. This did not include Grey's force at Attaree and Littler's force at Ferozepore. The artillery now consisted of 108 guns of various calibre, including eighteen heavy howitzers and mortars and six eighteen-pounder guns. The army was to be divided into three divisions. Sir Harry Smith would command the British right adjacent to the Sutlej. Maj.-Gen. Walter Gilbert would command the middle. Sir Robert Dick was given the responsibility of leading the initial assault on the vulnerable northern Sikh defences with the British left. To facilitate this, Dick's division and the left of Gilbert's division were strengthened with five of the nine European regiments. Added to these were six of the twelve native regiments in the British first line. Both Gilbert and Smith's divisions had the roughly equal strength of two European regiments and three to four native regiments.

The Battle

In addition to receiving reinforcements, Gough had been waiting for the state of the Sutlej to change to his advantage. A few days earlier, heavy rains had fallen upstream and these had now swollen the normal placid river, raising its level by seven inches. The fast current made the river impassable from the various fords close to the Sikh camp. The only communication and source of reinforcements the Sikh contingent in the entrenchment would now have with the army on the north bank would be via the bridge. In the afternoon of 9 February, Gough informed his division leaders, brigadiers and heads of department that the battle would be fought the next day and the order of battle was discussed. They were also advised that the Sikh garrison in the entrenchment needed to be annihilated as a campaign in Sikh territory on the north bank was undesirable. The night before the attack, Sir Henry Hardinge rejoined the force at Sabraon from Ferozepore in anticipation of the assault the next morning.

On 10 February 1946, a Tuesday morning, British troops were woken up at 3.00 a.m. No bugles or drums were sounded and the soldiers were ordered to take off the white cap covers of their shakos so as not to draw attention to British preparations. The Gurkha regiment was advanced forward to the Sikh outpost of Sabraon but it was found to be empty. By 4.00 a.m. the entire British army had moved out silently and taken their positions, ringing the Sikh entrenchment at around 800 metres distance. Smith, as ordered, lined up his forces between the Sutlej and the village of Guttah. Gilbert's division began west of Chote Sabraon and faced the long stretch of Sikh defences running along the south *nullah*. Dick's forces on the British left wheeled round in a clockwise fashion towards Aleewala village before taking up positions in the western portion of the southern *nullah* for protection. The cavalry under the command of Thackwell was divided in two. While the 3rd Light Dragoons would support the left, the 9th Lancers were stationed on the left of Smith's division to support the British right flank. Capt. Campbell's cavalry was located between Gilbert's and Smith's divisions. At the Harike ghat, behind Smith's division, were stationed the 16th Lancers and a troop of horse artillery under Brigadier Cureton both to oppose any Sikh cavalry crossing and to threaten a crossing of their own. Further back at Rhodewalla, another European regiment, HM 80th, was kept in reserve.

The British big guns had already been moved into position by midnight along with their crews and several regiments for protection. The heavy artillery was placed largely in two locations. Eight guns, composed of five twenty-four-pounder howitzers and three twelve-pounders (originally nine-pounders reamed up to twelve-pounders) were located between Smith's and Gilbert's division. They faced the eastern section of the Sikh defence, where the line left the east *nullah* and curved south-westwards to meet the south *nullah*. This was one of the more formidable areas of the defence. The bulk of the artillery – twenty-five heavy guns comprising of six 5.5-inch howitzers, fourteen eight-inch howitzers and five eighteen-pounders – was placed between Gilbert's and Dick's division where the defences were ordinary trenches and breastworks. The No. 19 field battery faced the centre of Sikh lines. On the British right, horse artillery flanked Smith's division. In addition to this, a rocket battery was also being used. The larger siege pieces were placed around 1,300 yards from the

entrenchment with the smaller pieces placed at around 800 yards.
It was now a matter of waiting until the start of hostilities.

Artillery Duel

The night had been by all accounts extremely cold but the weather
clear and there was no dust in the air. A mist hung over the Sutlej,
however, delaying the British attack until between 6.30 a.m. and
7.00 a.m. when the sun rose and the mist vanished to give a clear
view of the battlefield.

The artillery on the British right opened up first, commencing
with one of the big twenty-four pounders. British guns in the
middle and the left then followed suit. Despite a silent approach
by the British, there appears to have been no element of surprise.
Sikh infantrymen sounded the kettle drums as the first salvos
landed in the entrenchment and a few moments later the Sikh guns
began replying. Harry Burnett Lumsden of the 59th Bengal Native
Infantry, situated on the British extreme left, watched the opening
of the cannonade:

> Exactly at seven o' clock in the morning the Seikhs were saluted
> by a salvo from our heavy gun batteries, near the tower in front of
> Rhodewalla, which was instantly returned, with interest, from every
> battery along their front. The cannonade thus commenced was carried
> on both sides for upwards of three hours, the enemy serving their guns
> with wonderful rapidity and precision, knocking our horse artillery
> (which had gone out to the front very boldly, and given them several
> rounds of grape) back to the line in no time.

The cannonade was continued by both sides for over two hours
reaching its peak at 9.00 a.m. before British ammunition was
exhausted. Despite the lengthy contest, there seemed to have been
little initial success for both sides. The defences and trenches made
an effective shelter from British guns for the Sikh troops and no
significant damage is recorded on any of the Sikh defences. On
the British side, Dick's forces on the left flank used the south
nullah as a makeshift trench with most of the Sikh shot flying
over their heads, while British infantry along the middle and right
also kept their heads well down during the duel. As the gunners

found their mark, occasional successes were chalked up. After the battle, it was found that a few of the Sikh trenches and large foxholes had received direct hits, killing thirty to forty men at a time. Another British success was the damaging of two cannon on the north bank. The Sikh artillerymen manning these guns were seen promptly crossing the river to help their comrades man the batteries in the entrenchment. Sikh gunners meanwhile observed a convoy of ammunition hackeries pulled by bullocks destined for the British mortar batteries. Gunfire at the column caused a fire among the carts with an inevitable stampede of the cattle through British lines. Another Sikh volley aimed at the mortar battery brought down two or three men. The Sikh artillerymen had increasing problems to face as time wore on. It was difficult to operate the guns in the sandy soil and consequently many of the shells were flying past the British lines. It was also noted that many of the shells were defective, exploding in mid-air, a result of the sabotaged munitions sent from Lahore.

For the infantry on either side, however, there was little to do at this stage but experience the grand contest between the heavy guns. The sheer noise and spectacle of the occasion left an indelible impression on all those present. William Humbley would write later:

> Let the reader pause and imagine the thunder of 120 guns on both sides reverberating for a length of time 'as if the clouds their echo did repeat' and he will have but a very faint conception of the mighty grandeur of those awe-inspiring sounds. Never shall I forget the majesty of the whole scene.

British soldiers stood up in the *nullahs* in awe and Sikh infantry manning the barricades climbed onto the parapets of the defences to watch the mighty duel of the big siege guns and heavy artillery, the likes of which had not been seen since Waterloo.

Advance of the British Left

Gough and Hardinge had meanwhile spent the previous two hours surveying the proceedings from the watchtower at Rhodewalla. As the British guns began to fall short of ammunition, Gough sent the word for Dick's division to advance. Thackwell, riding past the Rhodewalla tower, was reminded by Hardinge, 'When you get into the entrenchment, don't spare them.'

At 9.00 a.m. Dick ordered his division forward. From the south *nullah*, where they were sheltering, the division swivelled to the east to face the northernmost portion of the Sikh line. In front of the line moved the horse artillery. Following close behind was Stacey's brigade in the lead with Wilkinson's brigade around 200 yards behind. With no guns facing them apart from the *zambarooks*, the only initial fire against the British line came from the Sikh guns from the north bank. This was too inconsequential to have any effect. The British line halted frequently to correct their line before moving on. As the British horse artillery moved within 300 yards of the Sikh trenches, the small force of Sikh cavalry adjacent to the river launched an attack on the left of the division held by HM 53rd Regiment but the combined fire from the guns and muskets proved too much and the cavalry retreated.

How much resistance and how many defenders were met differed drastically along the line and accounts vary considerably as to what happened next. Some accounts say the weakly defended trenches on the extreme right of the Sikh line were quickly captured. Stacy's brigade marched through around 1,200 yards of open space before entering the Sikh defences. Herbert Edwardes, aide-de-camp to Gough later wrote that Dick's division found defences 'weak and easily surmountable' and that HM 10th Regiment marched in 'totally unopposed with their firelocks at their shoulders'. The whole British division had penetrated some way before Sikh reinforcements from the centre and left drove them back. This would seem to suggest that Tej Singh had either posted few soldiers here or had deliberately withdrawn them.

Harry Lumsden, in the front line of the advance with the 59th Native Infantry on the left of Dick's division near the Sutlej, describes a rather different and more difficult encounter as they moved out of the south *nullah*:

> The instant we moved out of our cover in the *nullah* we were saluted with an awful discharge of well directed shot, which did great mischief in our line; and this sort of amusement the enemy kept up for us with great effect until we reached within 800 yards of their batteries when

our troop of horse artillery [fired] a few shells while the infantry closed up their half-broken line and once more moved forwards to the charge. The enemy now changed their round shot for quilted grape which caused even greater loss than the former, but could not stop our men who were by this time driven half mad with seeing so many of their companions killed round them and having reached 200 yards of the entrenchments we gave the Seikhs the benefit of a round of musketry from the whole line and with three cheers regularly raced into the trenches with the bayonet killing all the gunners on the spot.

The Sikh cannon fire he describes may have been from the north bank of the river or from the array of *zambarooks* as no Sikh heavy guns were stationed in this sector. Henry Conran, present with the artillery on the British left behind Dick's division, recorded a different picture of the proceedings. As the British advanced, the Sikh defenders put up a stiff resistance to repel Stacy's attack:

As though disdaining the shelter of the heavy batteries, the British column steadily advanced against a fire of artillery, such as none but Sikh gunners could pour forth; our men progressed until within two or three hundred yards of the enemy, when musketry, *jinjals* and what-not, intensified the murderous storm poured upon their devoted heads. Soon we remarked that some of them began to straggle from the rear of the column; the pace slackened in front; presently they halted; and then, to our dismay, we saw them recoil, shattered and dispersed, over the plain; while the triumphant Sikhs, jumping over their entrenchments, pursued and cut the wounded to pieces. A general officer of artillery standing near me exclaimed, with an oath, 'The fellows, they will have to do it all over again'.

In yet other accounts, the British line managed to reach and advance past the entrenchment before being thrown back. As Dick's forces forced their way into the north, Sikh gunners on the parapets immediately to the south of the captured lines turned some of the artillery towards the British columns, enfilading them for a short time before a determined attack on the guns by HM 80th and 10th silenced them.

What is certain is that a Sikh counterattack made up of units defending the south and east sectors drove back the British line past the entrenchments that had been captured. Dick, commanding the division, had been killed. This was a desperate measure, however. The Sikh defenders had been forced to remove significant numbers of units from the south, leaving that area considerably weaker. The British attack would be repulsed a second time before the division managed a permanent breach in the Sikh line with reinforcements of Wilkinson's brigade, including HM 80th, and the 63rd and 33rd Native Infantry, joining HM 9th Regiment in the advance.

The capture of the north compromised the Sikh position. British forces could now wheel round to the right and attack the main defensive line from the rear. In addition, the bridge and the heart of the Sikh camp was less than 800 metres away to their left. Meanwhile, as Dick's division initially faltered and retreated, Gough had ordered the British divisions in the centre and right to advance to relieve pressure on the left. Sir Harry Smith, commanding on the right, moved forward the first line of troops under Brigadier Penny, comprising HM 31st and the 47th Native Infantry. They found two or three Sikh cannon firing upon them from the north bank. These were silenced after an hour by British horse artillery before the advance could continue. The ranks of Sikh defenders had thinned considerably in the south as reinforcements were sent northwards. Nevertheless, they put up a fierce fire in the face of the British advance. The first brigade, led by Penny, was beaten back. As they retreated, Smith ordered Hick's brigade to advance as reinforcements. This was composed of HM 50th Regiment, the 42nd NI and the Nusseree Ghurkas. This second attack was also repulsed. Col. Robertson, fighting in HM 31st in Penny's brigade advancing adjacent to the river, described the reception the advance received:

> They kept up a terrific fire on us for the men were all picked shots and as fast as a man fired he handed his musket to the men behind him when a loaded one was handed back in return. Three times we got close up to the works and three times we were driven back.

After a severe contest, the combined weight of Smith's division managed to penetrate the defences on the fourth attempt and crossed the parapets. This was not without heavy casualties, however. As HM 31st Regiment, closest to the river, climbed over the ramparts, Sikh soldiers sprang a mine directly beneath them, causing many casualties and chaos in the British line. Nevertheless, with the entrenchment crossed, the British line advanced into the camp, slowly pushing back the defenders. As they moved forward, however, they found themselves under fire from behind. Sikh gunners had managed to get behind the British line and had moved the Sikh guns to fire into the rear of the advancing British line. HM 50th Regiment had to be sent back again to recapture the guns.

In the middle, facing the south *nullah*, Gilbert's division had also advanced at the same time as Smith's. As they moved forward, the Sikh gunners scored a hit on a British ammunition wagon supplying the guns between Smith and Gilbert's divisions. The wagon, fully ablaze and pulled by startled horses, passed through British lines and into the *nullah* while the battle raged all round. Approaching the *nullah* themselves, Gilbert's men on the right found the banks were too high. Because of this, part of the line had to file to the left where the bank was lower before forming up line inside the *nullah* and continuing the advance. The attack had as much initial success as the ones on the left and right, HM 29th having to charge three times at the Sikh line. The wooden fortifications on the British right were too high to be crossed without ladders. In one of their rare contributions, some Sikh cavalry charged out of the Sikh line attacking and killing twenty-nine of the now retreating infantrymen. Gough had to call in the 3rd Light Dragoons as reinforcements. Further to the centre, where the Bengal European Regiment was positioned, the situation was similar. Ensign Percy Innis of the regiment described the British attack at this point:

> Now on rushed the Bengal European Regiment with a determination which promised to carry everything before it; soon reaching the ditch which formed the outer defence, and springing into it, they found themselves confronted by the massive walls, which in the distance had appeared less formidable, for they now found these works too high to escalade without ladders. To retire again was to encounter the storm of fire through which they had passed, to remain in their present position was annihilation; therefore the regiment mortified and chagrined was forced to seek shelter under cover of the bank of the dry river which it had left but a short time before.

Both HM 29th and the Bengal European Regiment were eventually ordered to move a few hundred metres to their left where the entrenchments were much less formidable. Here British soldiers mounted on each other's backs to clamber over the top of the barely manned barricades.

Along the strongest and well-manned sections of the Sikh line, fighting continued for half an hour on the parapets before the sheer weight of British numbers began to tell and the Sikh line was forced away from the barricades and towards the river. British sappers now created gaps in the defences to allow British cavalry to pass through and form up on the other side with British horse artillery being brought in from the extreme north through the gap between the entrenchment and the river.

Flight of Tej Singh

The situation for the Sikh army was critical, but Tej Singh had already fled, bolting across to the north bank as the first British troops entered the camp. Accounts vary on the Sikh commander's conduct during the hours before and during the battle. It is said that the night before the attack, Tej Singh had come to Sham Singh Attariwalla advising him to flee. This would suggest Tej had some inkling as to the British attack in the morning. Another account has Tej Singh trying to induce Attariwalla to abandon the army as the first guns fired and accompany him across to the north, which Sham Singh gallantly refused to do. Still another has Sham Singh sending a messenger asking Tej to leave his tower and help marshal the troops. Tej sent the messenger back with the message that he would come but needed to first secure the bridge. Soon after this, he slipped away across the river with some horsemen to secure his passage to the north. As he crossed the bridge with his escort, he had a boat sunk in the middle of the bridge making the bridge unusable for the Sikh troops now retreating towards the river. On the north bank had been stationed around eight to ten cannon. Once across the river, Tej Singh now ordered these to be pointed at the bridge itself to stop Sikh troops retreating to safety. Lal Singh, meanwhile, commanding the troops on the north bank, had stayed with his cavalry in a state of unreadiness, making no visible attempt to put the troops on the north bank on a war footing despite the heavy fighting to the south.

Earlier in the day, Sham Singh, as the first artillery shots signalled the start of the battle, had dressed in white and sent his syce back to Attari, the general's home village with the message that Sham Singh would not be coming home. Mounting his horse 'Shah Kabutar', he rode tirelessly along the Sikh lines, constantly encouraging his men to die rather than turn their backs. As the tide gradually turned against the defenders, he gathered together the few cavalrymen at his disposal in the entrenchment, around fifty horsemen who had attacked HM 29th earlier. Rallying these horsemen behind him, he charged HM 50th Regiment on the British left, falling under the furious musket fire of the advancing column. He was later found riddled with seven shots. Hardinge later compared his attack to that of the charge of the Light Brigade, writing that 'with Sham Singh fell the bravest of the Sikh generals'.

Retreat to the River

Once the bulk of the British army had entered the barricades, the nature of the fighting changed. In danger of being attacked from the rear by Dick's division on the right, the Sikh line began the retreat in orderly fashion towards the bridge and river. The British units also largely avoided hand-to-hand fighting. Instead they advanced in disciplined order, firing volley after volley from their muskets at close range. Thomas Bunbury, fighting with the 80th Regiment on the British left, described the scene within the entrenchment:

> It was an extraordinary sight to see the Sikh battalions with the mounted officers march past us at pistol shot distance. Not a man of them increased his pace or attempted to run. They eyed us with looks of bitterness and hatred, keeping their formation whilst crowds of our disorganized stragglers were firing into them as they passed.

An organised withdrawal was only possible up to the riverbanks, however. As the Sikh units all along the line pulled back, the area at the riverbank began to get more and more densely packed and effective resistance became impossible. Army units now became hopelessly intermingled with each other. Pte Joseph Hewitt in the 62nd Foot, fighting a few hundred metres away to the right of Bunbury, painted a similar picture of the desperate situation the Sikh soldiers found themselves in:

> We followed them at about twenty paces distant and did not close with them again but kept firing at them as fast as we could. They went slowly, for those in front would not run and those behind could not. They were a dense crowd moving forward towards the river, their only way of escape. Now and then a few turned and rushed at us with their *tulwars* only to be caught on our bayonets or to be shot down. The slaughter was terrible. Our front rank had to go along stooping for a careless shot from behind might hit them as we were four five deep. Europeans and sepoys mixed. When a rush came, down went the butt of the muskets in front rank like resisting cavalry.

Some five or six Sikh regiments were seen retreating to the riverbank only to find the bridge had been damaged by Tej Singh. They then tried to march through to the south side of the entrenchment in the hope of using the Harike ford two kilometres to the southeast; it was the only available option. The regiments then proceeded to cut their way through under heavy fire from the British lines. Opposing them were two troops of British horse artillery, firing almost point-blank into their ranks, and the massed ranks of ten regiments of British infantry, both the divisions of Smith and Gilbert.

Along the southern end of the entrenchments, the retreat of the Sikh regiments followed the same fashion as in the north. Col. Robertson of the 31st Regiment, advancing next to the banks of the river, observed the Sikh soldiers opposing him 'marching, not running with their arm sloped in a most defiant manner'. Here again individuals would break ranks and would run at the British line, sword in hand, only to be bayoneted.

Destruction of the Bridge

Gradually, the mass of Sikh soldiers were pushed back onto the banks of the river and onto the damaged bridge. Some accounts say a crowd of Sikh troops was seen on the bridge, wavering in their attempts to cross because of the cannon on north bank readied to fire upon any Sikh troops. British sources largely agree that the bridge had been sabotaged. William Edwardes, Under-Secretary to the British Government, wrote:

> The Sikhs made a gallant and desperate resistance, but were driven towards the river and their bridge of boats which, as soon as the action had become general, their leaders Rajah Lal Singh and Tej Singh had, by previous consent broken down, taking precaution first to retire across it themselves, their object being to effect, as far as possible, the annihilation of the feared and detested army.

Both Cunningham of the Engineers, and Mcgregor, the British army doctor at the battle, wrote similar accounts. William Gould of the 16th Lancers, fighting close to the bridge, mentions seeing the centre boat of the bridge filled with combustibles; Tej Singh had possibly contemplated burning the bridge. While it was never set on fire, the combustible material proved an obstacle to those trying to cross.

Nevertheless, the bridge still stood despite the sabotage, with a mass of soldiers now crowding the bridge in a frantic attempt to cross. Under fire from British horse artillery, which had reached points along the riverbank, and due to the weight of soldiery, sections of the bridge began to disintegrate. Col. Robertson happened to be fighting close to the river, a few hundred feet upstream of the bridge and with a good view of it. In his account, he mentions parts of the bridge giving way due to the weight of the men attempting to cross. Arthur Hardinge, another son of the Governor-General, was also present near the bridge, and related a similar story:

> I saw the bridge at the moment overcrowded with guns, horses and soldiers of all arms swaying to and fro, till at last with a crash it disappeared in the running waters, carrying with it all those who had vainly hoped to reach the opposite shore. The river seemed alive with a struggling mass of men. The artillery now brought down to the water's edge, completed the slaughter. Few escaped; none, it may be said, surrendered.

The accounts of Sitaram, a sepoy, and Sgt Pearman, both fighting close to the bridge, are remarkably similar to Hardinge's. Pearman was with the 3rd Light Dragoons, approaching the riverbank from the north:

> The bridge was broken and on fire and being choked up with a mass of soldiers, camels and horses with some artillery and carriages. Some of the boats got loose, the river being rapid at the time, the whole mass was turned into the river.

The state of the bridge and cause of its destruction is largely a moot point. As large a body as the 10-15,000-strong garrison would, under ordinary circumstances, take several hours to cross the narrow pathway of the bridge in organised fashion. In the confused and desperate situation that prevailed at the banks of the river, it is doubtful whether more than a few thousand at best could have crossed to the north in the closing minutes of the battle, even if the bridge had been intact.

With the bridge unusable and the flooded river unfordable, Sikh soldiers fought and died by the river while others entered the water en masse and attempted to swim across. Soon the river was crowded with thousands of Sikh soldiers.

End of Battle

Gough's command to his men not to spare any Sikh soldier turned what had been a battle into a massacre. A long line, many ranks thick, of British soldiers now crowded round the banks along with horse artillery, shooting at close or point blank range at the Sikh soldiers. So fierce was the gunfire that Joseph Hewitt, present at the riverbank, would describe it later as sounding like 'all the drummers of the British army were beating a roll together'. Thousands of soldiers attempting to reach the north bank died, their bodies packed closely together in the water. In some areas, the bodies were so thick it seemed to British soldiers that they could cross the river by stepping upon the bodies. In other less congested areas, however, Sikh units kept their discipline and close ranks in the water. Colonel Bhoop Singh crossed the river with his regiment largely intact despite having two horses shot underneath him during the crossing.

There were instances of mercy as well: British soldiers sick of firing at their helpless counterparts offered help to wounded or drowning Sikh soldiers. The Sikh soldiers, as in previous battles, invariably preferred death. One of the more poignant scenes of the battle was recorded by Charles Hardinge at the riverbank:

> We stopped one man who was levelling his musket at a dying Sikh in the river, to whom we promised protection if he would come ashore. The dying man shook his head as much to say he would never give in to the *Feringhees* [British] and floated down the stream.

As in the other battles, any Englishmen or Europeans fighting for the Sikh army were given harsh treatment. The sepoy Sitaram of the 52nd Native Infantry, fighting near the riverbank, described the fate of an Englishman in the Sikh army:

> I remember, when I was close by the head of the bridge (at Sabraon) seeing an English soldier about to bayonet what I thought to be a wounded Sikh. To my surprise, the man begged for mercy, a thing no Sikh had ever been known to do during the war, and he also called out in English. The soldier then pulled off the man's turban and jacket, and after this I saw him kick the prostrate man and run him through several times with his bayonet. Several other soldiers kicked the body with great contempt and ran their bayonets through it. I was told later that this was a deserter from some European regiment who had been fighting for the Sikhs against his comrades.

What was curious to many of the British soldiers, unaware of the Sikh commander's duplicitous intentions, was that no Sikh cannon or musket fire came from the north bank in support of their dying comrades in the water. Cust commented later that the British advance could never have approached so close to the riverbanks had a cannonade ensued from the north bank, the Sikh guns being more powerful than the British horse artillery brought to the riverbank. Richard Pelvin of the 16th Lancers, stationed at the Harike ford, saw the same behaviour at the ford, writing that the Sikh gunners fired a few shots before they 'ceased firing and remained watching us until Sobraon was taken'. By 11.00 a.m. the firing ceased and the battle was over, bar a nominal cannonade from a nine-pounder battery at Harike ford ordered by the Sikh commanders before commencing a retreat from the Sutlej northwards.

Looting of the Camp

Looting of the camp had already begun before the last shots of the battle, British soldiers spreading out and searching the corpses for valuables. Few items of value were found in comparison to Ferozeshah, however, the Sikh soldiers having only brought their weapons across the river. Shortly after the battle, British camp followers also began flooding into the camp in search of plunder. Among the more notable possessions found with many of the dead Sikh soldiery were well-thumbed *Gootkas*; the soldiers evidently had spent much time in prayer. In several places in the entrenchment, fires now began spreading, igniting gunpowder reserves near the Sikh guns. Loud explosions could be heard at intervals through the camp. As at Ferozeshah, Sikh soldiers had also taken care to lay mines around the camp, which British soldiers and camp followers found to their cost as they searched for their fortune. Capt. Humbley recorded the scenes in the camp immediately after the fighting:

> At about two o'clock ... I rode leisurely through the enemy's entrenchments and witnessed the horrible slaughter that had taken place; even at that time, a few determined artillerymen occasionally sent a ball across the river to the dismay of our plundering camp followers. A mine too would now and then explode and hurl the heedless and inquisitive into eternity for the entrenchment was completely undermined and during the following night and morning explosions were every now and then heard in the camp.

The explosions were powerful enough to be heard at Ferozepore, over thirty kilometres away. Gough, meanwhile, anxious to deprive the Sikh army of the means to fight, declared a significant reward of four rupees, up from the usual one rupee, to local villagers for the retrieval of Sikh muskets from the river.

Casualties

The Sikh army is estimated to have lost up to 10,000 men at Sabraon. In addition to this, the sixty-seven guns stationed on the south bank and 200 or so *zambarooks* were also captured along with nineteen Sikh standards. The total number of guns captured now amounted to 320 pieces. Eighty of these guns had a bigger calibre than anything seen in Europe.

Notable casualties were Sirdar Kishen Singh, son of late Jemadar Khooshyal Singh and cousin of the Commander Tej Singh; Gulab Singh Kooptee; Heera Singh Jopee; Mubarak Ali; Ellabec Baksh; and Shah Nawaz Khan. Also among the dead was General Sham Singh. His servants on the north bank would swim over after the battle. Gough, in deference to the Sikh general, generously allowed his followers to search for his body after the battle without any hindrance. Permission to take the warrior away was also given and his body was transported to the north bank in a raft before being taken to Attari. His widow had already immolated herself. Many of the Sikh soldiers stayed on the north bank for a day and a night before crossing south again to find their comrades, who were either cremated or thrown in the river.

The vast majority of Sikh casualties were in and around the river where retreat was impossible. In the entrenchments, the Sikh dead and dying were found in the trenches and large foxholes dug in the perimeter. As in the other battles, the Sikh gunners were always found next to their cannon, bravely refusing to part with them.

The casualties on the British side were 2,383 in total with 320 fatalities. Notable casualties were Sir Robert Dick, commanding the British left wing, a veteran of the Peninsular War and Waterloo. Brigadier Taylor also died. Brigadier Penny and Brigadier McLaren were wounded, as were Colonels Ryan, Petit, Gough and Barr.

Disposal of the British dead began in the afternoon. The bodies were collected in rows and buried in mass graves on the battlefield. The outpost of Rhodewalla was converted into a field hospital with the main army camping in the same position as the night before. On the evening of 10 February, Sikh magazines around the camp were blown up. This, and the fact that mines around the camp continued to explode the next day, made the work of recovering the dead difficult and dangerous for both sides. Most of the Sikh heavy guns were taken back to the British camp in the afternoon.

End of the War

Events moved quickly after Sabraon. On the afternoon of 10 February, Hardinge returned to Ferozepore, ordering Sir John Grey, stationed at Attaree ford, to commence the crossing of the river. As agreed with Lal Singh, the crossing would be unopposed. By the late hour of the same day, six regiments had crossed with advance elements of Grey's force having already reached Kasur, fifteen kilometres west of the Sutlej. The bridge had still not been fully readied, many of the sunken boats having sustained damage, and considerable numbers of troops crossed by boat. The main British force rested in camp at Sabraon for two days before moving to Ferozepore to join Grey's force on 12 February. By the 13th, the whole of the British army had crossed, a total of 24,000 men, 100,000 camp followers, 68,000 baggage animals, and artillery including 40 heavy guns. Hardinge himself joined the army on the same day along with all his staff. On 14 February, the entire British army had reached Kasur, fifty kilometres from the Sikh capital; the city's fort was occupied. Gough kept the force here for a further two days, allowing more British units to cross the Sutlej.

News of the disaster at Sabraon was brought back to Lahore by a *sowar* from Gulab Singh's own Kashmir army, which had been held back from the contest. He was stopped at the palace gates by a certain Hanooman Singh, a soldier of Jewan Singh's battalion who asked him what news he brought from the battlefield. The *sowar* had replied triumphantly that the Khalsa army had lost its power. Angered at his insolence, the soldier had killed the *sowar*, cutting off his head. The soldier was brought before Maharani Jindan, who ordered his hands to be cut off as well.

Notwithstanding the recent setback at Sabraon, the Sikh army had sufficient strength to be able to continue the campaign. The 20,000 troops at Sabraon had thirty-six guns in their possession. Scattered around Lahore and various forts and garrisons round the country lay over 300 cannon, which could be obtained at short notice. In addition, Sikh regiments stationed at Lahore and throughout the rest of the country could have reinforced the army.

Ranjodh Singh's force, now lying idle, was moving westwards to join up with the main army. However, continuing the campaign was never considered by the Sikh leadership and no ammunition or supplies of any kind were sent to the army. As far as they were concerned, the army had been dealt a blow from which it would find it difficult to recover; now was the time to sue for peace. After Sabraon, Lal Singh ordered the Sikh army to Patti, around fifteen kilometres north of the Sutlej, followed by Cheema (Jinha) and then Bharranah, east of Lahore. As the British army marched towards Lahore, strict orders were issued for the Sikh army to keep its position. Negotiations were commenced and orders given not to allow any Sikh soldier into the capital.

Within the Sikh army the mood was sombre but defiant. There was considerable debate as to whether to continue the fight with the general consensus being to fight and die rather than submit. But ammunition was required to continue the struggle and none was forthcoming from Lahore. A few were more apathetic given the support being provided to the troops and thought it of little use to continue. The *punchayats* at the camp met and it was finally decided to wait for Ranjodh Singh's army to join up with them before a final decision would be made. Ranjodh Singh had meanwhile also absented himself from his troops, travelling to Noorpore, so his troops would arrive at Amritsar under Raja Ajeet Singh Ladwa. He was, however, compelled to attend the meeting of the *punchayats*. The mood among these troops was similar; to die gloriously in battle would be better than face the disgrace that would be heaped upon them. The soldiers in the *punchayats* also feared expulsion from the army by a more empowered court after a surrender. During the meetings, much scorn was poured on the Sikh rulers who had engineered the defeat. There was also considerable anger among the troops that assistance from Gulab Singh had not been forthcoming and that he was already negotiating the handing over of the Jullunder Doab territory to the British. On 19 February, the same day that the British would reach Lahore, the Sikh army camp was rocked by a series of explosions; the remaining reserves of ammunition of the Sikh army had been blown up. Treason was the likely cause, although the cause was given as an accident. Nevertheless, it left the army bereft of what ammunition had remained, rendering further resistance impossible.

Tej Singh had meanwhile absented himself from the army by going to Amritsar, under the pretext of being present at the cremation ceremony for his nephew who had died at Sabraon.

At Lahore, meanwhile, on 15 February, Gulab Singh released all British soldiers, giving them ten rupees each and sending them to the British camp, escorted by Sikh soldiers. This included the prisoners taken at Bhudowal who had been transferred from Phillour fort and put under the charge of the European doctor John Martin Honigberger. Gulab Singh, nominally a vassal of the Lahore state, had become an influential figure after Ranjit Singh's death among the nonentities that populated the Lahore government. He had requested, and been given, carte blanche by Maharani Jindan for negotiations with the British. On 16 February, at 2.00 p.m., Gulab Singh reached the British camp for negotiations. He was received coldly and the presents he brought – 5,000 rupees, twelve horses and two elephants, among others – were refused by Hardinge. When he raised the issue of a truce with the Governor-General, he was referred to Frederick Currie, his secretary, and Major Henry Lawrence, the political agent with whom discussions were commenced. Gulab Singh agreed to all British demands.

The British resumed their march to Lahore on 17 February, marching ten miles. On the 18th, a slow advance was ordered in battle order as reports came in of movements of the Sikh army close by as the British moved to within sixteen miles of Lahore. On the 18th, while en route to Lahore, Dhuleep Singh, the young Maharaja, arrived at Lullianee at a few minutes past 3.00 p.m. to pay submission. He was greeted with a guard of honour from HM 31st and 50th and the 9th and 16th Lancers, who formed a double line. A royal salute was ordered from the twenty-four-pounders. Dhuleep Singh would accompany the British army to Lahore.

On 19 February, the British reached the capital, camping in front of the Sikh barracks. Maharani Jindan had summoned the remaining *punchayats* in the city and told them to spread the news around the city that the British were to be treated as friends. The *punchayats* were sent away with presents of silk cloth. As the British approached the city, the Maharani ordered salutes of five guns to be fired with all cannon subsequently removed from their embrasures in the fort walls. The Sikh army cantonment houses in Anarkalee had been ordered to be readied for the British. The Badshahi Masjid, opposite the fort and palace, was also prepared for the British troops, although they would at first camp at Meean Mir. Orders were given that any insults offered to British officers, who would be allowed into the city and fort, would be punished in the severest way and that their servants and attendants were to be treated politely. Meanwhile, all Sikh troops were expelled from the city and the Muslim Najeeb militias, raised by Lal Singh previously to counteract the Sikh forces in the capital, were given control of the city.

The British occupied the fort and part of the palace on 22 February, also taking control of the Badshahi Masjid and Hazuri Bagh in front of the fort. One of the first actions of Sir Henry Hardinge on entering the city was to visit the *samadh* of Ranjit Singh where he offered 250 rupees.

Assured of their positions, Hardinge's terms, which would break up the Sikh Empire, were readily agreed to by the ruling clique in a series of treaties. The Treaty of Lahore (see Appendix A) was signed on 9 March 1846. The Jullunder Doab, the considerable tract of land lying between the Sutlej and Beas rivers, would be ceded to the British as well as all territories of the *durbar* south of the Sutlej. In addition, a punitive one and a half *crores* (15 millions) of rupees were demanded as war reparation. British forces would occupy Lahore for a year at the expense of the Sikh government. The British army could also pass through the Punjab as and when desired. The Sikh army would be reduced to around a third of its size; only 20,000 soldiers and 12,000 cavalry could be maintained, and any artillery used in the campaign – that is, the remaining thirty-six guns – had to be surrendered. The state was effectively banned from employing European soldiers and civilians. The war reparation demanded was well beyond the capacity of the state to pay, and in consequence Kashmir was seized. Recognising that the occupation of the distant territory was beyond their capabilities Hardinge gave the province as a reward for his neutrality to Gulab Singh for a nominal 75 *lakh* rupees. The sale of Kashmir was ratified shortly thereafter on 16 March 1846 as part of the Treaty of Amritsar (see Appendix B), and Gulab Singh became finally independent of Lahore.

The Sikh army followed orders to surrender, and the remaining guns of the army were handed over to the British with, it was said, 'many groans' from the Sikh troops. The high pay that had been extorted from the court was also reduced. The previous pay of fifteen rupees was reduced to between six and eight rupees, depending on seniority, with those soldiers in the capital who had received the higher pay ordered to repay it. Any troops refusing the reduction in salary were to be discharged; their muskets were also to be taken. If they refused or claimed their weapon had been lost, they were to be charged for its cost. It was suggested that the troops were to pay one month of their salary to pay for the demands of the British and ultimately to pay one year's salary four months at a time, although this was never pursued. Four companies of two battalions at Lahore were given outstanding pay and the men in the *punchayats* of the companies were stripped of their arms and turned out of office as a public signal that the reign of the soldier committees was at an end.

The independence of the powerful Sikh kingdom that Ranjit Singh had constructed effectively came to an end and with little fanfare with the signing of a third treaty at Bhyrowal on 16 December 1846 (see Appendix C) whereby the British Resident was awarded complete authority over the internal administration of the state by the compliant ruling clique. This would largely be the state of affairs until the outbreak of the Second Anglo-Sikh War two years later.

7

A Temporary Peace

*They hope traitors like Lall Sing will not always command, and
therefore my expectation is to see the fragments of the Sikh army unite
again in mass.*

– Sir Charles Napier, 1846

The policy of the chiefs of the Lahore state to rely on foreign
support while weakening the army never sat well with the fiercely
independent people of the Punjab. Order had been established but
at the overwhelming price of loss of independence. The Punjab
for the next two years entered into an uneasy period of peace.
The British increasingly controlled the state but the Sikh army
remained unbroken and its soldiers not in the least despondent at
the recent setbacks. The common feeling among the Sikh troops
was that the Khalsa was still young and that the setbacks against
the British were but temporary. Much of the Sikh army stationed
throughout the state and in Lahore had not actually been called
on to fight in the war, and there was the perception that the British
had not faced the full strength of the Khalsa: if they had the result
would have been very different. The consequent reduction of the
Sikh army left many ex-soldiers with no paid employment and
little to do. Many of them would rejoin the army with alacrity at
the outbreak of the Second Anglo-Sikh War in 1848.

Among the common population, there was a sense of humiliation,
and the dismemberment of the state angered many. The state had
not, after all, suffered invasion; the campaign had been fought

outside Punjab proper and the common people had not been impacted. Among the aristocracy, the leading *sirdars*, and officials who had held positions of power, there was a general objection to taking orders from junior British administrators who now fanned out over the country. The feeling of defiance was widespread. A British reporter for *The Times* on 20 April 1846 wrote that the people and soldiers of Lahore 'say it [is] all very well for the British to walk into the Punjab as they did into Afghanistan but that the day will come when they shall be hunted out as they were from that country. They speak in the highest terms of the bravery of Sirdar Sham Singh Attariwalla who was killed at Hurrekee'. The reference to Afghanistan referred to the disastrous British retreat of 1842, which was still fresh in everyone's minds.

On 2 August 1847, the Maharani Jindan, anxious at the level of control slipping into British hands and showing signs of independent thought, was ordered to be removed from Lahore and her son Dhuleep Singh separated from her. She had been ordered by the then British Resident, Henry Lawrence – who had effectively become the successor to the Sikh Maharaja – to stay in purdah and refrain from interfering in matters of state. The royal family were held in high esteem by the common population, and the incident confirmed in the minds of the Punjab public that the British were achieving their ultimate aim of gaining the Punjab by stealth, aided by a supine Sikh leadership.

That the gradual erosion of the state would trigger another military contest was not generally perceived by the British until the actual outbreak of the Second Anglo-Sikh War. However, Sir Charles Napier, the conqueror of Sind and future Commander-in-Chief of the British Army in India, was one of the few to gauge the feeling across the Punjab correctly. Commenting on the mood around the country, he wrote:

The natives believe, truly, that we owe our victory to treason. It is known to all that Lall Sing wrote to poor Nicholson thus – 'I have crossed with the Sikh army. You know my friendship for the British. Tell me what to do.'

Prophesying a second war with the Sikhs, he later commented that the Sikh soldiers at Lahore 'hope traitors like Lall Sing will not always command, and therefore my expectation is to see the fragments of the Sikh army unite again in mass'. This echoed the general feeling of the Punjab population following the conclusion of the war. The infidelity of the Sikh leadership was a frequent topic of conversation in the streets and bazaars of Lahore as British soldiers confidently walked around the capital. Sitaram, a sepoy stationed at Lahore following the end of hostilities, recorded the mood on the streets as he walked around town:

> Their cavalry never came near any battlefield so far as I could make out, and when I was in Lahore I heard many Sikhs loudly proclaim that Sirdar Tej Singh was a traitor, and that he well knew, at the time he gave out that an English army was in his rear (after the feint attack at Ferozeshah which I have already mentioned) that the said army was miles away.

As the work of disbanding Sikh army units was carried out, soldiers would burn effigies of Tej Singh. According to Honigberger, the European doctor at Lahore, there seems to have been moves afoot within army circles to try and kill both Tej Singh and Lal Singh for their treachery as well as Gulab Singh for refusing to assist in the war, although these plans came to nothing.

Sir Henry Hardinge publicly rewarded the Sikh commanders for their co-operation during the campaign, reinstalling Lal Singh and Tej Singh as Vizier and Commander-in-Chief respectively. Their disinterest in the fortunes of the country under their control did not endear them to their new masters, however, and more privately a sense of chivalry demanded that they be treated as traitors. Sir Charles Napier was never one to veer away from uttering stinging remarks about their conduct. As late as November 1849 in Lahore, after the annexation of the Punjab following the Second Anglo-Sikh War, he pointedly refused any conversation with Tej Singh. Meeting various dignitaries during an event, he avoided Tej Singh, loudly exclaiming, 'Tej Singh! I won't sit by him; he's a traitor!' while warmly greeting Amir Sher Muhamad Talpur of Sind, a more honourable adversary during the Sind campaign of 1843.

The Sikh leaders would have mixed fortunes under the new masters of the Punjab. Lal Singh, anxious about his position in the

Punjab, wrote frequently to Henry Lawrence, the then Agent for the North-West Frontier, reminding him of his service to the British and requesting written documentary proof of his goodwill. The letter requested was eventually sent by Lawrence after approval from the Governor-General. Initially reinstalled as Vizier of a now puppet state, his love of intrigue would eventually prove his downfall. Lal Singh quickly lost British patronage when it came to light that he had sent written instructions to Sheikh Imam-ud-Din, the governor of Kashmir, to thwart the occupation by Gulab Singh of the valley granted him by the British after the Treaty of Lahore. Lal Singh was tried by a Court of Inquiry and found guilty. He was removed from his high office and expelled from the Punjab with a pension of 12,000 rupees per annum. Banished to Agra, he left Lahore on 14 December 1846 with four females of his household under a strong guard and a large retinue. He eventually reached Agra on 30 January 1847. He was given temporary shelter at the fort but deprived of all but seventy of his followers, only unarmed people being allowed to enter. The rest of the small army of followers and those with arms and horses and elephants were made to find alternative accommodation. A large house on the banks of the Jumna River, formerly occupied by a British general, was recommended for his incarceration. The rent for the house was a hundred rupees per month to be deducted from his monthly pension. Here the ex-Vizier would be guarded by a company of sepoys and some irregular horsemen for the foreseeable future. He was allowed to travel within five miles of his residence and further if he requested permission on the condition that he returned within twenty-four hours to his residence. Lal Singh continued to keep a large retinue with him, amounting to 250 people (including 15 armed men, 90 unarmed and 138 servants), and he lived in some style. But a close eye was kept on him and his actions were reported on a daily basis. He spent two years in Agra during which he whiled away his time by going for walks and drives round the city accompanied by a guard, and would frequently visit Hindu temples and the Taj Mahal. With the end of the Second Anglo-Sikh War came the annexation of the Punjab. The Lahore state being no more, pensions would from now on be paid by the British government and a general review of the pensions being paid by the Lahore state was instigated. This included Lal Singh's pension, and one of the last documented notes regarding the ex-Vizier, written by a Major H. P. Burn, deputy secretary to the board overseeing the transfer of Lahore pensions, and dated 24 April 1849, gives us a sense of British attitudes towards the ex-Vizier:

> Raja Lall Singh moreover has no hereditary claim on the Punjab, he is a man of yesterday, whom fortune, not merit, raised in a time of convulsion into power. The claim on British generosity for the maintenance of large numbers of deserving men in this country will be great. We may well save to meet such calls, a portion of Lal Singh's allowance.

Lal Singh's pension was reduced to 1,000 rupees a year. Finally, on 9 June 1849, those guarding him were made redundant as he was no longer considered in any way a danger. But he was told in no uncertain terms to continue to obey the directions of the British authorities. Lal Singh later moved to Dehra Dun, where he died in 1866.

Tej Singh, the Commander-in-Chief of the Sikh army, had somewhat better fortunes. As ambitious as Gulab Singh, Tej Singh had offered the sum of 2.5 million rupees to Hardinge in return for land carved out of Lahore territories. His offer was refused. He was used by the British to put down resistance being offered by Sheikh Imam-ud-Din Khan to the sale of Kashmir to Gulab Singh. Suitably compliant, he was made head of the Council of Regency after the Treaty of Bhyrowal and continued as the Commander-in-Chief of the Sikh army. He was made the Raja of Sialkot on 7 August 1847. During the Second Anglo-Sikh War, he refused to join the war against the British and at its conclusion helped disband the Sikh army. By the time of the annexation of the Punjab, Tej Singh's personal *jagirs* provided 92,779 rupees per year, of which the British agreed 20,000 could be inherited by his ancestors. During the uprising of 1857, he gave good service to the British, helping raise cavalry regiments in the Punjab for which he received a reward of a thousand rupees. He was nominated a member of the committee for the management of the Golden Temple at Amritsar, Sikhism's holiest shrine, and was also given the full powers of a magistrate in his estates. He was given a new title, the Raja of Batala, in 1861 when his *jagirs* were consolidated in that region. Tej Singh, a very wealthy man by this point, died of a chest infection on 2 December 1862. Harbans Singh, an adoptive son, inherited his considerable estates.

Ranjodh Singh, the commander at Bhudowal and Aliwal, came from the village of Majithia around ten kilometres north of Amritsar. There was some disagreement between Ranjodh Singh and his brother Lehna Singh after the war. Lehna Singh, an intelligent man had served under Ranjit Singh, making munitions and cannon. Having left the Punjab during the First Anglo-Sikh War, Lehna Singh had returned after two and a half years. The land he had left behind in the care of Ranjodh Singh now became a point of contention. Ranjodh Singh became a somewhat unenthusiastic accomplice in the new British-controlled government. He was sent unwillingly to Kangra by the British to coax the governor of the province to surrender after the end of the war. He also became a member of the Council of Regency formed after the deposition of Lal Singh as Vizier. The Treaty of Bhyrowal gave away what little state control still remained to Ranjodh Singh and the other *sirdars*. Ranjodh had meanwhile also been appointed a judge at Lahore by the British. However, suspicions were raised about his fidelity to the British and he was found to be in possession of some artillery, specifically a large mortar, two twenty-four-pound howitzers and a six-pounder. This resulted in him being stripped of his status as a judge. During the period of the Second Anglo-Sikh War, he was also suspected to be in communication with Diwan Mulraj, the governor of Multan, who was fighting against the British. He was incarcerated during the war and his *jagirs* were confiscated. However, his brother Lehna Singh came to his aid, providing a pension of 2,500 rupees a year for his benefit. After the death of Lehna Singh, the British gave Ranjodh a pension of 3,000 rupees, but refused to return his *jagirs*.

The royal family would suffer the greatest loss from the transfer of power to the British. Maharani Jindan, the Queen Regent, was stripped of all influence over the state with the signing of the Treaty of Bhyrowal and given a pension of 150,000 rupees a year. In August 1847, she showed her unwillingness to countenance Tej Singh being installed as the Raja of Sialkot for his assistance to the British. Later accused of plotting to kill the British Resident, she was removed from the palace and held at Sheikhupura, thirty kilometres north-west of Lahore in the September of that year, while her pension was reduced to 48,000 rupees per annum. Lord Dalhousie, successor to Hardinge as Governor-General, then ordered her removal from Punjab altogether, sending her to Benares in British territory where her allowance was further reduced, citing the reason that she might use it for 'improper' purposes, alluding to her attempts to instigate an uprising against British control of the Punjab. Accused of communicating with Mulraj, one of the Sikh leaders during the Second Anglo-Sikh War, she was incarcerated in Chunar fort. Escaping from the fort dressed as a maid, she reached Kathmandu, Nepal on 29 April 1849 but her jewellery – worth 900,000 rupees – was confiscated. She was granted asylum by a not altogether happy Nepalese government. Nepal had also fallen under the sway of the British and the British Resident at Kathmandu, stopping short of asking for her return, had nevertheless warned the Nepalese government to take steps to avoid the Maharani becoming an embarrassment to the British government. Maharani Jindan stayed in Nepal until 1860 when the British granted her a meeting with her son, Dhuleep Singh, at Calcutta. He would take her to England, where she would die on 1 August 1863 at the age of forty-six. Dhuleep himself ended up in England, living his life as an English aristocrat on the pension given him as a deposed monarch. Later in his life, he would contest the occupation of the Punjab. Conscious of the affection in which the son of Ranjit Singh was held by the Sikh nation, and wary of the numerical strength of Sikh troops in the British army, he was never allowed to return to India.

PART TWO
BATTLEFIELD GUIDES

8

Mudki Guide

*... piles of whitened bones and skulls of the slain ... had been gathered
by the cultivators and thrown in heaps ... Such is the soldier's end who
falls on the battlefield and such is the honour and glory.*

– James Gilling, 9th Lancers, Mudki

Mudki Past

Sir Hugh Gough had been anxious to unify his army with the
force under Littler at Ferozepore after the Battle of Mudki and
the focus moved on swiftly to Ferozeshah, allowing little time for
the disposal of the dead. However, Mudki would stay as British
headquarters until several days after Ferozeshah. The fort was
used as a makeshift hospital. Its small size was nowhere near
adequate and conditions rapidly deteriorated as more wounded
were brought in. Sick and wounded occupied every corner of the
fort, even more so after the battle at Ferozeshah when some of the
wounded were brought back to the fort. Gough had outmarched
his supplies quite considerably. With no medical equipment, the
surgeons did as best they could. Work was done in darkness with
only two rush lights available to illuminate the hospital. Robert
Cust, wounded in the battle and a resident of the fort himself,
provides a graphic description of conditions during the days
immediately after the battle:

Never shall I forget the complicated horror of those two days at

Mudki. I have made no mention of the discomfort and the dirt of the mass of men and beasts crowded in a confined spot. This was not all. It was the accumulation of suffering of which I was a spectator on all sides. In the tent next to which I slept with Mr. Currie was a wounded officer who was calling out 'For God Almighty's sake spare me this torture, spare me I cannot bear it!' There was the wounded sepoy at the door exclaiming in broken accents 'Duhai Colonel Sahib, maro maro!' (Mercy colonel, kill me kill me!). There were the mangled bodies of those killed in action lying side by side. There was even the more painful sight within – the senseless heap of clothes in the doolie ready to be conveyed to the grave all that remained of a gallant officer and valued friend. Death indeed became familiar. There are days in the chapter of many never to be forgotten.

Two large pits were dug near the village for the British dead, excluding the officers who were buried in separate graves in the quieter areas of the camp. The pits were marked by inner walls surrounded by a wall enclosing both walls. Other corpses as they came in were buried in shallow graves with frequently more than one body to a hole. Little ceremony was shown – a clergyman would simply read a short service before earth was thrown on them.

Meanwhile the village of Mudki was deserted after having been forcibly emptied of both camp followers and local villagers. An army officer noted only three village inhabitants during the period between December 18 and 21, all British. The wife of an officer had decided to commandeer one of the *havelis* for her own needs, while an army surgeon was performing amputations in the open street. The only other occupant of Mudki was a commissariat officer who had requisitioned a shop in which to stock his supplies. James Gilling of the 9th Lancers, passing through the village in the new year, found it to be in a very melancholy state:

On the 5th January 1846, we marched to Moodkee and encamped near the village of that name. Everything here presented an awful aspect of havoc and devastation. The evils of relentless war were depicted in the whole scene around us. The village was partially destroyed and deserted by all except a few old and decrepit men and women, and troops of pariah dogs, which had become bloated and fattened on the bodies of the dead on the field.

Several poignant records of the field of battle were left by passersby over the next few months. These were soldiers from both Gough's army and the considerable reinforcements from British territory now marching to join Gough under Sir John Grey from Meerut and beyond. Grey used the same thoroughfares as Gough and thus men from his columns would pass by the fields of Mudki and Ferozeshah. Charles Hardinge, son of the Governor-General, visited the field of battle the day after hostilities and commented on the Sikh dead:

> We visited the field of battle in the morning. Heaped round the captured cannon, fifteen in number lay the stalwart forms of the Sikh gunners, locked in death's last embrace. How the native reveres his guns was well exemplified. There were few that had not fallen near the pieces they worshipped. Over the field itself there was the usual mingling of the dead. The Khalsa soldier, the European linesman, the young officer, with groups of horses and camels, all lay in one shapeless mass.

Looting of the considerable number of dead littering the field of battle began quickly. By 21 December, as Gough's column left Mudki and passed over the southern end of the battlefield, corpses had been stripped clean of their arms, boots and clothing by camp followers and villagers. Bodies of Sikhs and Europeans lay well past Lohaum indicating the confused nature of the fighting on the night of 18 December. Robert Cust, recovering from the wounds he received at Mudki and having missed the action at Ferozeshah, hastened to rejoin Gough's force now at Sabraon. Passing through the field on 23 December, Cust recorded the state of affairs still prevailing between Mudki and Ferozeshah:

> We got on our horses and rode over the battlefields of Mudki to Ferozepore. We passed heaps of dead bodies: some barbarians had cut off the heads of the English soldiers. We skirted the scene of the battle of Ferozeshah: the village was burning, we overtook hundreds of stragglers of our broken regiments for without doubt, we suffered a defeat in the afternoon attack.

Two days after Cust, Pugh of the 47th Native Infantry Regiment, rushing to join his regiment at Sabraon, passed through Mudki. The stench of the hundreds of rotting bodies on the battlefield was now great enough to be apparent some way off. The odour of the corpses grew more terrible as he passed through the battlefield and had the effect of making passersby faint:

> Weapons of war, corpses of Sikhs, Europeans and Sepoys littered the ground undisturbed from the time of the battle a week earlier from Mudki to Ferozeshah save for the fact they had been stripped, all the bodies, of their clothes and possessions of any value by looters. Alongside the corpses lay the carcasses of camels and horses. At various points small heaps of bodies lay where the conflict had been particularly uncompromising. At other points hastily dug trenches indicated the location of some corpses. Scraps of soldiers clothing and personal possessions of little value were apparent everywhere.

Henry Babbage with the 55th Native Infantry Regiment would travel through on 28 December, ten days after the battle. Taking time to walk through the battlefield, he recorded further evidence of the recent contest:

> We passed over the battlefields, only a few miles apart about a week after Ferozeshuhur. The ground was covered with signs of battle; some of the bodies had been buried, but many were still lying unburied, both Europeans and natives; nearly everyone was perfectly stripped; long trenches had been dug, and the dead thrown in and buried hurriedly, but in places heaps lay just as they had fallen – but all stripped. The camp followers and the villagers and others had carried off all they could find, and left scarcely a vestige of clothing or anything worth taking. The ground was covered with bush jungle and low trees not very close anywhere, and the tracks of the gun-wheels were visible everywhere as they had passed over the ground here and there, in one place there were marks where some military man had climbed up a tree and had been cut down; sword marks were visible in many places on the branches. The smell was awful everywhere. It is true that the Sikhs retired from Ferozeshuhur with heavy losses, but the loss on our side was great and the retreat of the Sikhs was as much owing to our good luck as to anything else.

According to a sergeant of the 16th Lancers moving up from Meerut to Mudki on the first day of the new year, the village had become a most uncomfortable place to stay on account of the unbearable stench now emanating from the field. Several fresh large mounds and a great many shallow graves sprung up in the immediate vicinity of the village, hasty burial sites for the wounded that had expired in the fort and for the corpses being brought in from day to day. Thomas Malcolm, a soldier in the 10th Foot passed both Mudki and Ferozeshah having marched from Meerut on 16 December. His regiment had reached Mudki in the first week of January. Setting up camp at Mudki for the night, he and his fellow soldiers were given the unpleasant duty of interning more of the British dead before setting off for Sabraon the next day. Two weeks after the battle, the field was still covered with fragments of soldiers clothing, carcasses of men, horses and camels now half-eaten by jackals. James Gilling, passing through at around the same time commented on 'numbers of dried, blackened and shrivelled bodies, both of men and cattle' strewn along the way from Mudki to Ferozeshah.

The last account from the stream of reinforcements heading towards Sabraon was left by William Edwardes, Under-Secretary to the British Government, who was accompanying the siege train that would pass the battlefield in the first week of February 1846, over six weeks after the battle. Edwardes later recalled how as he pushed through the jungle:

> My horse shied violently on passing a bush; on looking down I saw a bare-headed European soldier lying under it, as I thought asleep. I pulled up, and saw that it was the dead body of a soldier of the 31st regiment, who had been shot through the chest. Shortly after we came upon many bodies of Sikhs, Hindustani sepoys and European soldiers lying about among the bushes, and we found that we were traversing the scene of the late battle of Moodkee. The dead bodies were strewed here and there all along the road until we reached the scene of the action of Ferozeshuhur.

A year after the battle, and with the Treaty of Lahore (see Appendix A) ending hostilities, the area was returning to normality. On 21 January 1847, James Coley, the chaplain to the Governor-General, would chance to pass through Mudki again. He had accompanied the Governor-General through a tour of the Punjab and was now making his way back to Ambala in British territory. Traces of the battle were fast vanishing although the hastily constructed British graves still made themselves apparent:

> Between two and three miles from Moodkee is the village of Loham, where the battle ended, being about a mile and a half from where it began i.e. from the entrance into the thick high bush-jungul, which covers most of the intervening ground: so that last year's accounts were exaggerated, which stated that we pursued the enemy four or five miles, But what a place for a field of battle! I see no remains on the ground except bones of beasts. Our camp is pitched on nearly the same spot which it occupied last year. A cluster of little mounds close by marks the burial place of some of our brave brethren.

Two years after the campaign, James Gilling arrived at Mudki. Gilling was making his way to the Punjab, this time to fight the Sikh army in the Second Anglo-Sikh War. Much of the ravages of war had already disappeared. Gilling describes corn, indigo and sugarcane fields growing where two years earlier there had been so much bloodshed:

> Happily hardly a vestige of the former fearful devastation was now visible save the clustering graves and the piles of whitened bones and skulls of the slain which had been gathered by the cultivators and thrown in heaps together as encumbering the ground. Such is the soldier's end who falls on the battlefield and such is the honour and glory.

In 1870, the British authorities would erect a large obelisk to mark the battle. The location chosen was the position where the British lines were drawn up immediately prior to hostilities on the road from Mudki to Lohaum. Made of burnt brick and seventy-five feet high, the obelisk was set in a square garden, forty metres in length and breadth. A caretaker or *chowkidar* residence was built in the corner of the square plot.

During the first decade of the twentieth century, the railroad arrived with the construction of the line from Ludhiana to

Ferozepore passing six kilometres north of the battlefield. In 1914, Major Sandys of the Royal Horse Artillery visited the site. He commented that 'the site can only be reached either by riding or walking, but the cart track is none too good and it is heavy walking in places'. By the time of Sandys' visit the plaster covering the Mudki monument was already wearing away. A low brick wall had also appeared around the enclosure by this time. He continued: 'It is all very bare, there is no garden and only a few shisham trees adorn the enclosure and even the ubiquitous *chowkidar* was not in existence'. The sand hills and high pampas grass which characterised the battlefield still remained, especially at Lohaum, and the area retained its difficult nature, sand piling up at the walls of the monument. The construction of a large canal cutting through the north of the field accelerated the fast-changing nature of the area.

Visiting Mudki

Mudki lies on the NH15 national highway running south from Amritsar to Faridkot. The village is also close to the NH95 running eastwards from Ferozepore to Moga and Ludhiana. The intersection of the two highways at Talwandi Bhai is seven kilometres north of Mudki. From Amritsar, Mudki lies around 100 kilometres to the south, from Ferozepore 40 kilometres to the east and from Ludhiana 100 kilometres to the west. The crossroad junction of the NH15 with the road from Bhaga Purana to Lohaum in the north-west of Mudki is an ideal point from which to reach the battlefield and explore the village. The road to Lohaum takes you to the battlefield.

The Battlefield Today

The old road running from Mudki to Lohaum used by British troops to reach the battlefield still exists with the two roads from the fork in the road running to Lohaum through the centre of the battlefield. The two roads effectively cut the battlefield into three sections. The northern section of the site lies due east of Lohaum. The centre of the site lies in the substantial area between the north and south roads, with the southern section lying southeast of

Lohaum. The Mudki site is now largely cultivated land. The jungle of tamarisk trees, prickly thorns and hedges which was prevalent in this area has disappeared. Tamarisks only survive lining the roads in the area, including the Mudki to Lohaum road itself. Fortunately, the site has escaped the increasing trend for locals to move out of the confines of the villages and construct new property on farmland. Therefore the only obstruction to a clear view of the whole battlefield site is the tree-lined south road from the fork to Lohaum. Thus the visitor can get an uninterrupted view of either the north or the south of the battlefield from different vantage points.

A few of the sandy hillocks, which previously dotted the landscape, obscuring the view of the battlefield, still survive. Some of these can be found on both sides of the road from Mudki to the battlefield. Only one hillock survives on the northern part of the battlefield proper, the others having been levelled by local farmers. The southern section of the battlefield, south of the road to Lohaum, still contains several, although the long line of hillocks separating the two forces has disappeared. The area west of the battlefield has changed less over the years. The land between Lohaum and Shukoor – eight kilometres to the west and south of Ferozeshah – where Gough and Littler's forces met, contains scores of hillocks, leaving the terrain much as it would have been at Lohaum during the battle.

To the north of the battlefield, the Phidda canal, running parallel to the Mudki road, now cuts its way in a southeast direction and along the northern limit of the battlefield site. The old road running north-east of Lohaum from Mudki to the village of Jaid, which is shown in contemporary maps of the battle, has been affected by the construction of the canal. The road has now disappeared completely south of the canal while the section of the road to its north still survives. A new road from Lohaum to Pathali and Jaid north of the canal runs through the north of the site. Close to Lohaum it runs through what would have been the middle of the Sikh lines. Nearer the canal, it runs almost equidistant between the former positions of the Sikh and British cavalry to the north. A small drainage canal now intersects the fork in the road, running along the same location as the British lines prior to the battle.

To the south of Lohaum, the road leaving the village runs

through what would have been the middle of the Sikh lines southeast of Lohaum before running to a point equidistant between the former positions of the British and Sikh cavalry in the south. Where the road intersects the drainage canal is a good approximation of the southern limit of the battlefield with the drainage canal approximating the location of the British left flank.

One of the most important consequences of the canal construction in the area is the disappearance of the old road from Khulkhurdh to Lohaum. This was part of the direct road from Ferozeshah village used by the contingent of the Sikh army marching to Mudki. Three kilometres west of Lohaum, the twin Rajasthan canals now pass southwards intersecting the old road. Only the stretch from Ferozeshah to Khulkhurdh now survives.

The village of Lohaum marked the point where the bulk of the fighting ended, a few hundred metres behind the original Sikh lines. Little of the old Lohaum remains, unfortunately. The village has grown eastwards, overrunning some of the areas along which the middle of the Sikh line was stationed. Like Mudki, the village is now surrounded by cultivated land.

Modern-day Mudki has grown much larger since the war, spilling out of its old walled perimeter southwards and eastwards onto the other side of the NH15 highway. Most of the village is modern yet important parts of the historic quarter still exist in close proximity to the village lake. The village lake was a welcome sight to the British army as they marched into Mudki. Hundreds of soldiers, their mouths parched with thirst after the gruelling walk from Chirruk, crowded into the lake before the alarm for battle was sounded. The present-day lake is considerably smaller than it used to be. The remains of the Mudki fort and some large *havelis* lie in stately ruins or have been incorporated into newer buildings south of the lake. Unfortunately, little is being done to protect the remains and these are being progressively dismantled by locals who use the ancient bricks for more modest village projects and dwellings. No trace of the burial mounds used to dispose of the British dead adjacent to what used to be the old village perimeter now exist as the village has expanded considerably. Nor is there any sign of the walled enclosure holding the collection of British graves outside the fort. However, village elders recall British graves being found within living memory. Three British graves still survive in an identifiable state although their occupants are unknown. One of the early nineteenth-century wells still exists in the village just south of the lake and close to the British graves. The British war monument lying two and a half miles from Mudki stands at the fork in the road from Mudki. As with the other war monuments, it receives little maintenance, but the well-built nature of the structure has ensured its survival. Just a few metres away from the monument, a Gurdwara has been built in honour of the Sikh soldiers who died in the battle.

Points of Interest

Mudki Village (30°46'53.38"N, 74°52'51.51"E)

The most convenient way to explore the village is to travel by car to the southern end of the village lake. From here, the remaining historic sections of the village are easily accessible by foot. Some of the graves and sections of Haveli A (see below) are located on private property and permission from owners is required.

A. Mudki Fort (30°46'48.51"N, 74°52'51.86"E)

One of the few surviving descriptions of the fort was left by Daniel Mackinnon who described it as 'a small compact fort, situated on a mound commanding the country, which is open and sandy for a circle of about three quarters of a mile radius, taking the fort as a centre'. Large sections of the fort still survive although in much ruined state.

The fort was a sizeable and well-built two-storey building. Currently, the portion which survives is around thirty metres in length. The outer walls and the adjacent area up to five or so metres (seen from the road) is missing, exposing what would have been the middle section of the fort. However, the remains are impressive. At one end, part of a corner tower still remains. Many of the architectural features, doorways and alcoves of the inner rooms are now exposed to the elements and little artwork survives. The fort is neglected and the ground floor inner rooms are largely filled with large amounts of debris from the upper floor. A staircase survives to the right of the building, although it is blocked. Some of the British fatalities were buried inside the fort compound.

B. Sikh Havelis

Haveli A (30°46'51.05"N, 74°52'53.03"E)
Haveli B (30°46'51.00"N, 74°52'49.09"E)
Haveli C (30°46'49.05"N, 74°52'49.05"E)

Sections of three old *havelis* still exist. The sole remnants of Haveli A are beautiful and well-built arches constructed with Nanakshahi bricks that open up into two small rooms. The area is currently used for keeping livestock by the owners. The remains of Haveli B are more substantial. Most of the front wall to the right of the doorway has been destroyed revealing the stairway to the second floor. A lot of the plaster work has survived on the upper floor. From the street and to the right of the building, original decorative wall paintings and artwork on the second floor have survived, albeit exposed to the elements. Some of the original doors and door frames remain and small alcoves are visible on the walls. Also visible are the old drainage wells on the second floor beside the old door. It is possible to get to the upper floor of the house via the narrow staircase, although it is difficult to say how safe the structure is at the moment. On the upper floor, there are small decorative recesses normally on both sides of doorways and larger ones elsewhere in rooms. The remains of Haveli C are still more substantial although in a similarly neglected state. They consist of a ground floor with second floor area sealed off. It is unclear how long the remains of these *havelis* will survive as the remaining sections are unprotected.

C. British War Graves

Grave A (30°46'52.57"N, 74°52'53.33"E)
Graves B and C (30°46'52.71"N, 74°52'52.69"E)

There are three known British graves in Mudki. All are situated in the same private dwelling close to the southern end of the village lake. The occupants of the grave are unknown as none of the grave covers or headstones have survived. Village elders recount tales of other British burial places in and around the village. These were gradually removed or destroyed as the village expanded. The residence containing the graves lies just a few feet from the lake. Situated in the middle of the courtyard, Grave A has a new exterior now acting as a seating area. The owner recalls the grave previously being topped with a small obelisk. The grave has never been opened. There is a local legend surviving of the ghost of a Sikh soldier from the Mudki battle having haunted the area until the grave was renovated. This is despite the grave being British. Two other graves, B and C lie together in a separate section of the house where livestock are kept. These are much less visible with barely any brickwork visible above the ground. The space is used for storage of firewood and forage, further obscuring any detail.

D. *Village Lake* (30°46'54.08"N, 74°52'52.07"E)

The village lake is sizeable, around 200 by 100 metres, although according to villagers, it used to be considerably larger, covering the entire north of the village up to the road to Lohaum. It lies in the north of the village near the road leading to the battlefield. The muddy waters did not bemuse British soldiers as they plunged in after a long day's march in the intense heat. A graphic description of the soldiers around the village pond was given by James Coley, the army chaplain, upon reaching the village:

> There is a large pool here, which was quite a picturesque sight when filled with soldiers who rushed into it up to their middles the moment they arrived to quench their thirst. Most of them looked fagged and exhausted and some of the Europeans as of readier for the hospital than for the field.

As the lake gradually shrank, a considerable number of dwellings sprung up between the lake and the Lohaum road, obscuring the view of the lake.

E. *Ancient Well* (30°46'52.09"N, 74°52'51.03"E)

Situated in one of the wider thoroughfares of the village, just south of the lake, is the oldest well in the village, dating back to the period before the war. The well is now disused. The well lining is made from Nanakshahi bricks, although the brickwork around the well is modern. Curiously, an underground entrance to the well, now blocked, can be seen just above the water level. This entrance belonged to an underground passage connected to the nearby *haveli*, allowing the patrician ladies to bathe or draw water without venturing into the open. When this underground passage was blocked and whether this passage has been investigated is unclear.

F. Mudki to Lohaum Road (30°46'53.09"N, 74°53'10.73"E to 30°48'14.81"N, 74°51'0.95"E)

The road used by the British troops to march to the battlefield four kilometres from Mudki goes direct from its intersection with the NH15 highway. The road is now a modern tarmac road. The road leads directly to the Mudki Gurdwara, the monument and the battlefield.

G. Ferozeshah to Mudki Road (30°52'40.75"N, 74°47'25.72"E to 30°50'42.99"N, 74°48'45.81"E)

Less than half of the old road used by the Sikh army to march from Ferozeshah to Mudki still exists, specifically the 3.5-kilometre section from Ferozeshah to the village of Khulkhurdh and a little section beyond. This still survives largely in its original guise as a dirt track, which has preserved its charm. However, the Rajasthan canals passing to the east of Khulkhurdh village, the large Phidda canal passing north of Lohaum and the GT road along with other new roads have caused considerable changes in the area and the original road from southeast of Khulkhurdh to Lohaum has subsequently vanished. Instead of the old direct route, one must go to Vara Bhaika village a mile to the south along the canal bank after crossing the canal before heading to Lohaum. Closer to Ferozeshah, a small 250-metre section of the road fell victim to the construction of the GT road, requiring visitors to use the main thoroughfare for part of the way.

H. British Monument (30°48'14.75"N, 74°51'3.27"E)

The monument stands just a few metres away from the Mudki to Lohaum road fork. The general condition of the monument is good although the outer facade of this structure is now crumbling away at the base. The original plaques no longer exist and some rather inferior replacements have been put in place recently. The date of erection is clearly shown on the plaques as 1870, twenty-five years after the battle. The level of the square plot is said to be higher than the surrounding fields owing to the locals depositing any surplus earth in the area of the monument over the years as they levelled the surrounding fields for cultivation.

J. Mudki Gurdwara (30°48'8.26"N, 74°51'11.42"E)

Mudki Gurdwara stands on the Mudki–Lohaum road, three kilometres from the outskirts of Mudki and just 300 metres from the war monument. The building is a modern one. The entrance of the Gurdwara contains stone statues depicting some of the important events in Sikh history, including some episodes of the Anglo-Sikh Wars. The Gurdwara is well worth a visit for the *langar* (free communal food) and chat with local elders who are always eager to discuss the battles with the British. The name of Gough, the British Commander-in-Chief is not recognised. Hardinge, the Governor-General, is remembered by his sobriquet Tunda Lat – Tunda meaning crippled and Lat being a corruption of the English word Lord (Hardinge had lost his left hand at the Battle of Ligny in 1815). In front of the Gurdwara is a metal plaque with details of the battle and the treacherous part played by the Sikh generals during the war. The Gurdwara is located just east of what would have been the front line of the British prior to the battle.

The Battlefield
K. Lohaum Village (30°48'49 N, 74°50'25"E)

The battle ended at Lohaum as the outnumbered Sikh infantry and artillery made a slow retreat to this village over the course of the evening. A small village during the battle, Lohaum remains less than a quarter of the size of Mudki.

L. The Sikh Lines

The Sikh battle lines were formed around two to three hundred metres east of Lohaum village. Lohaum has since expanded eastwards and the outskirts of the village on the north and south roads to Mudki now form a good approximation of the location of the centre of the lines. The Sikh infantry line would have been shorter than the British, most of the line being formed of Sikh cavalry on the flanks. The left flank of the Sikh army would have occupied the area to the left of the road running north-east to the village of Pathali up to around the location of the Phidda canal. The road heading south from Lohaum is a good approximation of the location of the Sikh right wing, occupied by half of the Sikh cavalry. The line ended around 1.5 kilometres south of the village.

1 **Middle of the Position of the Sikh Lines prior to Battle** (30°48'45.73"N, 74°50'34.16"E on north road and 30°48'38.92"N, 74°50'22.03"E on south road)

The middle of the line was held exclusively by the infantry and artillery. From the middle, the war monument can clearly be seen marking the location of the initial British line.

2 **Northern Flank of Sikh Army** (30°49'25.27"N, 74°51'0.80"E)

The location can be reached by travelling along the Phidda canal side road. Travelling towards Pathali, north-east of Lohaum, the canal lies 1.5 km away. Taking a left and travelling along the canal for 0.5 km takes you to the location of the Sikh left flank.

3 **Southern Flank of Sikh Army** (30°48'2.18"N, 74°49'47.13"E)

This location can be reached by taking the road leaving Lohaum to the south and travelling 1.5 km southwards. The Sikh position would have been a few hundred metres on the right (west).

M. Middle of the Battlefield (30°48'33.57"N, 74°50'45.77"E on north road and 30°48'28.63"N, 74°50'39.08"E on the south road)

Both Sikh and British lines straddled the two Lohaum roads. The trees lining the south road make it difficult to see the whole battlefield. The middle of the north road provides a good view of the northern half of the battlefield and the south road for the southern section. Looking west at the village and east at the monument gives a good indication as to how small the battlefield and how fierce the fighting was, the battle lines moving little during more than eight hours of fighting. A single hillock survives near the middle of the battlefield a few metres from the north road, one of the many that dotted the landscape.

N. The British Lines

The small canal intersecting the Mudki to Lohaum road at the fork in the road now runs where the British lines were formed up immediately prior to hostilities. A dirt track running adjacent to it is wide enough to allow vehicles. The British line was just over two kilometres in length.

1 Middle of British Lines (30°48'15.53"N, 74°51'0.27"E)

The fork in the road was the centre of the British position held by the 2nd Division commanded by Major-General Gilbert. This division was the weakest, both the brigades in the division being composed exclusively of sepoy troops.

2 Old Mudki to Jaid Road North of the Battlefield (30°48'52.34"N, 74°51'30.77"E)

Contemporary maps show the British right flank ending just south of the road from Mudki to Jaid, two kilometres north of Lohaum. The road passed around 1.5 km north of the Mudki to Lohaum road. The construction of the Phidda canal, which intersected this road, means the southern section from Mudki to the canal has disappeared although the path of the road is still visible in aerial images of the site. North of the canal, the remnants of the road to Jaid still survive.

3 *Right Flank of British Lines* (30°48'47.43"N, 74°51'26.77"E)

Two of the three British cavalry brigades fought on the right flank comprising the 5th Bengal Light Cavalry and the Governor General's bodyguard under Brigadier J. B. Gough, and HM 3rd Light Dragoons and one wing of the 4th Bengal Light Cavalry under Brigadier White. Three to four hundred metres south of this position was the 1st Infantry Division under Lt-Gen. Sir Harry Smith.

4 *Southern Flank of British Army* (30°47'41.21"N, 74°50'31.67"E)

The cavalry brigade under Brigadier Mactier held the left flank comprising the 9th Bengal Irregular Horse and one wing of the 4th Bengal Light Cavalry. Around three to four hundred metres to his right was the 3rd Infantry Division under Major-General McCaskill.

9

Ferozeshah Guide

[There was] a cloud of ravenous birds darkening the sky in our vicinity, with sundry beasts of prey prowling amongst the jungle.
– Henry Conran, 7 February 1846, Ferozeshah

Satiety had made them [jackals and vultures] epicures.
– Daniel Mackinnon, 16th Lancers, Ferozeshah

Ferozeshah Past

Ferozeshah and its environs stayed deserted until the latter part of March 1846 when the end of hostilities signalled the drifting back of the local villagers. The village itself had been devastated by the fires that swept the camp on the second day. During this period, several makeshift memorials for the more notable of the British dead had sprung up, constructed by the British army prior to leaving Ferozeshah for Sabraon. Among these were ones for Majors Broadfoot and Somerset. Both of these were simple pavements of brick with the name inscribed on the top. Broadfoot had been found near a Sikh battery to the south of the camp by a British doctor and was later reburied at Ferozepore. Somerset's corpse had already been buried in an unmarked grave and a number of graves were reopened to identify his body prior to reburial. Meanwhile, the camp and village had continued to burn until 23 December.

Despite the prolonged stay at Ferozeshah by the British and

efforts to bury their dead, many hundreds of European as well as Sikh bodies – along with the carcasses of camels, bullocks and horses – continued to litter the battlefield well into March 1846, three months after the battle. W. Gould of the 16th Lancers was one of the first to reach the field of battle after Gough's army had departed towards Sabraon. Bivouacking at Mudki, he had ridden to Ferozeshah on 1 January 1846, eleven days after the battle:

> Making a reconnaissance with my captain, we entered a kind of park-like enclosure [the entrenchment], and here we found traces of the fearful work of Gough's engagement. Men, horses, and camels lay in heaps unburied, vultures in hundreds feasting on them; none had been touched, all lay as they fell. The Sikhs lay in heaps under their guns, the Light Dragoons as they fell from their horses, the tents of the blind half-hundred still standing, knapsacks around in all directions. The guns we secured and fatigue parties performed the sickening duty of burying the dead.

The clearing of the field seemed to have been performed poorly as the battlefield would remain much as it had been since 22 December. James Gilling's account a few days later on 5 January mirrors Gould's. On his way to joining Gough's force, he took a detour to the village of Ferozeshah:

> [But] on reaching the entrenchments which had surrounded the Sikh camp, a more melancholy spectacle presented itself, and told of the fierce struggle that had been made. In many places the trenches were literally filled with arms, legs and bodies; side by side, and pile on pile, Briton and Sikh were mingled together; their arms, which had been raised in battle against each other, were now powerless and shrivelled. Numbers of broken gun-carriages, limbers, military belts, dress caps, epaulettes, broken swords and firelocks, were strewed confusedly over the 'field' while whole strings of gun traces, with horses, lay just as they fell.

A few local villagers could be seen shifting through the battlefield looking for cannon shot. The British had offered a bounty for expended ammunition as their supplies were most critical at this time. Many Sikh and British corpses were being discovered nearly naked, their clothes taken as trophies by locals. On 21 January, Robert Cust visited the battlefield along with Henry Lawrence, the future Resident at Lahore. Despite some recent burials, most of the bodies of British soldiers still lay exactly where they had fallen a month before, so much so that, he remarked, a traveller who was ignorant of the battle could ascertain accurately which regiment had been positioned where and how many casualties each unit had suffered. To the south-west of the village, some new and makeshift British graves could now be seen between the gap where Littler's division on the British left and the Governor-General's division in the centre had stood. The occupants of the graves had evidently been buried extremely hastily as arms and legs could be seen protruding from the ground. Corpses of humans, horses and camels were exciting much interest from scavenging animals; hundreds of feral dogs and jackals roamed the battlefield. On 7 February, as the British siege train passed by Ferozeshah, Henry Conran, accompanying the convoy, commented on a 'cloud of ravenous birds darkening the sky', signalling their proximity to the battlefield. William Edwards, also with the siege train, took time to examine the battlefield:

> That battlefield presented an awful scene of havoc and slaughter. Neither side had been able to take efficient measures for the burial or removal of the dead who lay just as they had fallen some three weeks before. Vultures and other birds of prey were collected in numbers, and so gorged that they barely noticed us or moved out of our way. It was easy to trace by the heaps of dead men and horses where the struggle had been most severe. The centre of the Sikhs' entrenched position was heaped up with bodies of our soldiers and of the enemy, mixed up with the carcasses of animals and fragments of tents and gun-carriages. The scene was one calculated to impress the mind most deeply of the horrors of war.

W. Gould would pass the battlefield a second time, after the war had been concluded, his regiment returning to its barracks in March. Visiting the battlefield and village on 8 March, he confirmed that the village was still deserted. Several weeks after Gould, Robert Cust, returning to Ferozeshah on 27 March, this time accompanied by the Commander-in-Chief, made the following observations:

At length, the trees and villages of Ferozeshah, a name, that will not soon be forgotten, came into sight, and we rode over the field, still covered with the bodies of the slain. The month, or rather six weeks, which had elapsed since my former visit, had worked a change, and the shining white skeletons had now assumed the place of the dark decaying corpses, which had met my gaze on my former visit. Still time and decay, had been fanciful in their ravages, and many bodies retained their consistency and some of their colour. The European was clearly distinguishable from the Native. The long flowing hair marked the Sikh and the cropped forehead the Hindu sepoy. Many of our poor fellows had been disinterred, but the buttons of their jackets or the stripe of the pantaloons told us to what regiment they belonged. Many graves had burst from the expanding of the bodies beneath, the effects of gunshot wounds, and head and legs, and occasionally a grinning skull, were seen protruding from the grave and produced a most ghastly effect. The people had returned to their fields and villages and but for the bones of the slain all traces of the great and memorable fight were being effaced.

On 20 January 1847, a year after the battle, James Coley reached Ferozeshah on his journey from Lahore, returning to Kalka in British territory. By this time the more obvious signs of the battle had disappeared, as he wrote:

Traces of the great battle are still perceptible in skulls and bones and rags and fragments of red jackets strewed about the plains. I could discover no remains of the trenches, though some, who were in the engagement, say they might be traced. In one spot there is a cluster of graves where some of our countrymen must have been buried. A quantity of dried skin, like leather lies scattered about, which I am assured by the natives is human skin parched and hardened by the sun. I found one skull partly covered with skin and hair, the skin being in the state just described. I was amused by some of our seepahees [sepoys] who were looking at one of the skulls and showed it to me as something very wonderful: for, pointing out the serrated sutures, they declared that it was writing and though not legible to them nor me, whom they asked to interpret the writing, God had engraved it there at his first formation to mark the man's destiny in letters on his skull.

With the return of the villagers, Ferozeshah village had been rebuilt and the fields were already under cultivation. Charles Hardinge, visiting shortly after Coley, was probably the last to see the field prior to the disappearance of all evidence of the battle:

> The field of Ferozeshahar is scarcely capable of being recognized as the scene of the late contest. Nothing remains to mark the different points of attack except the bleached skeletons of men and horses which are scattered in that spot where the fire was hottest, and the plough has turned upon the soil where many a gallant spirit fell.

Prior to the Second Anglo-Sikh War, a memorial obelisk had already been constructed at Misreewalla village for a Lt Peter Lambert who had expired on the second day of the battle. The memorial, an obelisk twelve feet high on a pedestal six feet square, was made of white *chunam* (plaster) by his fellow officers of the Bengal Horse Artillery. The more notable casualties of the British had been buried at Ferozepore cemetery. A British officer visiting Ferozeshah in 1876 noticed a small obelisk about four feet high constructed a few hundred metres to the north of the village. It bore no inscription. He was told by some village elders who remembered the battle that it was the grave of 'Judge Sahib' who fell in the thick of the fight. The title of 'Judge Sahib' would suggest that somebody distinguished was interred there. He had apparently been hit in the thigh before dying, so the story went, a fate which befell Broadfoot the political agent. However, Broadfoot died near the south face of the entrenchment and was buried at Ferozepore.

In 1869, the war memorial at Ferozeshah was erected by the British. Similar in style to that at Mudki, the three-sided obelisk was made of burnt brick and stood seventy-five feet high with a base of around fifteen feet long. A square garden was later erected around it with a caretaker's hut. Ferozeshah and its surroundings were used for encampment by the British army a number of times during the nineteenth and early twentieth centuries, its proximity to the Ludhiana to Ferozepore thoroughfare proving useful. In April 1911, the British Viceroy of India, Lord Hardinge of Penshurst, grandson of Sir Henry Hardinge, visited the battlefield during his first year in office and a grand military parade was held in front of the British monument.

The construction of the Sutlej canal with large trees planted on its banks had considerably changed the nature of the area by the time of Major Sandys' visit in 1914, by which time the jungle round the village had been cleared. A *chowkidar* was now present at the monument handing out pamphlets detailing the battle, the British units who took part, their casualties and also a portion of Sir Hugh Gough's dispatch to the Governor-General on the second day of the battle.

Visiting Ferozeshah

Ferozeshah lies ten kilometres from the Mudki battlefield as the crow flies. The NH95 highway running from Ferozepore to Moga and Ludhiana runs a kilometre south of the village. Ferozeshah lies twenty kilometres from Ferozepore and forty kilometres from Moga.

The Battlefield Today

The passage of time has been unkind to the battlefield, which has been afforded little protection from modern development. The site suffers from the presence of several new roads and canals along with the train line from Ferozepore to Moga, all of which traverse the battlefield. These, along with the unsympathetic new construction of buildings and dwellings to the south of the village, now mar the site.

To the south, the NH95 highway cuts through what was the initial position of the British centre commanded by Hardinge and what became the British bivouac during the night of the battle. The location is also scarred by the construction of an electricity substation at the junction of the NH95 and the access road leading to the village from the highway.

As the village expands, dwellings being built on the external perimeter of the village are now in some places close to covering what would have been the position of the Sikh entrenchments. Other dwellings now springing up largely between the village and the NH95 are obscuring what would have been the no man's land between the Sikh entrenchments and the initial British lines. As the original village was destroyed in the battle, nothing of note now survives. However, just outside the village one of the old village wells that served the Sikh army still exists. The other historic wells of the village were built over within living memory.

To the west of the village, a large canal now runs where the left wing of the British lines, commanded by Major-General Littler, was situated. The construction of the canal has had the effect of cutting through the old road running due west to Ferozepore, the only surviving section now being the 1.5-km stretch from the village to the canal. The former road from Ferozeshah to Misreewalla has also disappeared. This makes it impossible to travel from the west of Ferozeshah direct to Misreewalla village, the line of retreat used by Littler and Smith's divisions during the battle. To reach Misreewalla, one must travel west from Ferozeshah on the NH95. To the north-west of the village the canal cuts through the area where the second Sikh army under Tej Singh was positioned on the second day of the battle.

The railway line from Ferozepore to Moga runs approximately half a kilometre north of the village. The line, along with the canal, cuts through the former position held by Tej Singh's army to the west of the village and also what would have been the northern end of the Sikh entrenchments. The line also cuts through the old road to Itaanwalla, the old village two kilometres to the north and shown in contemporary maps. To the north-east of the village, a new road to the village railway station traverses through what would have been the eastern face of the entrenchments. South-east of the village, the road running to Mudki used by the Sikh army still exists as a dirt track as far as the village of Khulkhurdh.

None of the British graves that had sprung up round the village after the battle survive. However, both the British obelisks at Misreewalla village and Ferozeshah still stand. The Ferozeshah monument in the south-west of the village now stands a few metres away from the modern village Gurdwara. The expansion of the village means the monument is now close to the outskirts of the village. The Anglo-Sikh War Museum situated on the NH95 highway two miles east from the village is a recent and welcome addition to the area and contains a collection of weapons and paintings related to the Anglo-Sikh Wars.

Points of Interest

Ferozeshah Village (30°52'45.28"N, 74°47'16.51"E)

Ferozeshah was a small village of less than ten houses during the battle and formed the centre of the half square mile Sikh camp. After being captured by the British, the village was retaken by Sikh forces during the night of Ferozeshah following fierce fighting, only to be abandoned after Lal Singh's retreat. The British retook it the following day, this time with nominal effort.

Wells of Ferozeshah

Ferozeshah was well supplied with water for the Sikh army. A map drawn by Capt. Sackville-West map shows nine wells ringing the village, five to the east and four to the west. Desperate British troops swarmed round these wells after the battle – having gone a day and a half without water – causing a number of deaths as some soldiers were inadvertently pushed in. Joseph Hewitt of HM 62nd Regiment was amid the chaos:

> Seeing a big crowd near the village we went to see what was up and found they were round a big well about 4 yards diameter, flush with the ground. It was a risky job to get to the water but we were bound to have some so I took a firm grip of taffy's belt behind with my left hand and the water skin in my right hand; he soon crushed in, I keeping well behind him. Down went the jumbo and soon we had what we wanted. He told me when we got clear of the crowd that there were many dead bodies down the well and I believed it for there was such a crowd of all sorts round the well, crushing and struggling to get the water many must have been pushed in as no protection whatever was round the well. Any how we had a good swig and thought it very good.

The locations of the wells, several being close to the Sikh lines around the village, provide the best way of understanding the position of the Sikh entrenchment.

Well A (30°52'34.48"N, 74°47'11.35"E)

The only surviving historic well lies around a hundred metres to the south of the outskirts of the village. Standing on a small square of waste land, the well is disused now and filling up with debris. The well was just within the southern stretch of the entrenchment and would have serviced Sikh troops stationed just a few metres to its south, facing Hardinge's division in the centre of the British line.

Former Position Well B (30°52'39.26"N, 74°46'59.98"E)

This well no longer survives. Ferozeshah Gurdwara now stands on its location. This well along with Well A serviced the Sikh soldiers stationed on the south-west of the entrenchments.

Well C

The location of this well has not been identified. The well was situated to the southeast of the village around the centre of the bivouac of the Sikh army.

Well D

The location of this well has not been identified. The well, near to Well E and south of the old road to Ferozepore, was close to the western side of the entrenchments and around where Littler's attack took place.

Former Position Well E (30°52'49.32"N, 74°47'5.58"E)

This well, formerly lying between the old road going to Ferozepore to the west of the village and the road to Sodhi Nagar (Sultan Khan Walla), no longer survives. On its former location is sited a small village pond. The well lies behind the residence of Gurdial Singh Sarpanch, a well-known village elder. The well was close to the western face of the Sikh entrenchment.

Well F

The location of this well has not been identified. The well was close to the northern section of the western face of the entrenchments and lay between the British lines and Tej Singh's army on the second day of the battle.

Former Position Well G (30°52'57.20"N, 74°47'32.30"E)

This well no longer survives. The northernmost of the wells, this lies on a large extension of the village to the north-east in the house of one of the village elders, Sarban Singh. The well was well north of the Sikh tents in the entrenchment near the belt of forest to the north of the village. The well serviced the Sikh troops in the north-east of the entrenchment.

Former Position Well H (30°52'49.50"N, 74°47'24.00"E)

This well no longer survives; a village barn now stands in its place. The well lay just east of the former village and its position marked the end of the tents and bivouac of the Sikh army. The location of this well lies on what is now the village ring road round Ferozeshah between the junctions of the roads going to Itaanwalla village and Ferozeshah train station.

Former Position Well J (30°52'49.00"N, 74°47'25.20"E)

This well no longer survives. It was located just a few metres away from Well G, opposite the road leading to the train station.

The Gurdwara (30°52'39.10"N, 74°46'59.91"E)

The Gurdwara is a new construction. A modest building, it stands just outside the south-west section of the village adjacent to the British monument. A climb to the top of the Gurdwara affords the visitor a good view of the western and southern sections of the battlefield.

Sikh Positions

North-west of camp (30°53'18.91"N, 74°47'19.55"E)
South-west of camp (30°52'36.49"N, 74°46'52.44"E)
South-east of camp (30°52'29.08"N, 74°47'21.30"E)
North-east of camp (30°53'12.02"N, 74°47'53.26"E)

The Sikh camp and area of most of the fighting formed a rough rectangle around the village. The cultivated farmland around the village makes it difficult now to walk along the exact line of the entrenchment, but points along the former line a few hundred metres outside the current village perimeter can be reached using the roads leading out of the village. Visitors can travel more freely through what would have been the north of the camp and where the last of the fighting took place by travelling north along the road to Itaanwalla up to the railway line.

Tej Singh's Position Facing the British (30°52'47.98"N, 74°46'42.00"E to 30°53'24.35"N, 74°46'55.18"E)

The Sikh army position north-west of the village ran from north of the old Ferozepore road and cut across the Sultan Khan Walla road where the railway line now runs.

British War Monument (30°52'37.86"N, 74°46'59.17"E)

The Ferozeshah war memorial situated to the south-west of the village is the most elegant of the four obelisks built by the British. The structure remains in good condition although the original plaques that decorated the structure have disappeared. The word 'Ferozeshah' is written in large letters in English, Punjabi and Persian on the three sides. The location of the monument is just a few metres north of what would have been the south-western corner of the Sikh entrenchment, the location of some of the fiercest fighting on the first day. The structure stands in its own square plot, around twenty-five metres in length and breadth.

British Original Position on Day 1

Littler's Position (30°52'45.51"N, 74°46'12.29"E to
30°52'17.47"N, 74°46'31.77"E)
Hardinge Position (30°52'14.66"N, 74°46'36.77"E to
30°52'3.83"N, 74°47'9.98"E)
Gough's Position (30°52'2.95"N, 74°47'25.37"E to
30°52'21.22"N, 74°47'58.20"E)

Littler's division occupied a position south of the old road to
Ferozepore approximately where the canal west of the village now
runs. The British centre, commanded by Sir Henry Hardinge, was
situated close to the junction of the NH95 highway with the access
road to the village. Gough's division was situated to the south-east
of the village.

British Position Facing Tej Singh on Day 2
(30°52'48.89"N, 74°47'18.01"E to 30°53'17.48"N,
74°47'30.02"E)

The railway line north of the village cuts through the location of
the British position on the second day of the battle. British infantry
lined up north of the village facing west, with the cavalry and horse
artillery still further north across from where the railway line now
runs.

The Anglo-Sikh War Museum (30°51'46"N, 74°49'0"E)

The museum was opened in 1976 and contains large paintings
depicting scenes from the First Anglo-Sikh War along with maps
of the battles. The artwork was created by the noted painters
Jaswant Singh and Kirpal Singh. Also of interest is the collection
of weapons dating to the wars. Muskets, swords and pistols are on
display. Outside the museum stand two horse artillery cannon of
the period. In order to take photographs, visitors must have prior
permission from The Director of Cultural Affairs, Archaeology
and Museums, Punjab, Plot No. 3, Sector 38A, Chandigarh.

Misreewalla (30°52'11"N, 74°45'30"E)

Misreewalla lies three kilometres south-west of Ferozeshah as the crow flies. The village can be reached by driving west towards Ferozepore on the NH95 from the junction for Ferozeshah for two kilometres. This village was passed on the left by the British as they approached Ferozeshah and used for bivouac by Smith's and Littler's divisions after the British retreat during the night.

British Memorial at Misreewalla (30°52'12.64"N, 74°45'36.90"E)

A war memorial is situated to the east of the village in memory of a British officer, the twenty-five-year-old Lt Peter Lambert, killed by Sikh artillery fire on the second day of the battle. A scaled-down version of the other monuments, it has its own square plot with a caretaker's hut. Most of the white plaster and whitewash that originally covered the monument has disappeared. The inscription on the plaque, almost illegible now, reads:

> Sacred to the memory of Sir Peter Colnett Lambert, 3rd troop 3rd brigade horse artillery who fell in action at Ferozeshah on the 22nd December 1845. This is erected over his remains by his brother officers. *Requiescat in pace.*

Sultan Khan Walla (30°55'58.86"N, 74°46'26.90"E)

Sultan Khan Walla has now been renamed Sodhi Nagar. The village lies seven kilometres north of Ferozeshah. The Sikh army passed through the village on the way to Ferozeshah and again in the morning of 22 December on their way to Harike after Lal Singh's order to retreat. The road to Sodhi Nagar leaves the ring road of Ferozeshah on the north-west of the village and passes the village of Bhambalanda. The considerable amount of gunpowder abandoned by Lal Singh at Ferozeshah was transferred to Sultan Khan Walla and destroyed by the British.

Shukoor (30°49'54"N, 74°45'25"E)

Shukoor was the location of the junction of Gough's and Littler's forces prior to the battle. It lies six kilometres to the south-west of Ferozeshah.

10

Bhudowal Guide

Our camp followers soon made the place a wreck ... they set fire to several villages in the vicinity, and nightfall exhibited a long series of conflagrations marking their track.

– Daniel Mackinnon, 16th Lancers, Bhudowal village

Bhudowal Past

Ranjodh Singh's force departed Bhudowal on 23 January 1846. The following day, the village was occupied by Smith's contingent returning from Ludhiana. The battlefield was as it had been left a few days earlier, the town and fort deserted save for the British corpses from the previous conflict strewn around the village and nearby sand dunes. Sikh troops had done a thorough job of sacking the British baggage; wreckage of the British equipment, supplies and *dhoolies* for carrying the British wounded were littered everywhere along with letters, official papers and documents blowing in the wind.

Angry at the reverse they had suffered, British soldiers began sacking the village and other hamlets in the vicinity. Nearby villagers were accused of aiding the Sikh army and of robbing the remnants of Smith's army that had effectively been abandoned during the battle. A Sgt Pearman recorded the destruction of the village:

Many of the men killed on the 21st were found and buried and some of the men were found dead in the village of Badowal where they had been plundered and no doubt killed as they were naked. We found some of the men's things and the hospital stores of the 16th Lancers broken up and destroyed. This made the men very angry – and it soon spread at last. Some of the men of the artillery set fire to some of the houses which were soon on the ground. In fact we destroyed the place.

Other dwellings were burnt during the evening for the sole purpose of allowing the British soldiers to dry their wet laundry in the extreme cold of the winter night. Mackinnon was also present during the destruction and looting of the village fort:

Buddewal was speedily and thoroughly ransacked, but very little was found worth carrying off. Tents, empty trunks, and crazy furniture abounded in and around the palace (as it was called) of our friend the Ladwa Rajah, the author of the Sikh expedition into this neighbourhood, and a quantity of grain and cattle were found in the town [...]

Our camp followers soon made the place a wreck; nor did their vengeance stay here, but, wandering in parties about the country, they set fire to several villages in the vicinity, and nightfall exhibited a long series of conflagrations marking their track.

While condemned by Sir Harry Smith, little was done. The plundering of the neighbourhood continued uninterrupted for the next three days as more troops and British camp followers trudged in from Ludhiana and Jagraon. William Gould of the 16th Lancers, taking part, was one of the few who found anything worthy of sequestering:

When we got to the fort it was deserted – they had the start of us. Ordered to dismount and enter the fort, we found they had burnt the bedding, money-chests and tents, taking with them all of value, and it was quite apparent they hurried away, fearing we would come down on them from Loodianna. The town also bore the marks everywhere of a quick departure. On entering the palace, we found it undisturbed, profusely furnished with European furniture; and on going into one of the best rooms, my comrade and I heard some women scream. Rushing to where the sound proceeded from – an adjacent room – we saw some of our native cavalry ill-treating two women – Circassians who had belonged to the Rajah's harem. They were forcing their jewellery off them. On seeing two white soldiers, they ran to us. By persuasion, and at times by threats, they showed us where some money was hid. Taking us into the Seraglio, they pointed out a black stone near a fire stove. The floor of this apartment was made of marble, chequered black and white. On lifting the stone pointed out, we discovered two bags containing rupees. Counting them in camp, one had three hundred, the other four hundred and fifty. The girls were beautiful Circassian slaves, and could not have cost less than one thousand rupees each. They were much obliged to us, saying, 'Company Dewoy, thank you, thank you.' We had great fun that night in camp, appropriating anything found of use. We killed cows and sheep, made cakes, had plenty of milk, and, besides, the two young Circassians attended on us.

The British corpses were buried during the British stay at Bhudowal and Smith ordered the destruction of the Bhudowal fort shortly after the Battle of Aliwal.

Visiting Bhudowal

Modern Bhudowal lies less than five kilometres west of the metropolis of Ludhiana and around twenty-five kilometres from the town of Jagraon further to the west. The village lies one kilometre south of the NH95 highway connecting Jagraon and Ludhiana.

The Battlefield Today

Nothing of note exists in modern Bhudowal, the old village having been destroyed. The village itself has expanded considerably and risks becoming a suburb in the future with the similar expansion of the nearby city of Ludhiana. The road from Jagraon to Bhudowal and Ludhiana, along which the Sikh army was arrayed and which ran adjacent and to the south of the village, no longer exists. It is quite likely that the railway line from Jagraon to Ludhiana, which now runs past Bhudowal, may have been built over the old road with the new Bhudowal being built south of its original position and thus the NH95 taking its role as the main thoroughfare.

The battle was largely ignored by the British and no monument was constructed. According to village elders, British graves were found just east of the village of Pamali lying four kilometres south of Bhudowal many years ago. This is in accordance with the battle as some casualties were inflicted well to the south after the rout of the British rear column.

The sand dunes to the south of the village, which characterised the battlefield, have been replaced by cultivated land. To the north of the village, a formerly wooded region, a large military area close to the GT road has been constructed. A monument dedicated to the Raja of Ladwa, ruler of the area who fought at Bhudowal and was later imprisoned by the British, now stands close to Pamal village.

Points of Interest

Bhudowal Village (30°51'38.55"N, 75°44'43.39"E)

The village is largely a modern construction although some nineteenth-century period houses remain. The battlefield lies to the south of the village and is traversed by the roads to Pamal and Lalton Khurd. It is likely that the railway line now occupies the former road to Ludhiana and hence it is difficult to walk along what would have been the former Sikh lines.

The Battlefield

Bhudowal to Pamal road (30°51'11.75"N, 75°44'35.52"E)
Bhudowal to Lalton Khurd road (30°51'22.73"N, 75°45'13.26"E)

The battlefield lies between the village of Bhudowal and the rough semicircle of villages comprising Hassanpur to the west, Pamal to the south-west, Lalton Khurdh to the south-east and Jandeh to the east. The best place to see the battlefield is the roads from Bhudowal to Pamal and from Bhudowal to Lalton Khurd, which cross the former battlefield.

Monument and Museum (30°50'29.03"N, 75°43'39.88"E)

A monument dedicated to the Sikh soldiers of the campaign is situated on the road between Bhanohar and Pamal villages, around three kilometres south-west of Bhudowal. The monument was constructed in 1995, the 150th anniversary of the battle. A museum adjacent to the monument is being constructed by a retired army officer, Capt. Amarjit Singh Sekhon, who lives in the vicinity.

British Wartime Base (30°49'22.72"N, 75°44'57.22"E)

Six kilometres south of Bhudowal lies the village of Pamali, close to the similar-named Pamal to its immediate north. A British-built *haveli* lies just outside the village to the south, on the road to Mansurah, past a canal as ones leaves the village. The building was occupied by the British during the Second World War for military purposes.

11

Aliwal Guide

[A] splendid plain of hard ground, expressly manufactured by the devil for men to murder one another upon.
  – Lord Dalhousie, Governor-General of India, Aliwal, 2 January 1849

Aliwal Past

Robert Cust, confidential assistant to the deceased Major Broadfoot, returned to Aliwal after departing from the Commander-in-Chief's camp at Lahore on 30 March 1846, two months after the battle. Travelling eastwards from Lahore, he had witnessed the long train of Sikh guns being taken to Delhi before being transferred to Calcutta. Sir Henry Hardinge had decided on a calculated show of power to awe the other kingdoms of India, there still being disbelief among the villages and towns of India that the Sikh army had been defeated. The deliberately slow procession of the captured Sikh artillery from Punjab through the towns and villages of the northern provinces to Calcutta was calculated to impress the British victory upon the locals, as Cust recalled:

> These guns were being dragged along in a species of triumph, three of them yoked together behind oxen, without limbers, and guarded, as if in derision of the Sikh artillerymen, by a few ragamuffins, burkundazes, and custom house guards.

He was soon joined by the Commander-in-Chief at Aliwal.

Touring the battlefield, Cust found much of the evidence of battle had already begun to vanish:

> We rode on about five miles, and on arriving at the slightly elevated village of Poundri [Bhundri] commanded a fine view of the whole field, and a fairer scene and a prettier plain for an action cannot be imagined and could not be wished for. The horizon was bounded to the north-east, east and southeast by a gently swelling line of hills dotted with villages and groves of trees from the midst of them Sir Harry Smith with his force emerged [...]
>
> The green crops had now sprung up, and very little traces of the slaughter could be found, but a few skeletons here and there reminded us that a battle had been fought here. At the door of my tent I found the skull of a European, known to be so by the red hair, and arms and legs were strewed here and there through the encampment, brought thither by dogs. In the evening I again rode over the field and visited the graves of three young officers who had been killed in the engagement. The sun was then setting and melancholy reflections rose in my mind as I gazed on the three small heaps that marked the last resting place in a strange land, and a solitary spot of three young Englishmen.

Lord Dalhousie, successor to Sir Henry Hardinge as Governor-General of India, travelled to the battlefields of Aliwal and Sabraon during his journey from Calcutta to the Punjab in late December 1849, after the outbreak of the Second Anglo-Sikh War. Dalhousie, anxious to keep the British government close to Gough, who was again conducting the campaign, proceeded to station himself in close proximity to Sikh territory at Ferozepore. Upon reaching Ludhiana, he rode out to Aliwal. Already the Sutlej, in heavy flood, had washed away most reminders of the battle. Dalhousie curiously mentions an early British monument already constructed on the site. From his camp at Makhu, a village near Sabraon turned into a British cavalry station, he wrote on 2 January 1849:

> On my march here I rode over the field at Aliwal. It is a splendid plain of hard ground, expressly manufactured by the devil for men to murder one another upon. The river has cut a great part of it away already. The monument to the officers killed has sunk, and in all probability within two years there will be no such place as Aliwal.

The severe flooding of the Sutlej and consequent damage in the preceding year had changed the field so much so that Colonel Angelo, an officer accompanying Dalhousie's entourage who had commanded a regiment at the battle, could scarcely recognise the battlefield and the positions the armies had taken. Dalhousie wrote:

> The rivers had cut in on the field so deeply that the tombs of the officers who had been buried near the centre were, as far as they remained at all, across the river in the Jullunder Doab; and the village of Aliwal itself, which had been in the very middle of the position, was now not fifty yards from the Satluj. The whole of the district was burnt up and desolate. The carcases of cattle, dead from starvation, lay in heaps near every village, and the gaunt forms of the poor beasts that still wandered weakly round the huts were 'just perfect veesions'.

In 1870, the Aliwal war memorial obelisk was constructed between the villages of Gorahoor and Aliwal. Similar to the others, the monument was situated in a small square area, formerly a garden with a caretaker's hut. Originally constructed closer to the river, it was later moved to its present location, possibly to protect it from the flooding of the river. The profile of the obelisk was similar to the Mudki monument and was positioned where the Sikh lines were drawn up during the battle. The names of the British dead were inscribed on a tablet in Ferozepore church. A tombstone destined for the battlefield was instead put in a garden in Ludhiana.

The area remained something of a backwater, unfrequented by roads, until the early part of the twentieth century. Major Sandys of the Horse Artillery wrote upon visiting the battlefields in 1914: 'Riding is the best way of getting there, the ground is sandy and heavy and there are only cart tracks.'

Visiting Aliwal

Aliwal is fifteen kilometres north-west of Bhudowal as the crow flies. The nearest major city to the Aliwal battlefield is Ludhiana. The battlefield can be reached from the village of Baran Hara, a few kilometres north-west of Ludhiana from where a road leads directly west to Aliwal. The site can also be reached from

Jagraon by travelling north on the NH71. At Sidhma Bet, the road commonly called the GT road travels east towards Aliwal.

The Battlefield Today

The site suffers from the same problems caused by modernity as those of Ferozeshah and Mudki. What was once a grassy expanse is now heavily cultivated land with local farmers having extending their land holdings up to the riverbank.

Both Aliwal and Bhundri villages have grown substantially, Bhundri expanding up to the banks of the Bhudha *nullah* to its north. The village and its environs were the scene of the heaviest fighting, including the stand taken by the Avitabile regiment. Many of the British casualties were buried where they fell. Indeed, village elders recall the digging up of British corpses in the village as recently as the 1950s as the settlement underwent expansion.

A number of roads now traverse the battlefield and its vicinity. The GT road from Baran Hara and Ludhiana reaches the village of Bhutha Dua (Bultatoa) before proceeding westwards to Bhundri and Sidhma Bet, cutting through the battlefield and the initial Sikh and British positions in an east-to-west direction. Another road from Porein moves in a northerly direction to the village of Aliwal, cutting through the position of the initial British lines and passing through the middle of the battlefield eventually reaching the position of the Sikh lines. Just over a kilometre further west, a road leaves the GT road to the village of Gorahoor running almost exactly along the location of what was the Sikh army's right flank. A new road from Bhundri now runs north-westwards connecting the village to the area of the Sikh encampment on the banks of the Sutlej and cutting through the area where fighting took place in the latter stages of the battle. A road now runs round the Porein ridge overlooking the battlefields, connecting the villages of Bhutha Dua, Ranuke, Kotlee, Porein, Chote Purewal, Leehan and Gorahoor.

Several small villages have sprung up in and around the battle site. To the north of Aliwal and Bhundri, between the Sikh lines and the Sikh camp, the villages of Kulghena, Kot Umbraa and Numberdhari occupy the area. On the Porein ridge east of Aliwal, the villages of Gorahoor, Leehan, Chote Purewal and Ranuke now crowd round the ridge.

The area between the initial Sikh and British lines is a patchwork of small separate landholdings by local farmers. The slight incline or ridge on which the Sikh army was drawn up, mentioned in most firsthand accounts, no longer exists having fallen victim to the farmers' enthusiasm for levelling their landholdings for cultivation. Other landmarks survive, however. The Bhudha *nullah*, a large dry water channel crossing the battlefield north of Bhundri village, is too substantial to disappear. In addition, the large shallow *nullah* enclosing the Sikh camp close to the banks of the river can easily be discerned. However, some of the smaller *nullahs* north of Bhundri and shown on contemporary maps have disappeared. The British monument still stands on the battlefield. The area of the Sikh camp is now under cultivation. A modern dyke has been built on the south side of the Sutlej in this area for flood protection. North of Bhundri, the dyke cuts through what would have been the centre of the Sikh encampment. Further west it separates the area where the Sikh army retreated across the river from the battlefield.

Points of Interest

The Battlefield (30°56'22.57"N, 75°36'46.32"E)

The junction of the GT road from Humbran and Bhutha Dua villages to Bhundri with the road from Aliwal to Porein is a very good approximation of the centre of the battlefield. A half-kilometre to the north lies the village of Aliwal, garrisoned by a small force of Sikh mercenaries prior to the battle while the main Sikh line was less than a kilometre to the west, towards where the monument stands. Two kilometres to the south lies Porein, from where the British force approached. The British line, after descending the ridge, stretched from below Porein to beyond Bhutha Dua, directly east of the junction.

The Sikh Lines (30°57'8.21"N, 75°36'26.68"E to 30°55'57.02"N, 75°35'23.61"E)

The Sikh line ran in a broad curve from the banks of the Bhudha *nullah*, north-west of Aliwal to the ridge at Gorahoor village. It is difficult to walk the length of the Sikh line in its entirety. The

Gorahoor road sits almost directly on top of where the right wing of the Sikh army was positioned. However, the position of the Sikh left, from the junction of the Gorahoor road with the GT road to the Bhudha *nullah*, runs through cultivated land. The left flank can be reached by driving north from Aliwal.

The British Lines (30°55'16.67"N, 75°36'10.42"E to 30°56'38.05"N, 75°37'58.21"E)

The initial British lines were formed directly underneath the ridge below Porein, Kotlee, Ranuke and Bhutha Dua villages. It is difficult to walk along these locations as this is now cultivated land. But three roads cut through this position. The Porein to Aliwal road, the GT road from Bhutha Dua towards Bhundri, and a small road between Kotlee and Ranuke villages connecting with the GT road, all pass through the area allowing for closer examination of the battlefield.

Aliwal Village (30°56'42.50"N, 75°36'46.01"E)

The village from which the battle takes its name is a nondescript village less than half a mile from the GT road to Bhundri. The village was a few hundred metres in advance of the Sikh line and therefore the first to be attacked by the advancing British. The village has retained its small size. Aliwal village also forms a good base to investigate what was formerly the Sikh encampment area on the banks of the Sutlej. The river is a distance of around three kilometres north of the village if one uses a dirt track leaving the village to the north. The camp lay a few hundred metres to the west and its location is reachable by travelling on the dyke adjacent to the river. The track also passes the Bhudha *nullah*, around one kilometre from the village, which marked the eastern wing of the Sikh positions.

Bhundri Village (30°56'35"N, 75°34'43"E)

Avitabile regiment position (30°56'50.69"N, 75°34'19.39"E)
Sikh regulars' stand (30°56'49.59"N, 75°34'52.74"E)
Sikh Gurdwara (30°56'31.54"N, 75°34'37.49"E)

Bhundri village is famous for the rearguard action the Sikh regulars took after the retreat from Aliwal. The town was garrisoned by Sikh soldiers with other units in the Bhudha *nullah* to the north-west of the village and the Avitabile regiment a few hundred metres west of the village. The British took most of their casualties at Bhundri while facing the Sikh regulars. The north of Bhundri is the most rewarding place to visit as the Bhudha *nullah* runs very close by. The *nullah* is dry and walkable, although hardly picturesque. A few hundred metres west of Bhundri, on the south bank of the Bhudha *nullah*, was positioned the Avitabile regiment. This can be accessed by taking the road to Kot Umbraan, a small village north of Bhundri. The road intersects the *nullah* half a kilometre from Bhundri from where it is possible to walk the rest of the distance. A road leaving the north-west of Bhundri for the village of Kulhgena passes close to the *nullah* north-east of Bhundri where a determined stand by around a thousand Sikh regulars was made. The road leaving to the north-east from the village leads directly to the location of the former Sikh camp on the banks of the Sutlej. The same *nullah* also anchored the Sikh left flank further to the east as the battle commenced six kilometres upstream. However, at Bhundri the channel was dry and posed no barrier for either side.

Sikh Camp (30°58'12.03"N, 75°35'47.07"E)

A shallow but wide *nullah* runs barely 200 metres south of the main stream of the Sutlej. To the north, midway between Aliwal and Bhundri, the *nullah* swings further south in a wide arc moving around 500 metres from the river before returning to its parallel course with the river. The area between river and *nullah* formed the main Sikh camp with the *nullah* bank forming a natural defensive line on its perimeter. The whole of this area is now under cultivation with the dyke cutting through what would have been the centre of the camp. The Sikh regulars made their camp adjacent and west of the main army, a location reachable by travelling along the dyke westwards.

End of the Battle (30°58'25.82"N, 75°35'36.26"E to 30°58'22.72"N, 75°33'7.83"E)

Battle raged through the villages of Goorsean and Kot Umbraan ending along the banks of the Sutlej, moving westwards along the river for a distance of approximately four kilometres. This entire stretch can be reached via the road running on the dyke or driving north from the villages of Kot Umbraan and Goorsean.

Porein Village (30°55'10"N, 75°37'5"E)

Porein village, overlooking the battlefield, was the location where the British army under Sir Harry Smith stopped immediately prior to the battle. Smith climbed to the top of the highest house in the village to gain a commanding view of the whole battlefield. Visitors to the village can also get a similar view from the higher parts of the village by asking a house owner for permission, or from the west of the village where it meets the ridge. Another alternative is to travel down the road to Aliwal and beyond the outskirts of the village. Having a pair of binoculars will help, as the British commander found; Aliwal and the former position of the Sikh lines are nearly three kilometres away to your north. The village of Bhundri is, at five kilometres, much further away to the north-west. Porein and the villages to its north-east on the ridge, Kotlee and Bhutha Dua, were used as a field hospital by the British after the battle. Gould of the 16th Lancers records the night-time scene along the main thoroughfare of Porein after the battle as the British casualties drifted in:

> In the evening I was ordered to take some wounded to the hospital at the village, two miles back. On getting there, the wounded were laid out on straw down the centre street, the surgeons busy in their shirt sleeves amputating arms and legs by the light of torches.

Most of the village is new but small parts of it still contain some areas of older buildings that date from the nineteenth century.

Porein Ridge

Although Porein lies on the highest point of the ridge, alternative views of Aliwal and the north of the battlefield may be obtained from Kotlee and Bhutha Dua, 1.5 and 3 kilometres north-east respectively from Porein. Many of the British dead were buried on the ridge, although no outward signs remain. West of Porein, the villages of Gorahoor and Leehan give a view of the battlefield from the south, the road running through these villages quite close to the ridge. The right flank of the Sikh army was established just a few yards north of Gorahoor on the western side of the ridge. A view to the north, towards the British monument, gives a good approximation of the Sikh lines.

The British Monument (30°56'16.10"N, 75°35'49.06"E)

Between Gorah Hoor and Aliwal stands the British monument. And although still standing, it is in the poorest condition of all the monuments. It is likely the current monument is a newer construction than the original monument, which probably collapsed at some stage in the past. The monument incorporates certain sections of the original. The lower five-foot base has disappeared along with the entire column section above, where the plaques were once installed. Much of the structure seems to be built of different brick than the original. Portions of the former obelisk still lie nearby. Similar to the other monuments, the obelisk is situated in a square plot, twenty metres in length and breadth. A caretaker's hut, now little more than four walls, is situated at the north-east end of the plot. The original plaques that decorated the four sides of the monument have vanished.

12

Sabraon Guide

*On the day following the action, many Sikhs came across to find
their dead and small fires were lit everywhere where dead were being
cremated. Two days after the battle, the strange sight was witnessed of
British and Sikh, Hindoos and Musselmen wandering indiscriminately
over the field where all had so recently been engaged in mortal contest.*

— Daniel Mackinnon, 16th Lancers, Sabraon

Sabraon Past

The day after the battle, a British party of farriers was dispatched to
destroy the wounded cavalry horses on the battlefield. This, along
with the funeral pyres of Sikh soldiers dotting the landscape, not
to mention the grave pits being dug by the British, gave the former
battlefield an extremely melancholic aspect. The body of General
Sham Singh Attariwalla was transported across the river by his
relatives. The many Sikh dead who were not claimed by their kin
would lie on the field for many months, food for the jackals and
wild dogs in the area. Many bodies on the field were difficult to
identify; the fires that had spread through the camp had burnt the
clothes off and charred the corpses horribly. The vast majority of
the Sikh casualties had been in and around the river, and sandbanks
downstream of the site were covered with the dead and the dying.
Days later, many bodies had floated miles downstream to the British
bridge at Khoonda ghat near Ferozepore, lodging themselves into
the bridge and forming a human barrier in the water. Many of

the British wounded, meanwhile, would expire while returning to Ambala and would be buried without coffins or clothes and with little ceremony in unmarked graves under trees along the roads.

Despite the punishing fire it had received during the battle, the bridge of boats still survived, albeit in much damaged form. On the morning of 11 February 1846, Gough ordered his engineers to burn one part of the bridge and sink another. Nevertheless, it remained in a recognisable form for several months. British troops also brought the remaining Sikh guns into the British base. Five days after the battle, under Gough's orders, much of the fixed defences in the Sikh entrenchments were destroyed.

Between 22 and 23 March, six weeks after the battle and with the war at an end, contingents of the British army occupying Lahore began returning to their cantonments in India. Among the men was Sir Joseph Thackwell on his way to Ludhiana. Thackwell visited the Sabraon battlefield on 27 March, recording his observations thus:

> I went over our old camping ground, and I paid a visit to the field of Sobraon and witnessed a horrid sight. The river line of the Sikh camp is about 2,750 yards and the line of the entrenchments is about 3,655 or perhaps more, and along its extent were some Europeans still unburied, and between 2,000 and 3,000 Sikhs in a state of fearful decomposition ... A poor Sikh horse with a broken leg was still alive, a skeleton, but I caused the coup-de-grace to be given him from a pistol.

Robert Cust passed by Sabraon the following day. He left a more detailed description of the state of the battlefield. The village of Rhodewalla by this time was returning to normality yet the battlefield seemed hardly touched. Surprisingly, significant portions of the Sikh bridge still survived in a half sunken state weeks after Gough had ordered its destruction:

> By a long detour of some thirty miles we managed to embrace the battlefield of Sabraon in our morning march. Starting at three o'clock, on elephants, we arrived by early dawn at the outskirts of the former position of our army. The cultivator had now resumed his ancient empire, and we directed our horses through abundant crops of wheat,

which had sprung up during our absence at Lahore. At length we reached the village of Rhodawala, then our fortified outpost, now again converted into a village. The inhabitants had returned, and roofs and out-houses were now conspicuous on both sides of the deep ditch and entrenchment which our engineers had constructed. Passing onwards we came to the watch-tower, or rather mound on which it stood. How changed was the dreary spectacle from the busy scene upon which my eye had rested when I last stood upon the spot. Forty thousand men were then engaged in deadly combat; The valley of the Sutlej was resounding with the roar of the cannonade, and the rapid and incessant discharge of musketry. Smoke then obscured the opposite bank, and to the rear glistened the swords and lances of our cavalry. The scene before me now was one of unbroken and uninterrupted silence and solitude. The fields were green with the springing harvest up to the entrenchments of the enemy, which rose in triple and quadruple strength between the spot where I then stood and the river. The opposite bank too was silent now. There were no tents whitening the ground; no busy crowds running about; no guns roaring defiance. Descending from the slight eminence, we moved down to the entrenchments and with difficulty induced our horses to enter them amidst the fetid masses of mouldering and corrupting dead bodies remaining there, not skeletons, as at Ferozeshahr. The vultures were satiating themselves and dogs gorging with human flesh. All garments had been carried away and weak mortal frames appeared in every attitude, in every stage of stinking and half-eaten corruption. Who can wish for war and its glories after witnessing such a scene? Still there remained some tokens to remind us that these miserable remnants of weak mortality had once been imbued with a spirit divine. Lying with outstretched arms, and dark flowing hair, we could pity the fate, we could glory in the defeat, but could not despise the bearing of our foe who still seemed to breathe defiance, who showed by the position in which he fell, that he had fought manfully and deserted his life rather than his colours. The more we examined into these defences, the more we were struck with the audacious boldness of the army which had ventured to cross in the face of our army. Immediately defending the bridge was a tete du pont; this was their first defence to protect the bridge of boats. Immediately after our foolish and unsuccessful cannonade early in January, they advanced and threw up more extensive works, taking in a large circuit. After we had deserted the watch tower, they erected a third line of works, stronger and more formidable than any of the previous ones and these we stormed and took. We advanced down to the river, which I had last seen choked with the dying and the dead. Some corpses lay half in and half out of the stream. The bridge of boats still remained, in a half sunken state. We crossed the stream in one of the ferry-boats and were surprised to find the high ground so far from the river. The village of Sabraon was at least [two kilometres] distant, and on the bank, on which were the batteries was at a distance which left unprotected the further portion of the camp, which we had supposed to be sufficiently protected and which was the most daring feature of our attack. We found entrenchments thrown up on the heights for eleven guns; but our guide assured us, that only seven were in position on the day of the battle. Entering our boats again we pushed over the wreck of sunken boats, which formed the bridge and returned as fast as possible to our camp, anxious to escape the heat of the sun, which was now becoming excessive after nine o' clock.

Almost a year later, on 16 January 1847, James Coley, the army chaplain, travelled to the battlefield on his way from Lahore to Ambala. The Sutlej, prone to flooding virtually every year, had already destroyed much of the evidence of battle:

> A considerable part of the entrenchments still remains, though a large portion of the field of battle has been swept away by the encroachments of the river. A great part of the wall has been knocked or worn down and is not now half the height it was; and a great part of the ditches has been filled up, perhaps with dead bodies, perhaps with alluvium from the ruins. I saw a pile of stones at one point of the battery, to mark the place where General Dick's division attacked and where he fell.

In the early part of January 1849, Lord Dalhousie, who had assumed the mantle of Governor-General in 1847, passing within three or four miles of the battlefield, expressed a wish to tour the site. Unfortunately for him, the Sutlej was in flood and much of the entrenchment area under water. Only a visit by boat, he was told, would be possible. Dalhousie, disappointed, remarked that it would be as 'going down the stream of time'.

This was one of several floods during the years after the battle.

In 1855, another flood inundated the area of the entrenchments, causing more of the site to be washed away. The Sabraon memorial was erected in 1868, the location selected being a few hundred metres south of the village of Rhodewalla, the former British outpost. The structure, an obelisk, was similar to the other memorials, although shorter in stature but having a larger base.

Visiting Sabraon

The Sabraon battlefield lies adjacent to the Sutlej a few kilometres west of the confluence of the Sutlej and the Beas rivers and around nine kilometres west of the Harike wildlife sanctuary. The nearest major road is the NH15 highway running from Faridkot through Zira to Amritsar. The closest towns are Harike itself on the north bank and Makhu south of the river. Sabraon lies around 40 km due north of Mudki, 55 km due south of Amritsar and 60 km from Ferozepore.

The Battlefield Today

The changes in the River Sutlej are much more dramatic at Sabraon than at Aliwal. The Rajasthan canals now divert the waters of the Sutlej southwards at Harike, two kilometres upriver from the battlefield, leaving the river beyond Chote Sabraon little more than a stream. During the dry season, the river now vanishes almost completely downstream from the Harike dam. Shepherds residing on the north bank routinely cross the dry riverbed to graze their animals on what were formerly the Sikh entrenchments south of the river.

The area of the Harike ford, to the immediate east of the Sikh entrenchments, has changed considerably due to the reduced flow of the Sutlej. The river formerly split into two channels at this point, the area of higher ground forming an island midstream. The reduced flow of the river has caused the north stream to dry up and consequently the island is now an extension of the north bank most of the time, only the southern channel being mostly wet.

The *nullahs* close to the Sutlej formed an important feature of this battlefield. The east *nullah* that marked the left flank of the Sikh entrenchments has over the years silted up with sand and disappeared – only aerial photographs provide proof of its previous existence. The south *nullah*, from which the east *nullah* diverges, is much too substantial to disappear. The *nullah* varies from 50-70 m wide with banks up to 2-3 m high. This *nullah* like others tends to be cultivated by local farmers at various points despite the likelihood of the riverbed flooding. Several other *nullahs* were featured on contemporary maps and sketches of the time. A shallow but wide *nullah* flowed to the west of Rhodewalla. Another *nullah* flowed along the villages marking the British front line. These have now disappeared.

Levees bordering the Sutlej have now been built both north and south of the river. The north bank levee veers north of where the Sikh camp was situated. Unfortunately, the levee south of the river cuts through the ground running between the former Sikh and British lines. Visitors therefore no longer have an uninterrupted view of the battlefield. However, the levee has a road running on top of it, allowing views of both north and south. The levee is a kilometre north of the former Sikh outpost of Chote Sabraon and follows a course due west from the confluence of the Sutlej and Beas rivers, turning south-west as it runs north of Rhodewalla.

Many roads connect the villages that formed the British line, which were Chote Sabraon, Aleewal and Rhodewalla. Further north, past the levee, the area is less well-developed. Two dirt tracks north of Chote Sabraon cross the levee and approach the south *nullah*. Travelling further north into what were the entrenchments needs to be done on foot. The eastern track stops at the southern *nullah* several hundred metres short of the eastern section of the Sikh position. The other dirt track leads to the middle of the Sikh lines along the south *nullah*.

Local farmers have brought all the area in the Sabraon bend under cultivation – in most areas to the edge of the river. Only the southern half of the Sikh entrenchment area cut through by water channels and small *nullahs* remains a wilderness used largely for grazing cattle. The land immediately south and west of the entrenchment is now dotted with small hamlets. The contraction of the river has revealed more of the *nullah* channels close to the river. Nothing remains of the original wooden defences of the entrenchment and frequent flooding of the area has washed away other features of the battlefield. However, interestingly enough, some of the trench works and foxholes adjacent to the north *nullah* have survived until the present time, although badly weathered. In addition, at various places inside the entrenchments large circular pits can still be seen.

Chote Sabraon is a large village now many times bigger than the walled area of the old village. The other notable villages of Rhodewalla, Aleewal, and Bootewalla remain relatively small. South of Rhodewalla, the British memorial stands in a quiet spot surrounded by fields. The base is in a state of disrepair, although the obelisk itself is in good condition.

Points of Interest

The Sikh Entrenchments

Junction of eastern stretch of line with Sutlej (31° 8'30.23"N, 74°53'17.24"E)
Line leaves eastern *nullah* (31° 8'26.77"N, 74°53'10.65"E)
Line joins southern *nullah* (31° 8'20.44"N, 74°52'52.61"E)
Middle of line along north bank of *nullah* (31° 8'34.35"N, 74°52'32.15"E)
Line leaves south *nullah* (31° 8'35.68"N, 74°52'15.13"E)
Bulge in line (31° 8'43.35"N, 74°52'2.90"E)
Junction of line with north *nullah* (31° 8'50.78"N, 74°52'1.51"E)
Line west of north *nullah* (31° 8'54.81"N, 74°52'4.84"E)
End of entrenchments (31° 8'59.20"N, 74°52'6.95"E)

The bulk of the area of the Sikh entrenchments and hence much of the battlefield was bounded by the east *nullah*, which has disappeared, and the sizeable south *nullah*. To the north-west, the line swept a few hundred metres west of the north *nullah* before nearing the Sutlej. This area can be reached by travelling north from the dirt tracks that intersect the road on the levee.

The Bridge of Boats (31° 8'57.77"N, 74°52'35.21"E)

The north bank, from Harike downstream until this point, is high and unsuitable for a bridge. However, a large sandy stretch on the north bank where an ancient *nullah* flowed into the Sutlej provided a place to build a bridge with ease. The few hundred metres to either side of the bridge were also the scene of the destruction of many of the Sikh army units during the final moments of the battle.

Chote Sabraon Village (31° 7'19.84"N, 74°52'59.95"E)

Sabraon formed the front line of the two armies. Little exists of the old village now. The village was used as an outpost by the Sikh army. On the day of the battle, the settlement formed a part of the British lines. Five twenty-four-pounder howitzers and three twelve-pounder reamers were stationed in the north of the village. The south and west of the village provide good views of the expanse where skirmishing took place.

Sikh Watch Tower (31° 7'26.74"N, 74°51'28.85"E)

A watchtower, along with the outpost at Sabraon, was used by the Sikh army to monitor British movements. A clump of trees north of Rhodewalla and 2.5 kilometres due west of Chote Sabraon, the only trees between the two armies, were used with platforms constructed among the higher branches. The watchtower was abandoned at night and then garrisoned during the day. The levee now runs through the location. The position can be reached via the road from Rhodewalla village running northwards towards the river. On the day of the battle, the British positioned many of their heavy guns here, six 8-inch howitzers and six 5.5-inch howitzers to the right of the watch tower and eight 8-inch howitzers and five eighteen-pounders to the left.

Harike Ford (31° 7'57.94"N, 74°54'55.58"E)

Downstream from Harike, but prior to reaching the Sikh entrenchments, the river splits into two shallow channels before rejoining three kilometres downstream, thus forming a small island. Harike ford was the only place where cavalry could cross with relative ease close to the battlefield and hence was an area of importance. Sikh cavalry regularly crossed for skirmishing in the south at this point. On the day of the battle, Brigadier Cureton was stationed here to make a show of force with HM 16th Lancers and the 3rd, 4th and 5th Light Cavalry. The Sikh army guarded the north bank with cannon preventing a possible British crossing to the north. The rise in the levels of the Sutlej on the fateful day would make the ford difficult to cross.

British Camp Ridge

Makhu village (31° 6'20.16"N, 74°59'1.79"E)
Nizamuddin (31° 7'7.23"N, 74°56'26.04"E)
Wuttoo (31° 6'53.71"N, 74°55'40.66"E)
Padree (31° 6'30.87"N, 74°55'25.91"E)
Nihalkee (31° 6'6.90"N, 74°53'55.88"E)
Killee (31° 6'5.18"N, 74°53'30.77"E)
Bootewala (31° 5'11.21"N, 74°53'39.13"E)
Jilewala (31° 5'45.19"N, 74°52'45.48"E)
Kamalwalah (31° 5'23.01"N, 74°50'52.70"E)

The British forces moved their position opposite to the Sikh lines across the Sutlej in early January. The area in front of the British camp was occupied by a wide shallow *nullah*, now vanished. The whole line stretched for around thirteen kilometres from Makhu in the north to Kamalwalah village to the south-west excluding the separate force under Sir John Grey at Nughar ghat.

British Cannon Park (31° 5'41.95"N, 74°53'43.14"E)

The triangular area between the villages of Nihalkee, Bootewalla and Killee was used by the British as an artillery park during the month-long period before the battle.

Rhodewalla Village (31° 6'46.42"N, 74°51'59.06"E)

The sleepy village of Rhodewalla was a British outpost during the day. During the battle, the British also stationed a strong garrison here. The rocky outgrowth on which the British constructed a lookout post has disappeared. A road leaves the ring road to the south of the village and leads to the British war monument a few hundred metres away. The village formed the edge of the no man's land between the Sikh entrenchments and the British encampment further south in which minor skirmishing became common prior to the battle. The British had dug entrenchments around the village to protect the outpost. Rhodewalla provides a good view of the area used for skirmishing, while the village of Sabraon, the southernmost Sikh army outpost, can be clearly seen just a mile away to the north-east. To the east and south can be seen the string of villages along which the British were encamped. Rhodewalla remains a small village in the present day.

British Outpost of Aleewala (31° 6'35.13"N, 74°50'41.21"E)

Aleewala remains the hamlet it was during the battle. It served as the most westerly outpost for the British. The construction of the levee now obstructs a clear view of the Sutlej and the area of the Sikh entrenchments to the north and west.

Gurdwara Sham Singh Attariwalla (31° 7'15.42"N, 74°52'36.76"E)

A little west of the village of Chote Sabraon, and around two kilometres south of the entrenchments where he died, lies the Gurdwara dedicated to General Sirdar Sham Singh, who died in the battle.

Sabraon Monument at Rhodewalla (31° 6'29.70"N, 74°52'5.20"E)

A short four-sided obelisk, the monument is in need of repair and attention now. The needle is set in a square area thirty metres in dimension. Unlike the other monuments, this structure has a high base on which the obelisk sits. A small caretaker's hut, similar to the ones built at the other battlefield memorials, also exists here. The monument is made of burnt bricks. It is situated just behind what was the British outpost of Rhodewalla.

Gutta (Cutta) (31° 7'27"N, 74°54'8"E)

Gutta is shown on British contemporary maps as at the river's edge. It now lies almost a kilometre away from the Sutlej. The British 1st

Division, commanded by Sir Harry Smith, was positioned between the villages of Gutta and Chote Sabraon, taking up a span of two kilometres prior to the battle.

Nihalkee Village (31° 6'6.30"N, 74°53'55.93"E)

This village along the British front line was used by the Governor-General, Sir Henry Hardinge, as his headquarters prior to the battle.

Bootewalla Village (31° 5'11.06"N, 74°53'39.52"E)

This village, around two kilometres further south of Nihalkee, was used by the Commander-in-Chief, Sir High Gough, as his headquarters prior to the battle.

Ferozepore Cemetery (30°55'39.08"N, 74°37'29.07"E)

Major George Broadfoot (30°55'36.08"N, 74°37'33.70"E)
Major-General Sir Robert Sale (30°55'36.09"N, 74°37'33.70"E)
Major William Fitzroy Somerset (30°55'36.70"N, 74°37'33.60"E)
Captain Jasper Trower (30°55'37.04"N, 74°37'33.50"E)
Lieutenant-Colonel Louis Bruce (30°55'36.60"N, 74°37'33.60"E)
Officers of the 31st Regiment (30°55'36.08"N, 74°37'33.05"E)
Captain William Hore (30°55'36.50"N, 74°37'33.80"E)
Colonel Vicomte Alexis de Facieu (30°55'36.96"N, 74°37'33.80"E)
Phillip Henry Van Courtlandt (30°55'36.50"N, 74°37'33.80"E)

The more notable of the British casualties during the campaign were buried in Ferozepore cemetery. These include Major George Broadfoot, the abrasive British political agent, who died at Ferozeshah. His grave is inscribed with the epitaph, 'The foremost man in India and an honour to Scotland', by a Captain Colin Mackenzie of the Madras army, which caused rather a stir in high British circles at the time due to Broadfoot's middling status. His assistant Peter Nicholson; Major William Fitzroy Somerset, Military Secretary to the Governor-General; Captain William Hore of the 18th Regiment and Assistant Secretary to the Government of India, who all fell at Ferozeshah, are also buried in the cemetery.

In addition to these men were buried Maj.-Gen. Sir Robert Sale, Jasper Trower, a captain in the 7th Light Field Battery, and Lt-Col. Louis Bruce – all killed in action at Mudki. Several officers of the 31st Regiment, including Capt. Samuel Bolton, are buried in a single grave. The cemetery also holds the grave of Colonel Vicomte Alexis de Facieu who served with the Sikh army for three years prior to his death in 1843, along with Phillip Henry Van Courtlandt, infant son of Colonel Charles Van Courtlandt, also with the Sikh army. The cemetery is to the east of Ferozepore, a few minutes' walk away from the Ferozepore Cantt bus station. It lies adjacent to the NH95 highway or Moga road as it leaves the city. The graves relating to the Anglo-Sikh Wars lie to the back of the cemetery.

APPENDIX A

The Treaty of Lahore

(9 March 1846)

Whereas the treaty of amity and concord, which was concluded between the British Government and the late Maharajah Runjeet Sing, the ruler of Lahore, in 1809, was broken by the unprovoked aggression, on the British Provinces, of the Sikh army, in December last; and whereas, on that occasion, by the proclamation, dated 13th December, the territories then in the occupation of the Maharajah of Lahore, on the left or British bank of the river Sutlej, were confiscated and annexed to the British Provinces; and since that time hostile operations have been prosecuted by the two Governments; the one against the other, which have resulted in the occupation of Lahore by the British troops; and whereas it has been determined that, upon certain conditions, peace shall be re-established between the two Governments, the following treaty of peace between the Honourable East India Company and Maharajah Dhuleep Sing Bahadoor, and his children, heirs and successors, has been concluded on the part of the Honourable Company by Frederick Currie, Esquire, and Brevet-Major Henry Montgomery Lawrence, by virtue of full powers to that effect vested in them by the Right Hon'ble Sir Henry Hardinge, G.C.B., one of her Britannic Majesty's Most Hon'ble Privy Council, Governor-General, appointed by the Honourable Company to direct and control all their affairs in the East Indies, and on the part of His Highness Maharajah Dhuleep Sing by Bhaee Ram Sing, Rajah Lal Sing, Sirdar Tej Sing, Sirdar Chuttur Sing Attareewalla,

Sirdar Runjore Sing Majeethia, Dewan Deena Nath and Fakeer Nooroodden, vested with full powers and authority on the part of His Highness.

Article 1

There shall be perpetual peace and friendship between the British Government on the one part and Maharajah Dhuleep Sing, his heirs and successors on the other.

Article 2

The Maharajah of Lahore renounces for himself, his heirs and successors, all claim to, or connection with, the territories lying to the south of the River Sutlej, and engages never to have any concern with those territories or the inhabitants thereof.

Article 3

The Maharajah cedes to the Hon'ble Company, in perpetual sovereignty, all his forts, territories and rights in the Doab or country, hill and plain, situated between the Rivers Beas and Sutlej.

Article 4

The British Government having demanded from the Lahore State, as indemnification for the expenses of the war, in addition to the cession of territory described in Article 3, payment of one and half crore of Rupees, and the Lahore Government being unable to pay the whole of this sum at this time, or to give security satisfactory to the British Government for its eventual payment, the Maharajah cedes to the Honourable Company, in perpetual sovereignty, as equivalent for one crore of Rupees, all his forts, territories, rights and interests in the hill countries, which are situated between the Rivers Beas and Indus, including the Provinces of Cashmere and Hazarah.

Article 5

The Maharajah will pay to the British Government the sum of 60 lakhs of Rupees on or before the ratification of this Treaty.

Article 6

The Maharajah engages to disband the mutinous troops of the Lahore Army, taking from them their arms and His Highness agrees to reorganize the Regular or Aeen Regiments of Infantry upon the system, and according to the Regulations as to pay and allowances, observed in the time of the late Maharajah Runjeet Sing. The Maharajah further engages to pay up all arrears to the soldiers that are discharged, under the provisions of this Article.

Article 7

The Regular Army of the Lahore State shall henceforth be limited to 25 Battalions of Infantry, consisting of 800 bayonets each with twelve thousand Cavalry – this number at no time to be exceeded without the concurrence of the British Government. Should it be necessary at any time – for any special cause – that this force should be increased, the cause shall be fully explained to the British Government, and when the special necessity shall have passed, the regular troops shall be again reduced to the standard specified in the former clause of this article.

Article 8

The Maharajah will surrender to the British Government all the guns – thirty-six in number – which have been pointed against the British troops and which, having been placed on the right bank of the River Sutlej, were not captured at the battle of Sabraon.

Article 9

The control of the Rivers Beas and Sutlej, with the continuations of the latter river, commonly called the Gharrah and the Punjnud, to the confluence of the Indus at Mithunkote and the control of the Indus from Mithunkote to the borders of Beloochistan, shall, in respect to tolls and ferries, rest with the British Government. The provisions of this Article shall not interfere with the passage of boats belonging to the Lahore Government on the said rivers, for the purpose of traffic or the conveyance of passengers up and down their course. Regarding the ferries between the two countries respectively, at the several ghats of the said rivers, it is agreed that the British Government, after defraying all the expenses of management and establishments, shall account to the Lahore Government for one-half the net profits of the ferry collections. The provisions of this Article have no reference to the ferries on that part of the River Sutlej which forms the boundary of Bhawulpore and Lahore respectively.

Article 10

If the British Government should, at any time, desire to pass troops through the territories of His Highness the Maharajah, for the protection of the British territories, or those of their Allies, the British troops shall, on such special occasion, due notice being given, be allowed to pass through the Lahore territories. In such case the officers of the Lahore State will afford facilities in providing supplies and boats for the passage of rivers, and the British Government will pay the full price of all such provisions and boats, and will make fair compensation for all private property that may be damaged. The British Government will, moreover, observe all due consideration to the religious feelings of the inhabitants of those tracts through which the army may pass.

Article 11

The Maharajah engages never to take or to retain in his service any British subject – nor the subject of any European or American State – without the consent of the British Government.

Article 12

In consideration of the services rendered by Rajah Golab Sing of Jummoo, to the Lahore State, towards procuring the restoration of the relations of amity between the Lahore and British Governments, the Maharajah hereby agrees to recognize the independent sovereignty of Rajah Golab Sing in such territories and districts in the hills as may be made over to the said Rajah Golab Sing, by separate Agreement between himself and the British Government, with the dependencies thereof, which may have been in the Rajah's possession since the time of the late Maharajah Khurruck Sing, and the British Government, in consideration of the good conduct of Rajah Golab Sing, also agrees to recognize his independence in such territories, and to admit him to the privileges of a separate Treaty with the British Government.

Article 13

In the event of any dispute or difference arising between the Lahore State and Rajah Golab Sing, the same shall be referred to the arbitration of the British Government, and by its decision the Maharajah engages to abide.

Article 14

The limits of the Lahore territories shall not be, at any time, changed without the concurrence of the British Government.

Article 15

The British Government will not exercise any interference in the internal administration of the Lahore State, but in all cases or questions which may be referred to the British Government, the Governor-General will give the aid of his advice and good offices for the furtherance of the interests of the Lahore Government.

Article 16

The subjects of either State shall, on visiting the territories of the other, be on the footing of the subjects of the most favoured nation.

This Treaty consisting of sixteen articles, has been this day settled by Frederick Currie, Esquire, and Brevet-Major Henry

Montgomery Lawrence acting under the directions of the Right Hon'ble Sir Henry Hardinge, G.C.B., Governor-General, on the part of the British Government, and by Bhaee Ram Sing, Rajah Lal Sing, Sirdar Tej Sing, Sirdar Chuttur Sing Attareewalla, Sirdar Runjore Sing Majeethia, Dewan Deena Nath, and Faqueer Noorooddeen, on the part of the Maharajah Dhuleep Sing, and the said Treaty has been this day ratified by the seal of the Right Hon'ble Sir Henry Hardinge, G.C.B., Governor-General, and by that of His Highness Maharajah Dhuleep Sing.

Done at Lahore, this ninth day of March, in year of Our Lord one thousand eight hundred and forty-six; corresponding with the tenth day of Rubbee-ool-awul, 1262 Hijree, and ratified on the same date.

(Sd.) H. Hardinge (L.S.)
(Sd.) Maharajah Dhuleep Sing (L.S.)
Bhaee Ram Sing (L.S.)
Rajah Lal Sing (L.S.)
Sirdar Tej Sing (L.S.)
Sirdar Chuttur Sing Attareewalla (L.S.)
Sirdar Runjore Sing Majeethia (L.S.)
Dewan Deena Nath (L.S.)
Faqueer Noorooddeen (L.S.)

APPENDIX B

The Treaty of Amritsar
(16 March 1846)

The treaty between the British Government on the one part and
Maharajah Gulab Singh of Jammu on the other concluded on
the part of the British Government by Frederick Currie, Esq. and
Brevet-Major Henry Montgomery Lawrence, acting under the
orders of the Rt. Hon. Sir Henry Hardinge, G.C.B., one of her
Britannic Majesty's most Honourable Privy Council, Governor-
General of the possessions of the East India Company, to direct
and control all the affairs in the East Indies and by Maharajah
Gulab Singh in person.

Article 1

The British Government transfers and makes over for ever in
independent possession to Maharajah Gulab Singh and the heirs
male of his body all the hilly or mountainous country with its
dependencies situated to the eastward of the River Indus and the
westward of the River Ravi including Chamba and excluding
Lahul, being part of the territories ceded to the British Government
by the Lahore State according to the provisions of Article IV of the
Treaty of Lahore, dated 9th March, 1846.

Article 2

The eastern boundary of the tract transferred by the foregoing
article to Maharajah Gulab Singh shall be laid down by the

Commissioners appointed by the British Government and Maharajah Gulab Singh respectively for that purpose and shall be defined in a separate engagement after survey.

Article 3

In consideration of the transfer made to him and his heirs by the provisions of the foregoing article Maharajah Gulab Singh will pay to the British Government the sum of seventy-five lakhs of rupees (Nanukshahee), fifty lakhs to be paid on or before the 1st October of the current year, A.D., 1846.

Article 4

The limits of territories of Maharajah Gulab Singh shall not be at any time changed without concurrence of the British Government.

Article 5

Maharajah Gulab Singh will refer to the arbitration of the British Government any disputes or question that may arise between himself and the Government of Lahore or any other neighbouring State, and will abide by the decision of the British Government.

Article 6

Maharajah Gulab Singh engages for himself and heirs to join, with the whole of his Military Forces, the British troops when employed within the hills or in the territories adjoining his possessions.

Article 7

Maharajah Gulab Singh engages never to take to retain in his service any British subject nor the subject of any European or American State without the consent of the British Government.

Article 8

Maharajah Gulab Singh engages to respect in regard to the territory transferred to him, the provisions of Articles V, VI and VII of the separate Engagement between the British Government and the Lahore Durbar, dated 11th March, 1846.

Article 9

The British Government will give its aid to Maharajah Gulab Singh in protecting his territories from external enemies.

Article 10

Maharajah Gulab Singh acknowledges the supremacy of the British Government and will in token of such supremacy present annually to the British Government one horse, twelve shawl goats of approved breed (six male and six female) and three pairs of Cashmere shawls. This Treaty of ten articles has been this day settled by Frederick Currie, Esq. and Brevet-Major Henry Montgomery Lawrence, acting under directions of the Rt. Hon. Sir Henry Hardinge, Governor-General, on the part of the British Government and by Maharajah Gulab Singh in person, and the said Treaty has been this day ratified by the seal of the Rt. Hon. Sir Henry Hardinge, Governor-General. (Done at Amritsar the sixteenth day of March, in the year of our Lord one thousand eight hundred and forty-six, corresponding with the seventeenth day of Rubee-ul-Awal (1262 Hijree).

(Signed) H. Hardinge (Seal)

(Signed) F. Currie

(Signed) H.M. Lawrence

APPENDIX C

The Treaty of Bhyrowal

(16 December 1846)

ARTICLES OF AGREEMENT concluded between the BRITISH GOVERNMENT and the LAHORE DURBAR on 16 December 1846.

Whereas the Lahore Durbar and the principal Chiefs and Sirdars of the State have in express terms communicated to the British Government their anxious desire that the Governor-General should give his aid and assistance to maintain the administration of the Lahore State during the minority of Maharajah Dulleep Sing, and have declared this measure to be indispensable for the maintenance of the Government; and whereas the Governor-General has, under certain conditions, consented to give the aid and assistance solicited, the following Articles of Agreement, in modification of the Articles of Agreement executed at Lahore on the 11th March last, have been concluded on the part of the British Government by Frederick Currie, Esquire, Secretary to Government of India, and Lieutenant-Colonel Henry Montgomery Lawrence, C.B., Agent to the Governor-General, North-West Frontier, by virtue of full powers to that effect vested in them by the Right Honourable Viscount Hardinge, G.C.B., Governor-General, and on the part of His Highness Maharajah Dulleep Sing, by Sirdar Tej Sing, Sirdar Shere Sing, Dewan Deena Nath, Fukeer Nooroodeen, Rai Kishen Chund, Sirdar Runjore Sing Majethea, Sirdar Utter Sing Kaleewalla, Bhaee Nidhan Sing, Sirdar Khan Singh Majethea, Sirdar Shumshere Sing, Sirdar Lall Sing Morarea, Sirdar Kehr Sing

Sindhanwalla, Sirdar Urjun Sing Rungurnungalea, acting with the unanimous consent and concurrence of the Chiefs and Sirdars of the State assembled at Lahore.

Article 1

All and every part of the Treaty of peace between the British Government and the State of Lahore, bearing date the 9th day of March, 1846, except in so far as it may be temporarily modified in respect to Clause 15 of the said Treaty by this engagement, shall remain binding upon the two Governments.

Article 2

A British officer, with an efficient establishment of assistants, shall be appointed by the Governor-General to remain at Lahore, which officer shall have full authority to direct and control all matters in every Department of the State.

Article 3

Every attention shall be paid in conducting the administration to the feelings of the people, to preserving the national institutions and customs, and to maintaining the just rights of all classes.

Article 4

Changes in the mode and details of administration shall not be made, except when found necessary for effecting the objects set forth in the foregoing Clause, and for securing the just dues of the Lahore Government. These details shall be conducted by Native officers as at present, who shall be appointed and superintended by a Council of Regency composed of leading Chiefs and Sirdars acting under the control and guidance of the British Resident.

Article 5

The following persons shall in the first instance constitute the Council of Regency, viz., Sirdar Tej Sing, Sirdar Shere Sing

Attareewalla, Dewan Deena Nath, Fukeer Nooroodeen, Sirdar Runjore Sing Majeethea, Bhaee Nidhan Sing, Sirdar Utter Sing Kaleewalla, Sirdar Shumshere Sing Sindhanwalla, and no change shall be made in the persons thus nominated, without the consent of the British Resident, acting under the orders of the Governor-General.

Article 6

The administration of the country shall be conducted by this Council of Regency in such manner as may be determined on by themselves in consultation with the British Resident, who shall have full authority to direct and control the duties of every department.

Article 7

A British Force of such strength and numbers and in such positions as the Governor-General may think fit, shall remain at Lahore for the protection of the Maharajah and the preservation of the peace of the country.

Article 8

The Governor-General shall be at liberty to occupy with British soldiers any fort or military post in the Lahore territories, the occupation of which may be deemed necessary by the British Government, for the security of the capital or for maintaining the peace of the country.

Article 9

The Lahore State shall pay to the British Government twenty-two lakhs of new Nanuck Shahee Rupees of full tale and weight per annum for the maintenance of this force, and to meet the expenses incurred by the British Government. Such sum to be paid by two instalments, or 13,20,000 in May or June, and 8,80,000 in November or December of each year.

Article 10

Inasmuch as it is fitting that Her Highness the Maharanee, the mother of Maharaja Dulleep Sing, should have a proper provision made for the maintenance of herself and dependants, the sum of one lakh and fifty thousand rupees shall be set apart annually for that purpose, and shall be at Her Highness' disposal.

Article 11

The provisions of this Engagement shall have effect during the minority of His Highness Maharajah Dulleep Sing, and shall cease and terminate on His Highness attaining the full age of sixteen years or, on the 4th September of the year 1854, but it shall be competent to the Governor-General to cause the arrangement to cease at any period prior to the coming of age of His Highness, at which the Governor-General and the Lahore Durbar may be satisfied that the interposition of the British Government is no longer necessary for maintaining the Government of His Highness the Maharajah.

This agreement, consisting of eleven articles, was settled and executed at Lahore by the Officers and Chiefs and Sirdars above named, on the 16th day of December, 1846.

(Sd.) F. CURRIE
(Sd.) H.M. LAWRENCE
Sirdar Tej Sing (L.S.)
Sirdar Shere Sing (L.S.)
Dewan Deena Nath (L.S.)
Fukeer Nooroodeen (L.S.)
Rai Kishen Chund (L.S.)
Sirdar Runjore Sing Majethea (L.S.)
Sirdar Utter Sing Kalewalla (L.S.)
Bhaee Nidhan Sing (L.S.)
Sirdar Khan Sing Majethea (L.S.)
Sirdar Shumshere Sing (L.S.)
Sirdar Lal Sing Morarea (L.S.)
Sirdar Kher Sing Sindhanwalla (L.S.)

Sirdar Urjan Sing Rungurnungalea (L.S.)
(Sd.) Hardinge (L.S.) & (Sd.) Dulleep Sing (L.S.)

Ratified by the Right Honourable the Governor-General, at Bhyrowal ghat on the left bank of the Beas, twenty-sixth day of December, One Thousand Eight Hundred and Forty-Six.
(Sd.) F. CURRIE,
Secretary to the Government of India

Glossary

Abattis	Line of defence made by felled trees, their tops pointing towards the enemy and with branches frequently sharpened.
Akali	Literally 'immortal'. Akali soldiers were asked to do the most dangerous missions in a campaign. Akalis were also called Nihangs.
Avitabile division	Troops in the Sikh army trained by the Italian General Paolo di Avitabile during the lifetime of Ranjit Singh.
Bheesty	Water carrier/provider for a regiment.
Brahmin	A member of the Hindu priestly class.
Chappus	Long slim boats with a high prow typically used by ferrymen on Punjab rivers.
Chowkidar	Employee assigned to guard an area or building.
Dhooly	Covered Indian litter or palanquin. Also used in India to transport sick or wounded soldiers.
Doab	The triangular area of land lying between two confluent rivers.
Durbar	Royal court of an Indian state.
Epaulement	A side work, made of fascines or bags filled with earth, or of earth heaped up, to afford cover from the flanking fire of an enemy.
Fascine	A cylindrical bundle of sticks bound together

	for use in the construction of fortresses and earthworks.
Fauj-i-ain	The regular brigades of the Sikh army.
Fauj-i-khas	The elite brigades of the Sikh army.
Ghat	A broad flight of steps on the bank of a river in India, used especially by bathers.
Gootka	Pocket-sized prayerbook containing chosen hymns from Sikh Scripture.
Gorchurras	Much feared irregular cavalry of the Sikh army.
Gurdwara	A Sikh temple.
Hackery	A cart with wooden wheels drawn by bullocks.
Haveli	A large house or mansion in India.
Jagir	A non-hereditary territory given by a ruler to a chief or high official from which the holder derives income through taxes.
Jinjal	A large musket, fixed on a swivel, used in Indian forts and fired with great precision.
Kardar	High official responsible for collecting tax in an area or province.
Khalsa	Literally 'pure'. Community of Sikhs who have undergone the sacred Amrit Ceremony initiated by the tenth Sikh Guru, Guru Gobind Singh.
Lakh	Indian word for the numerical amount of one hundred thousand.
Langar	Free communal meal served after a service at a Sikh temple or Gurdwara.
Lascar	An Indian sailor employed on a European ship.
Lota	A globe-shaped bottle or pot for carrying water.
Mahout	An elephant driver or keeper.
Mohur	A former gold coin used in India worth 15 rupees.
Moonshee	A writer or secretary.
Nanakshahi bricks	Long slim Roman-style bricks used up to the mid-nineteenth century in Punjab.

Nihangs	Also called Akalis.
Nullah	A gully or river channel that is often dry.
Punchayat	Council or committee selected by common soldiers from within their ranks to represent their interests.
Raja	King of an Indian state.
Razai	An Indian quilt or blanket.
Redoubt	Defensive emplacement outside a larger fort or defensive works usually relying on earthworks.
Ressalahs	A squadron of Indian cavalry.
Sahib	Term of respect for a European in British-ruled India.
Samadh	A mausoleum in India.
Sepoy	An Indian soldier in the service of a European power.
Shutur sowar	A camel rider.
Sirdar	A person of high rank and a title of respect used when referring to a Sikh.
Sirkar	The government or supreme authority in a state.
Syce	Horse groom or grass-cutter for army horses.
Sowar	A mounted soldier or cavalryman.
Tete-de-pont	Military works and defences thrown up at the end of a bridge nearest the enemy for covering communications across a river.
Tulwar	Curved sword or sabre used by Sikh soldiers.
Vedette	A mounted scout or sentinel employed to watch enemy movements.
Zambooruk	Also known as a camel swivel. A light-calibre gun mounted on and fired from a camel.
Zamindar	A landowner with extensive holdings.

Bibliography

PRIMARY SOURCES

Manuscripts and papers from the National Army Museum

Documents and letters relating to the service of Lt-Gen. Sir Hugh Gough as Commander-in-Chief in India, 1844-50.

Documents, letters and maps relating to the Indian military service of the Hearsey family, 1745-1900.

Documents relating to Lt E. A. Noel, HM 31st Foot, and Col. W. F. N. Noel, Royal Engineers.

Documents relating to Sir Charles Reid.

Documents, letters and papers relating to Sir Alexander Taylor, Royal Engineers, 1840-1873.

Extracts from the diary of Henry Davis Van Homrigh, January 1844 to December 1845.

Letter written by Lt G. Bidulph, dated 7 January 1846, relating his capture by Sikh forces.

Letters written by Robert Haviland, HM 62nd Foot in India, 1840-1848.

Manuscript journal of Sir Arthur Becher KCB, 9 December 1845 to 27 March 1846.

Manuscript letter of Frederick Abbott giving an eyewitness account of the battle of Sabraon, 1846.

Newspaper clippings relating to Maj.-Gen. Sir Henry George Smith KCB

Order Book No. 3 Company HM 9th Foot, 1845-1846.

Pen and ink plan of the Battle of Aliwal, 28 January 1846, by L. T. Sage, 30th Bengal Native Infantry.

Transcript of 'Memoirs of General J. B. Dennys', written in 1891.

Typed copy of the autobiography of Major-General J. R. Pughe, Bengal Staff Corps and 47th Native Infantry Volunteers, edited by Lt-Gen. Sir Alfred Bingley.

Books

Ali, Shahamat, *The Sikhs and Afghans in Connection with India and Persia*, London: John Murray, 1847.

Babbage, Henry P., *Memoirs and Correspondence of Major-General H. P. Babbage*, London: W. Clowes, 1915.

Baldwin, J. W., *A Norfolk Soldier in the First Sikh War*, Norwich: J. Fletcher, 1850.

Bancroft, Nathaniel W., *From Recruit to Staff Sergeant*, Calcutta: Thos S Smith, 1885.

Barr, William, *Journal of a March from Delhi to Peshawur and from thence to Cabul*, London: James Madden & Co., 1844.

Bingham, W. R., *The Field of Ferozeshah in Two Cantos with Other Poems*, London: Charles Edward Bingham, 1848.

Buckle, Edmund, *Memoirs of the Services of the Bengal Artillery, from the Formation of the Corps*, edited by J.W. Kaye, London: W. H. Allen, 1852.

Bunbury, Maj. Thomas, *Reminiscences of a Veteran*, London: C. J. Skeet, 1861.

Wade, Lt-Col. Sir C. M., *Journal of a March from Delhi to Peshawur*, London: James Madden & Co., 1844.

Cavenagh, Orfeur, *Reminiscences of an Indian Official*, London: W. H. Allen, 1884.

Cleveland, Cpl William, *Extracts from a Journal Kept on Board the Ship Madagascar*, Edinburgh: Summerhall Press, 1971.

Coley, James, *Journal of the Sutlej Campaign of 1845-6: And Also of Lord Hardinge's Tour*, London: Smith, Elder and Co., 1856.

Conran, Maj. H. M., *Autobiography of an Indian Officer*, London: Morgan & Chase, 1870.

Cunningham, Joseph D., *History of the Sikhs*, London: John Murray, 1849.

Cust, Robert N., *Linguistic and Oriental Essays Written from the Year 1840 to 1897*, London: Luzac & Co., 1898.

Description of a View of the Battle of Sabraon, London: Nichols, 1846.

Despatches and General Orders Announcing the Victories Achieved by the Army of the Sutlej, New Delhi: Nirmal Publishers, 1986.

Edwardes, Sir Herbert B., *Memorials Of The Life And Letters Of Major-General Sir Herbert B. Edwardes*, London: Kegan, Paul Trench & Co., 1886.

Edwards, William, *Reminiscences of a Bengal Civilian*, London: Smith, Elder & Co., 1866.

Gardner, Alexander, *Eye Witness Account on the Fall of the Sikh Empire*, Delhi: National Bookshop, 2007.

Hodson, George H., *Twelve Years of a Soldier's Life in India: Being Extracts from the Letters of the Late W. S. R. Hodson*, London: Boston, Ticknor and Fields, 1864.

Gilling, James, *Life of a Lancer*, London: Simpkin, Marshall & Co., 1855.

Grant, Hope, *Life of General Sir Hope Grant, Volume I: With Selections from His Correspondence*, London: William Blackwood & Sons, 1894.

Griffin, Sir Lepel Henry, *The Panjab Chiefs: Historical and Biographical Notices of the Principal Families in the Territories under the Panjab Government*, Lahore: Chronicle Press, 1865.

Griffin, Sir Lepel Henry, *The Panjab Chiefs, Volume II: Historical and Biographical Notices of the Principal Families in the Lahore and Rawalpindi Divisions of the Panjab*, Lahore: Civil & Military Gazette Press, 1890.

Hardinge, Charles Stewart, *Viscount Hardinge and the Advance of the British Dominions into the Punjab*, London: Clarendon Press, 1900.

Hardinge, Charles Stewart, *My Indian Peregrinations: the Private Letters of Charles Stewart Hardinge, 1844-1847*, edited by Bawa Satinder Singh, Lubbock, Texas: Texas Tech University Press, 2009.

Hardinge, Henry, *Letters of the First Viscount Hardinge of Lahore to Lady Hardinge and Sir Walter and Lady James, 1844-47*, edited by Bawa Satinder Singh, London: Royal Historical Society, 1986.

Hodson, V. C. P., *Historical Records of the Governor-General's Body Guard*, Charleston, SC: BiblioLife, 2009.

Hoffmeister, Werner, *Travels in Ceylon and Continental India including Nepal and Other Parts of the Himalayas, to the Borders of Tibet (1848)*, Whitefish, MT: Kessinger Publishing, 2009.

Honigberger, John M., *Thirty-Five Years in the East (1815-50)*, London: H. Bailliere, 1852.

Humbley, W. W. W., *Journal of a Cavalry Officer: with the 9th Queen's Royal Lancers During the First Sikh War, 1845-1846*, London: Longman, Brown, Green & Longmans, 1854.

Lumsden, Peter, *Lumsden of the Guides: A Sketch of the Life of Lieut.-Gen. Sir Harry Burnett Lumsden, K. C. S. I., C. B., with Selections from His Correspondence and Occasional Papers*, London: J. Murray, 1900.

Lunt, James, *From Sepoy to Subedar*, Lahore: Victoria Press, 1873.

Mackinnon, Lt Daniel H., *Military Service and Adventures in the Far East*, London: Charles Ollier, 1847.

M'Gregor, William L., *The History of the Sikhs, Volume I*, London: James Madden, 1846.

Napier, William Francis Patrick, *The Life and Opinions of General Sir Charles James Napier, G.C.B.*, London: John Murray, 1857.

Palmer, Gen. Henry, *Indian Life Sketches 1816-1866*, Mussourie: Mafasilite Printing Works, 1889.

Parshad, Dewan Ajudhia, *Waqai-Jang-I-Sikhan*, Punjab: Itihas Prakashan, 1975.

Pearman, John, *Sergeant Pearman's Memoirs*, London: Jonathan Cape, 1968.

Pearse, Hugh, *Soldier and Traveller. Memoirs of Alexander Gardner, Col. of Artillery in the Service of Maharaja Ranjit Singh*, Edinburgh: William Blackwood & Sons, 1898.

Robertson, Col. J. P., *Personal Adventures and Anecdotes of an Old Officer*, London: Edward Arnold, 1906.

Sandys, Major W. B. R., *A Visit to Some of the Battlefields of the Sutlej Campaign*, Godmanchester: Ken Trotman, 2005.

Smyth, George Carmichael, *A History of the Reigning Family of Lahore; With Some Account of the Jummoo Rajahs, the Seik Soldiers and Their Sirdars*, Calcutta: W. Thacker & Co., 1847.

Steinbach, Henry, *The Country of the Sikhs, Punjab: The Punjab Under Sikh Rule 1799 AD to 1849 AD*, London: Smith, Elder & Co., 1846.

The India Office Records From the India Office. Army of the Sutlej 1845-6 Casualty Roll, Uckfield: Naval & Military Press, 2002.

Tombs, Sir Henry, *Memoirs of Major-General Sir Henry Tombs*, London: Royal Artillery Institution, 1913.

Wylly, Col. H. C., *Military Memoirs of Lt.-Gen. Sir Joseph Thackwell GCB, KH Colonel 16th Lancers*, London: John Murray, 1908.

Articles, Journals and Magazines

Bentley's Miscellany, vol. 23, London: S. & J. Bentley, 1848.

Blackwood's Edinburgh Magazine, vol. 59, Edinburgh: William Blackwood & Sons, 1846.

Cumming, John, 'The night of Ferozeshah, 21st to 22nd December 1845', *The Army Quarterly* , vol. 33, London: William Clowes & Sons, 1936.

Murray, John, 'The Ludhiana Field Hospital', *The Medical Times*, vol. 19, London: W. S. Orr & Co., 1849.

SECONDARY SOURCES

Arnold, Sir Edwin, *The Marquis of Dalhousie's Administration of British India*, London: Saunders, Otley & Co., 1862.

Barrier, N. Gerald & Harbans Singh, eds., *Punjab Past and Present: Essays in Honour of Dr. Ganda Singh*, Patiala: Punjab University, 1979.

Beveridge, Henry, *A Comprehensive History of India, Civil, Military and Social, Vol. 3*, London: Blackie & Son, 1867.

Broadfoot, William, *The Career of George Broadfoot in Afghanistan and the Punjab*, London: John Murray, 1888.

Bruce, George, *Six Battles for India: The Anglo-Sikh Wars, 1845-6, 1848-9*, London: Arthur Baker, 1969.

Burton, Reginald George, *The First and Second Sikh Wars: An Official British Army History*, India: Government Central Branch, 1911.

Caine, Caesar, *Barracks and Battlefields in India*, New Delhi: Nirmal Publishers, 1986.

Taylor, Cameron, *Life of General Sir Alex Taylor*, London: Williams & Norgate, 1913.

Cannon, Richard, *Historical Record of the Fifty-Third: Or the Shropshire Regiment of Foot*,

Cannon, Richard, *Historical Records of the British Army: Comprising the History of Every Regiment in Her Majesty's Service*, London: HMSO, 1861.

Featherstone, Donald F., *At Them with the Bayonet! The First Sikh War*, London: Jarrolds, 1968.

Fortescue, John. W., *A History of the British Army*, 20 vols., London: Macmillan, 1899-1930.

Fyler, Col. A., *History of the 50th or (the Queen's Own) Regiment from the Earliest Date to the Year 1881*, London: Chapman & Hall, 1895.

Gambier, Parry E., *Reynell Taylor: A Biography*, London: K. Paul, Trench & Co., 1888.

Humphries, James, *The Hero of Aliwal: the Campaigns of Sir Harry Smith in India, 1843-1846, During the Gwalior War & the First Sikh War*, York: Leonaur, 2007.

Gough, Sir Charles & Arthur D. Innes, *The Sikhs and the Sikh Wars: The Rise, Conquest and Annexation of the Punjab State*, London: A. D. Innes & Co., 1897.

Kingston, William H. C., *Our Soldiers. Or, Anecdotes of the Campaigns and Gallant Deeds of the British Army*, London: Griffith & Farran, 1863.

Knight, Charles, *The Popular History of England*, London: Bradbury & Evans, 1865.

Lehmann, Joseph, *Remember You Are An Englishman: Biography of Sir Harry Smith, 1787-1860*, London: Jonathan Cape, 1977.

Lunt, James, *16th/5th The Queen's Royal Lancers*, London: Leo Cooper, 1973.

Marshman, John C., *The History of India, from the Earliest Period to the Close of Lord Dalhousie's Administration*, London: Longmans, Green, Reader & Dyer, 1867.

Murray, Hugh, *History of British India: With Continuation Comprising the Afghan War, the Conquest of Sinde and Gwalior, War in the Punjab*, London: T. Nelson & Sons, 1853.

Paget, George, *History of the British Cavalry, 1816 to 1919*, London: Leo Cooper, 1986.

Pearson, Hesketh, *The Hero of Delhi. A Life of John Nicholson, Saviour of India, and a History of the Wars*, London: Penguin, 1948.

Rait, Robert S., *The Life and Campaigns of Hugh, First Viscount Gough, Field-Marshal*, London: A. Constable & Co., 1903.

Rait, Robert S., *Life of Field Marshall Sir Frederick Paul Haines*, London: A. Constable & Co., 1911.

Raikes, Charles, *The Englishman in India*, London: Longmans, Green & Co., 1867.

Ramsay, B. D. W., *Rough Collections of Military Service and Society*, Edinburgh: William Blackwood & Sons, 1882.

Sandes, E. W. C., *The Indian Sappers and Miners*, London: Institution of Royal Engineers, 1948.

Sidhu, Kuldip Singh, *Ranjit Singh's Khalsa Raj and Attariwala Sardars*, New Delhi: South Asia Books, 1994.

Smith, Reginald B., *Life of Lord Lawrence, Volumes 1-2*, London: Smith, Elder & Co., 1901.

Stubbs, Francis W., *History of the Organization, Equipment, and War Services of the Regiment of Bengal Artillery*, London: Henry S. King & Co., 1877.

Taylor, A. C., *General Sir Alex Taylor, His Times, His Friends and His Work*, London: Williams & Norgate, 1913.

Taylor, Cameron, *Life of General Sir Alex Taylor*, London: Williams & Norgate, 1913.

Trotter, Lionel J., *The History of the British Empire in India, 1844 to 1862*, London: W. H. Allen, 1866.

Trotter, Lionel J., *The Life of Hodson of Hodson's Horse*, London: J. M. Dent & Sons, 1910.

Index

About the Author

Amarpal Singh was born in India in 1962 and moved to Britain when he was six years old. He has had a long-standing interest in both military history and the exploration and analysis of battlefields. He currently lives with his family in London. This is his first book, but he is already working on its sequel, *The Second Anglo-Sikh War*.

Praise for Amarpal Singh's *The First Anglo-Sikh War*:

'A valuable contribution to our understanding of an important but largely overlooked conflict. The sections on the battlefields today, which include vivid descriptions of the aftermath of combat by eyewitnesses, so often overlooked in works of military history, will help make this a key work for a long time to come' Dr Tony Pollard, battlefield archaeologist and co-presenter of BBC TV's *Two Men in a Trench*

'A remarkably well-researched work offering a refreshingly alternative perspective on the Anglo-Sikh wars and the surging imperial intrigues that presaged them' Harbinder Singh Rana, Director of the Anglo-Sikh Heritage Trail

'An extremely detailed study providing as definitive a narrative as is possible so many years later. I commend this work to military historians and enthusiasts everywhere' Dilip Sarkar MBE, military historian and Fellow of the Royal Historical Society